THE BANDIT ON THE BILLIARD TABLE

ALAN ROSS was born in India and spent his childhood in Bengal. He was educated at Haileybury and at St John's College, Oxford. During the war he served in the Royal Navy, initially on a convoy to Murmansk and later in the North Sea, a time memorably recalled in *Blindfold Games*, the first volume of his autobiography. After the war he wrote three Mediterranean travel books – the present volume, *Time Was Away* and *The Gulf of Pleasure* – before joining the *Observer* in 1950. As cricket correspondent he travelled extensively, writing several books on the cricket of his time, as well as a biography, *Ranji*, which have become classics. Since 1961 he has been editor of the *London Magazine*.

Together with D. H. Lawrence's *Sea and Sardinia*, *The Bandit on the Billiard Table* remains the only book available on this most alluring of Mediterranean islands.

By the same author

Cricket

AUSTRALIA 55
CAPE SUMMER
THROUGH THE CARIBBEAN
AUSTRALIA 63
WEST INDIES AT LORD'S
THE CRICKETER'S COMPANION (Editor)
RANJI

Poetry

POEMS 1942–67
THE TAJ EXPRESS
OPEN SEA
DEATH VALLEY

Autobiography

BLINDFOLD GAMES
COASTWISE LIGHTS

General

TIME WAS AWAY
THE GULF OF PLEASURE
COLOURS OF WAR
THE TURF (Editor)
THE EMISSARY

Alan Ross

THE BANDIT ON THE BILLIARD TABLE

A Journey through Sardinia

COLLINS HARVILL
8 Grafton Street, London W1
1989

Collins Harvill
William Collins Sons and Co Ltd
London · Glasgow · Sydney · Auckland
Toronto · Johannesburg

First published by Hamish Hamilton Ltd 1954
Revised edition entitled *South to Sardinia* published by
Hamish Hamilton Ltd 1960
This edition first published by Collins Harvill 1989

© Alan Ross 1954, 1960, 1989

ISBN 0-00-272020-5

All rights reserved. This book is sold subject to the condition that it shall not, by way of trade or otherwise, be lent, re-sold, hired out or otherwise circulated without the publisher's prior consent in any form of binding or cover other than that in which it is published and without a similar condition including this condition being imposed on the subsequent purchaser.

Printed and bound in Great Britain by
Hartnolls Limited, Bodmin, Cornwall

CONTENTS

	Introduction	vii
I	Corsica and the Straits of Bonifacio	1
II	Olbia—Cagliari	47
III	Cagliari and the South-West	93
IV	Oristano—Sassari	145
V	Alghero and Gallura	175
	Four Poems	195
	Index	201

INTRODUCTION

WHEN this book first appeared, in 1954, few English visitors had been to Sardinia. In village after village there had been none before us since 1939 and scarcely any before that. The bibliography is scanty: D.H. Lawrence's *Sea and Sardinia*, the result of a six-day visit, was published in 1923, and one has to go back nearly a century to find its predecessor.

The reasons for this were mainly to do with climate. Cicero, writing two thousand years ago, warned his brother Quintus, living in the Sardinian port of Olbia, 'Take care, my brother, of your health; although it is winter, recollect that it is Sardinia,' and this distrust of the climate has been echoed in the correspondence of most subsequent generations of residents, whether consuls, governors, humble soldiers or civilians. As a result, none of the island's conquerors devoted much time or energy to improving conditions or recording events. The island, stewing in its malarial fevers, was increasingly left to its own resources.

The 1939–45 war was responsible for a dramatic change in Sardinia's fortunes. Largely through American financial aid and research, malaria – which the Sards called *intemperie*, a term they tended to bestow on every ailment from the common cold and the hang-over to the pox – has been completely eradicated. Marshes were drained, hills reforested, and every house now bears its DDT spray-date.

The effects of this sudden discovery of health have been to add enthusiasm and vitality to the Sardinians' traditional qualities of independence and courage. After centuries of neglect, agriculture and industry have been revived over the last forty years on scientific lines. The Italian Government, made aware for the first time of the island's strange and beautiful landscape and undiscovered beaches, began to invest in small, modern hotels at suitable vantage points. The ancient sites and underwater cities of Carthaginian, Greek and Roman times have become the concern of well-subsidized archeologists. What for centuries had been an island of depression, if not despair, was now one of promise.

In the thirty-five years since my first visit these developments have been continued without much damage to the island's appearance or character. Sardinia remains more or less as I have described it, except for one small area in the north-east.

In 1962 the Aga Khan formed a syndicate to develop a wild, waterless, uninhabited and virtually uncultivated tract of land between Olbia and Arzachena. At that time it had no roads and was right off the beaten track. In the last twenty-five years, however, a port has been created at Porto Cervo and a number of architecturally adventurous, secluded and luxurious hotels built in the bays and inlets that separate Porto Cervo from Olbia. The most fashionable of these – *Cala di Volpe, Pitrizza, Romazzino, Le Ginestre* – rival in style and price anywhere on the Mediterranean. In their wake plots of land in the seven thousand five hundred acres of this Costa Smeralda have been sold off to suitably affluent clients, with the result that now, in the late 1980s, there are over two thousand five hundred villas, a golf-course and two marinas. What began as something very exclusive indeed can scarcely any longer be considered so. Agreeable though it may be if you like this kind of thing, it has no detectable relationship to the traditional Sardinia of the interior and the south.

As a spiritual travelling companion in the 1950s, I had an English barrister, John Warre Tyndale, author of the three-volume *The Island of Sardinia*, published exactly a hundred years earlier. Long-winded but informative, he was good to have around and were he not so bulky I would unhesitatingly recommend him again. What I do recommend unreservedly is the work of another lawyer, Salvatore Satta's *The Day of Judgement*, published in 1979 in Italy and in English translation in 1987. Set in Nuoro, Satta's wonderful novel, which bears comparison with Lampedusa's *The Leopard*, should be in the luggage of every discerning traveller to the island. Not only is it an absorbing work in its own right, but its description of family rivalry, provincial politics, agricultural struggle and landscape set the modern island in its proper historical perspective.

ALAN ROSS
London, 1988

I. MADDALENA
I. CAPRERA
S. Teresa
Palau
I. ASINARA
G. of Asinara
C. Falcone
Stintino
Castel Sardo
Sedini
Tempio
Olbia
Porto Torres
Sorso
Berchidda
Monti
Sassari
Tula
Tavolara
Oschiri
Chilivani
Ozieri
Porto Conte
Alghero
Benetutti
Bono
Bosa
Nuoro
Dorgali
SARDINIA
S. Caterina
(Cuglieri)
Macomer
Orgosolo
G. of Orosei
S. Leonardo
(S. Lussurgiu)
Seneghe
Tonara
Sorgono
MONTI DEL
GENNARGENTU
Aritzo
Arbatax
Tortoli
Lanusei
Oristano
G. of Oristano
Arborea
Ussassei
Mandas
Guspini
S. Gavino
Sanluri
Arbus
Gonnosfanadiga
S. Angelo
(Fluminmaggiore)
Muravera
Iglesias
C. Ferrato
Portoscuso
Cagliari
Carbonia
Carloforte
I. DI S. PIETRO
Villasimius
Calasetta
S. Antioco
G. of Cagliari
C. Carbonara
I. DI S. ANTIOCO
Teulada
G. of Palmas

THE BANDIT ON
THE BILLIARD TABLE

PART ONE

Corsica and the Straits of Bonifacio

I AWOKE with the smell of the *maquis* coming through the porthole: sweet, heavy and elusive. More nostalgic and haunting, for those who have succumbed to it, than almost any other smell in the world, it was possible to imagine what it meant to Napoleon on Elba, those clear mornings when a south-west wind came off a sea like scraped glass and the lonely exile climbed the chestnut-wooded slopes of Poggio to smell it. Perhaps he really did smell it, through the fisheries of Marciana Marina, the smoke of Portoferraio; perhaps it was simply desire and memory, rehearsed into something more powerful than reality. At any rate, he deserved to be refreshed by it, as he claims he was, on those days when the physical need to see his native island was so strong that he had to breast the western skyline of Elba and hope for the blue shadows of the hills above Bastia to greet him across forty miles of water. For these seas round Corsica are somehow specifically Napoleon's; though he rarely used them, and then badly, they bear the impress of his dreams and conquests, his failure, and his melancholy. Lower down, in the Straits of Bonifacio, we enter Nelson's territorial waters, but no one, coming past the Îles Sanguinaires into the great mauve bowl made by the mountains round Ajaccio, can fail to see it all in Napoleon's terms.

We had sailed from Nice in darkness the night before, edging out of the narrow Italianate port, where Garibaldi had been born, with the glow of sunset fading like transfers off the wharfside houses and the lights coming out in bars and restaurants along the quay. We swung across the Baie des Anges, the tinsel glitter of the Promenade des Anglais stretching out behind us like a lower and congested horizon of stars, and moved into a half-gale. The *Sampiero Corso*, eleven thousand tons and heavily loaded, met it easily enough, but the fourth-class passengers lying out along the holds under the creaking winches, caught the finest edge off the spray. All, as the blue-jowled and portly second mate bawled at them, included in the ticket.

By the time we were fully clear of the coast, it had begun to drizzle. I remembered how hot it had been when, at the exact date, mid-August, I had made the same journey five years ago. This time it was barely warm, and the rows of Corsicans going home for their annual leave huddled in their unrolled duffle-bags.

Now, as I went on deck, the swell of the night before had subsided and the sea had the pallid but relaxed look of hang-over. On the port beam the Îles Sanguinaires lay a mile or so distant, grey lumps of land like drowning camels as the water seemed to cut them off at the neck. Daudet has written about them, and de Maupassant, and they play their part in the small but select literature of Corsica, made up by Mérimée's *Colomba*, Boswell's uneven and somewhat pontifical Account, Edward Lear's endearing *Journal of a Landscape Painter*.

The sun had only just risen and we were sailing straight into it as it dipped its first rays like the beam of a lamp on the hillsides sweeping down to the wide, conical Bay of Ajaccio.

Ajaccio, as we grew near, seemed to have grown since I had last seen it. The suburbs looked to have climbed higher up the close green curl of the nearer hills and to have spread themselves further along the road towards the beaches to the west. Yet, as we swung round into it, with the sun clarifying perspectives against the central range of mountains, it was still recognizably the same town as rises with graceful symmetry from eighteenth-century engravings; a town beautifully shaped at the foot of high hills, encircled by mountains and within them, at water-level, the long arms of moles and jetties. Sailing-boats, with dawn on their sails like a painted colour, lay in neat rows: cobalt, saffron, emerald, pink, doubling their hulls in watered reflection. And, further along, under the palm-trees squatly planted by the old harbour walls, the fishing-boats seemed, like coarser children, to be segregated in their dark colours from the lifting elegance of the yachts.

On my last visit the heat had been suffocating. The sun beat down week after week from skies of a blue so transparent they seemed burned in bronze. The island had been becalmed, paralysed in all its faculties, except that of argument. Refuse and fruit had rotted in the streets because no one could be bothered to take it away. Corsica, in any case, was an island that people went away from, not a showpiece for visitors. This slight self-pity of the Corsicans, the provincial's or colonial's self-pity for the neglect of his *département*, combined with a natural pride of race, produced a curious alternation of arrogance and deprecation. Something had happened in the past, something would doubtless happen again; but in the meantime the absence of history had left a kind of apathy, an endemic nihilism.

I had experienced this feeling strongly in 1947. Corsica was then comparatively fresh from liberation, still full of heroic admiration for de Gaulle, who had strode magnificently through the streets a couple of years earlier, the first Allied General to set foot on Corsican soil. Then Ajaccio had been covered in political posters, the cafés and bars noisy with violent dialectic, obscure side-streets scrawled with *Vive de Gaulle* and *À Bas Thorez, le traître*. The memory of Napoleon had suddenly come alive and everyone was eager to tell stories about heroes of the past like Paoli and Sampiero, and to recount wild feats of recent resistance in the war just over. Here, they said, two Germans were shot; there, a British submarine landed secret agents on a moonless night and was provisioned by men of the Corsican *maquis*; and over in that bar an American had been strangled for making advances to a Corsican girl. For a moment the links of history seemed to have been joined up into some recognizable continuity; then just as suddenly they snapped. And my main recollection of the great Place de Gaulle, overlooking the western arm of the harbour, had been its perpetual sense of doomed expectancy, the feeling that everyone was waiting for something to happen and that they had been waiting so long that all other purpose had been drained.

But when I had been ashore for some hours this time, I could see other changes. Things seemed more prosperous, the streets cleaner and neater. Before, Ajaccio had seemed very much an outpost, a garrison town: a training-ground where soldiers came to do their military service, a post for a young officer to sweat away a few years on his way to promotion, perhaps dreaming of a Staff job in Paris or action in Indo-China. Mostly, it had seemed a convenient stopping-place for aircraft on the Marseilles–North Africa run, and as we lay stunned by the heat on the golden beaches of Calvi or Porto or Propriano, worn out by tiring journeys into the interior, we had seen so many aeroplanes, day in day out, that I had thought of calling the book I later wrote (under the title of *Time Was Away*) *The Airfield of Olives*—a title, like most author's original titles, rejected by the publisher.

Then, Ajaccio had seemed a perfect setting for a seedy novel about expatriates by Maugham or Simenon. There was a formidable black market, especially in drugs; and we had once got mixed up in a journey by lorry, paying the driver exorbitantly to take us to Piana when the normal transport had gone, only to find ourselves wedged amongst sacks of contraband flour, at that time the most valuable of all forms of barter or currency. We had, as a result, to wait in the mountains until nightfall before it, and we, could be safely unloaded.

Now de Gaulle's promise had failed to materialize, and the urgency had gone out of politics. Also the need for a black market. Doubtless the small white packages, with their magic powers, still went their rounds when the ships came in from Africa, but in the meantime there were more obvious diversions. A thriving tourist industry, its main centres at Calvi, Île Rousse, Bonifacio and Porto, had left its decisive traces on Ajaccio, and as a result the shops, and prices, were beginning to compete with those of Saint-Tropez and Cannes, Portofino and Capri.

It was all, no doubt, inevitable, if saddening. Perhaps the weather, too, contributed to my feeling of regret. For by now, clouds had hit the mountains with determined firmness and as they piled up a steady rain dripped through the plane-trees on the Cours Mirabeau under them. The hills were soon lost and by lunch-time mist had left the town as if floating on a fog-bound raft. The sea was a kind of mauve bruise and the coastline to the south could only be sensed under its moist and woolly blanket. Sometimes an occasional gust of *maquis* came through, purified and sweetened, to remind us that we were on an island.

★ ★ ★

Later that evening the weather cleared and we walked down through the exotic trees in the garden of the Grand Hotel, past rows of crowded cafés, their tables cluttered with brightly coloured ices, to where the buses left for the beaches—that string of superb sandy coves with beautiful names, Ariadne, Scudo, Marinella . . . and as good as any in the Mediterranean. In the bus I was reminded of the loveliness of Corsican girls, a curiously fragile loveliness nearly always left behind in early womanhood. It is a quite distinct beauty, hard-boned, erect, graceful in carriage and with arresting colour contrasts: blonde hair and brown eyes, black hair and eyes of clear, satiny blue, red-gold hair on the darkest of skins. I was reminded, too, of the heroic skill of the bus-drivers, pioneers of speed in an island where they form all the essential links in communication and whose daily routes, rarely less than six hours' solid driving, are over narrow, swinging ledges of rock. Indeed some of these drivers, dressed with a cowboy's nonchalant elegance, sometimes in black, with knotted black-silk neckerchiefs, have a true poetry about them, a cynical endurance, normally reserved in an age of speed for pioneers of flight. They have the qualities associated with a Saint-Exupéry, opening up the South American air route, and perhaps one day a Corsican poet, with the ear of a Marinetti, the eye of a Léger, will celebrate them in a deserved epic.

Meanwhile, we swung out under the soaking trees, past women walking in rows, their dresses the colours of boiled sweets, and past the offices of the airline company in the Rue Buonaparte, which John Minton and I had haunted five years ago when it had begun to seem as if we should never get off the island. Because of bad weather, the Air France planes, already heavily booked from Tunis, had missed several flights and in the hold-up we were forced to book places on a private line. The plane, a ramshackle eight-seater, had failed to take off the first time because of a storm, and the second time because the pilot could not be found. When we did finally get away, with a pilot whose lip was never free from a cigarette and whose hands shook like a dope-fiend's, the plane door immediately blew open and a square of blue sea came uncomfortably near as the concealed cargo of contraband on which we sat was sucked against the banging door.

Now we drove past the gigantic cemetery, hallmark in each

Corsican town of civic pride, and along by the hillside where I remembered the scrub used to smoke like sacrificial pyres, burned by the sun's heat. Camping-grounds had sprung up all the way along, turning the curved beaches, with their fringe of pine and olive, from the deserted playgrounds of a derelict paradise into the noisy lidos of an occupying army.

The succession of buses unloaded their passengers at the entrances to the three adjoining beaches, where already gramophone-jazz was blaring out over the sand, and sunblacked men and girls, in striped bikinis, played crepuscular ping-pong or drummed with sandalled feet at the bars. On tables pressed into the sand, glasses of *Cap Corse, Dubonnet* and *citron pressé* seemed to be composed of the colours a striated sky squeezed out from the last light of the day. Soon the darkness hunched over the mountains, leaving only the Sanguinaires, with their pines sticking up like the bristles on hair-brushes, visible against the silver slipstream of the moon. It was calmer and there was the promise of a good day ahead.

The husky music tinkled on until midnight, a new brand of longing, inscribed by Edith Piaf, replacing that of Tino Rossi, second only to Buonaparte in his fame as a Corsican. Otherwise it was as I remembered it. The waves lapped in the aromatic air with the same soothing gentleness, the whole island seemed to ride as easily at its moorings, and the Mediterranean night, flickering as it did over the jewelled coasts of the Continent, once more laid its benediction equally over the heeding and unheeding, the rich and needy. Only it seemed as though the pleasure centres might at last be changing, a subtle shift of fashion washing high and dry the famous and cosseted resorts of the recent past and substituting for them new ports and parades whose names were barely yet more than whispers.

* * *

The promise of the night before was not fulfilled. The weather, when we set off at seven the next morning for Bonifacio, was overcast and almost cold. The sea, as we drove eastwards along the bay, was the depressing drab colour the English Channel had been a week earlier, but without its movement or straws of sun. The rain, however, had brought a new greenness out of the landscape, settling the dust, and climbing past the aerodrome, up through winding avenues of ilex, olive and pine; it was in fact of Scotland that one thought. It had, I learned, been a bad summer, but the richness of the vegetation, the heavy green forests, was something quite unexpected. I remembered this journey southwards as one through gaunt rock, and desiccated scrub, in heat and dust. Now in the grey morning light the leaves were dust-free and the sun, when it gradually appeared through gaps in white scurrying cloud, had only a pale warmth.

The drive to Bonifacio is supposed to take five hours, according to the time-table, but I believe the bus never does it under eight. It is in fact a journey through loop after loop of superb romantic scenery, the great ranges of mauve, crested mountains backing away to the left and, in between them and the sea, deep valleys, thickly planted with trees, reaching down to wide sandy bays. The road clings to the side of bare rock for most of the way, swinging out to throw each gorge, its sea-edged cape and ridge of mountain into new perspective, and always at a different level.

At Sartène, which is just over half-way, we stopped for two hours, ostensibly for a wheel to be changed, in reality, it seemed, for the driver to have lunch and carry out pressing domestic duties. At any rate, this delay, never marked on the time-table, is a daily occurrence. At two o'clock, having leisurely lunched and drunk our coffee under the trees on the square, while a record of Edith Piaf singing *Jezebel* was put on over and over again, and a game of bowls was played at our feet, we rumbled downhill towards Bonifacio.

The last part of the journey is a steady, winding descent, through increasingly arid country. The scrub thins out, and the great grey-black volcanic rocks ripple under their sparse coverings like the scales of some prehistoric monster, whose snout lengthens into the flat promontory on which Bonifacio is perched. Some ten miles from Bonifacio you get your first glimpse of Sardinia. At Roccopina the road climbs to a crest of rock and, taking on a wider curve, offers a wedge-shaped view of the western end of the Straits of Bonifacio.

Although we had occasional intervals of sun during our lunch-time wait, the afternoon had already begun to go dead. White cumulus had given way to lower and heavy cloud, trailing moistly down from the mountains and spreading across from the east till the whole sky was a damp grey. In the distance, like a settling ship, Sardinia was nothing more than a dark outline, stern down in the water and with clouds dividing its black hills into three charred funnels.

* * *

Bonifacio had not changed much since I had last seen it. Perhaps it is too remote to be seriously threatened by the daily influx of tourists who stay a night there on their way round the island. Certainly the tourist agencies had organized their clients' time with military efficiency and there was even quite an orderly response by the fishermen and bar proprietors who benefit by it. At any rate the excursionists' routine is admirably clear-cut. The coach arrives from Porto Vecchio at four-thirty; at five, boats leave for the grottoes, returning at six and allowing an hour for a walk up to the citadel and an apéritif before dinner. This consists always of lobster mayonnaise, expertly prepared at the Pergola, and then at nine o'clock, leaving time for a stroll with a cigar along the port, fishermen start singing at a café called *Au Son des Guitares*. Again this is carefully done: the walls of the café are gaily painted, the singers romantically effective, the brandy adequate. Boats bob gently off the stone water-front, their masthead lights spilling over the sea as it ripples under them. The steep sides of the narrow bay loom forbiddingly up, seeming to isolate Bonifacio behind their impenetrable barrier. In the rocky fortress of the old town, aged crones sit out under plane-trees, and in the wine caves that drench the narrow streets with their musky perfume, men play cards. What goes on down below for tourists is like a performance at the theatre: it begins and ends at set times, and life outside it is untouched.

There were, of course, few tourists and no public singing when I had last been here. Yet there was a curious kind of puppetry about this orderly formula for entertaining visitors, a genuflection, as it were, to money, but without worship, that was rather pleasing. If Bonifacio had been anywhere on the mainland, it would by now be a thriving, fashionable resort. The two humble hotels, with stained fronts and dingy stone corridors, would have been painted, they would have bars and proper service. The heap of rusty scrap iron that has been lying immediately opposite them since the war would have been cleared away, the water-front road mended, the pavements washed, some lights put along the harbour's edge. None of this has been done: the road is full of huge pot-holes, discarded bicycle wheels, twisted machinery. At night the beautiful bay is in complete darkness, the only lights the headlamps of occasional lorries probing the mountain roads and the sweep of the lighthouse beam on the edge of the cliff. The spectacular, in fact, has been ignored; and the inhabitants—fishermen, a few customs officials, shopkeepers—look out in the darkness at a landscape they do not need illuminated. In lighted doorways the lobster-pots are woven, and the bare legs of children playing round the water-pump are cut off at the knees by pale rays escaping from interiors lit by single, yellow bulbs.

Apathy, in fact, will probably keep most of Corsica for the Corsicans: the long exhausting bus journeys, the only links between places, will limit exploitation to Calvi in the north and Ajaccio. Bonifacio, anyhow, seems likely, except for its brief set-piece that lasts from 4 pm to dawn, when the tourists depart, to remain much as it has been since Napoleon, as a young company commander, led his troops out against the Sardinians and in his first military engagement at Maddalena suffered a humiliating defeat.

The boat, next day, for Sardinia was due in at twelve and arrived at two. The clear, early morning skies had given way to low cloud, deepening the olive green of the inlet to heavy black. The rows of brightly painted boats now swung forlornly against the jetty, their colour drained out of them as the sun receded. A blustering wind tilted their masts, whipping up a creamy spray from the usually dark and placid water.

Beating its way against the wind the *Gallura*, when it arrived, was a clean, neat steamer, about half the size of a cross-Channel boat. It flew an Italian flag, and its officers in smart white uniforms and wearing dark glasses could be seen on the narrow bridge. Like nearly all Italian ships, whether warships, luxury liners or the coastal boats that ply from the various islands to the mainland, it had a rakish elegance about it, so that, when it tied up, one expected to see noisily experienced passengers come laughing down the gangway, instead of the carefully dressed peasants in incongruous blue suits and collarless shirts, bursting, string-tied suitcases in their hands, who finally emerged and who seemed to take root, like trees, in family heaps outside the customs.

It is at Bonifacio that the frontier formalities between France and Italy take place. In a small shed off the port, lined in front with palm-trees, and with the buff-coloured reflections of the straggling citadel glittering in the water all round it, French and Italian officials sit at tables placed in opposite corners of a map-lined room. Here passports are examined and stamped, luggage given a scant survey. Only peasants, in accustomed manner, are subjected to ruthless overhaul, the strings round the suitcases all untied, the paper parcels bared to supercilious gazes.

We waited while the incoming group went one by one into the shed and then came out to pile themselves into a battered taxi. Nine of them, six adults and three children, eventually wedged themselves in, stacking suitcases and parcels till they were sticking out of the windows like absurd ears. After a haggle with the driver, and after once being completely unloaded because one of them had filled a form in wrongly, they at last set off for Ajaccio, on their way to get hotel jobs in the south of France.

The French, especially in the south, have a genius for atmosphere, to which perhaps their films have made us over-susceptible. But a small, bare customs shed they manage to transform into something mysterious and fascinating. Sallow officials, their throats bare, *képis* pushed back, let their eyes play with bored indifference over the waiting people. The air reeks of wine and garlic and *Gauloise* cigarettes. The whole lazy performance exudes fatalism. Yet now and then an eye flickers into amused interest, a smile suggests depths and tastes altogether removed from the humdrum trivialities of visas and immigrant workers and currency exchanges. The French manage to convey by their inbred cynicism the absurdity of their official duties, even while they seem to exaggerate them, so that they produce an effect of sharing a secret behind it all, the secret that all civilized people share. They tend to look as though they have woken from recent participation in their particular vice, food or sex or drink, and are waiting to get back to it. They give off this strong sense of work being a rest from their sensual appetites, an impression whoever they come in contact with is tacitly expected to preserve. In the north of Europe, or in England, the life of pleasure is a life apart: work is work, no more. But the French manage to carry one into the other, so that a customs shed in an isolated French port seems essentially a symbol, an image so fertile in meaning, so stylized, that it conveys the totality of human life.

We in turn came under the casual charm of police, currency official, customs officer. Stamp, rhetorical interrogative, chalk scrawl. Were we travelling for pleasure? Yes, they had heard Sardinia was *gentil*, but, shrugging their shoulders as deferentially as possible, they had never conceived the idea of going there. People rarely did; except, of course, on business. Besides, *la Corse* was generally regarded as more beautiful. Still, if one had nothing better to do, perhaps it might be worth a visit. Not for long, though.

It had looked at first as though we would be travelling alone. But now, from on board, two dark Italian girls, in narrow black trousers, black jerseys and identical yellow scarves, came swinging ashore with male escorts and began to walk rapidly up and down alongside the boat. They had come, it appeared, for the trip; and we were now joined by two heavily loaded youths, eventually recognizable under their dwarfing shell of tents and camp accoutrements, as boy and girl. These, it turned out, were German students from Hamburg who, feeling stifled in the August heat of Paris, had decided to return through Marseilles, Corsica, Sardinia and Rome, hitch-hiking wherever possible.

Despite their unwieldy burdens, they could not have been further from the German travellers of caricature, knobbly-kneed, spiky-legged, equipped with Baedeker, Leica and thick glasses; but in recent years the once-familiar concept of the intelligent, good-looking, too smooth German, who, before the war, and, to some of us, since, has exerted his or her spell, has disintegrated under the superimposition of cold-eyed militarists and crude thugs. It now seems almost impossible to believe in the gay, liberal amoralists of the pre-Nazi era; and I remember, after the war in Hamburg, when elegant German naval officers, for a moment allowed to be equals, talked with such convincing and self-effacing brilliance, or sultry, bewitching women, products of a kinder past, spun their magic, while fireflies cruised through the pinewoods and magnolias laid their scent on the still, moon-washed surfaces of lakes—I remember how one regarded them with amused tolerance, entertained, attracted, but never believing them anything but suspect. Sometimes, listening to a German gramophone record salvaged from that period, Ilse Werner singing *Das Wird ein Frühling ohne Ende* or Eva Busch spilling *Ich Danke dir* from the luxurious, smoky divans of her throat, one had the *schwärmerei*, the regret for fragmentary moments of one's own past, but one had no longer affection or trust.

Now, however, there was another generation, and the two who followed us with rather more difficulty through the frontier ritual belonged to it, the sons and daughters of those subtle pre-war enchanters and enchantresses. Attractive Germans, perhaps because they are in such a minority, have a curious charm, quite unlike anyone else's: an individual, rather off-key *chic*, an elusive air of abandon. They are Babes in the Wood, real only so long as they escape identification. This role of innocence with suggestive undertones is, of course, assumed, but they play it so winningly that we surrender to the pervasive perfume of their egoism.

Watching them, I remembered a passage from Evelyn Waugh's preface to his book of collected travel pieces, *When the Going Was Good*. When I got back to London I looked it up. 'My own travelling days are over', he wrote. 'Never again, I suppose, shall we land on foreign soil with letter of credit and passport . . . and feel the world wide open before us. That is as remote today as "Yorrick's" visit to Paris, when he had to be reminded by the landlord that their countries were at war. It will be more remote tomorrow. Some sort of reciprocal "strength-through-joy", *dopo-lavoro* system may arise in selected areas; others, not I, gifted with the art of pleasing public authorities, may get themselves despatched abroad to promote "cultural relations"; the very young, perhaps, may set out like the Wandervogels of the Weimar period; lean, lawless, aimless couples with rucksacks, joining the great army of men and women without papers, without official existence, the refugees and deserters. . . .'

This vision of travel was, in 1945, real enough; it is barely less real today. But now, in fact, the *Wandervögel* of the very young were setting out with us, not travelling as a matter of course, as Waugh did, but for the first time. The world that, since childhood, always had locked doors, was cautiously opening them, testing the air.

The *Gallura* now made signs of departing and we went on board, up on to the boat deck. The four Italians were leaning against the stern rail, their hair blowing in the wind. The two Germans came and sat on the hatches near us. The girl must have been about eighteen, very pretty, with short dark hair, and wearing a white jersey and black trousers. The man, perhaps a year older, was tall and thin, in a crumpled khaki suit, and also very good-looking. They eased their great rucksacks off their shoulders, while under us the engines throbbed into action. We moved slowly out through the sharp bend in the rocks, the faded waterfront houses sliding away in the wake. Everything now looked insignificant against the steep battlements that jutted out into the sea and above which the honeycomb of shabby Genoese-built houses clustered precariously. Amongst them odd tufts of shrub thrust their way through crumbling stone, a few trees hung over tiny piazzas or marked the falling line of the road down to the port. Hens squawked about in the tombstones of the cemetery at the extreme edge of the cliff, and rusty guns pointed their muzzles straight down at the deep, bottle-green water.

Once clear of the sheer drop of coast the wind hit us. The low cloud had now swollen up over the dark peaks of Corsica, leaving Bonifacio in a final shaft of silver light, immediately withdrawn from it like a sword. For a moment the buff battlements glittered at the top of the gaunt, cracked rock, then the last rays of sun were cut off in cloud. The sea was a deep mauve between the islands, the sky over both coastlines barely lighter.

We began to roll a bit, gulls now hovering over the steamy wake or remaining poised between our swinging masts before beginning their screaming dive across the water.

It was almost impossible to believe we were going south, in mid-Mediterranean, at the height of summer.

At the eastern end of the Straits of Bonifacio, small rocky

islands stick out of the sea, increasing in size as they reach Sardinia. Almost the whole of the seven or eight miles is perforated by these grey crags, some oval and barely out of the water, others like sharp, pointed teeth.

We were now moving due south at the western end of the Straits, making for Santa Teresa, the nearest point on the Sardinian coast. Above us the solid black ceiling seemed to be only just clear of the masts. The sea, like dark *crêpe* in the distance, hissed round us, and with the wind on our port quarter we had constantly to keep our bows pointing at the open sea to the southwest. Occasionally a crack of light appeared, and then silver splashes lengthened over the waves, till the channel was a sieve of spilled reflections on the edges of which shoals of land floated. No green was visible anywhere: only sloping, fissured rocks, apparently uninhabited.

The Germans came over and asked us if we knew about boats from Sardinia to Civitavecchia. They had heard that a steamer left Olbia, on the north-east coast, at seven o'clock each night, but perhaps we would be too late, and the connection would have gone. They were, we learned, both originally from Stettin, in the east of Germany. Their parents used to have neighbouring estates. Naturally, they had lost everything. They lived in Hamburg, both families sharing flats with relatives. They were studying practical science: she, veterinary surgery, he, agriculture. In July they had gone to Paris, hitch-hiking all the way, intending to stay two months. But the heat had driven them out, and they had got lifts on night lorries thundering down the neon-lit Route Nationale through Lyons to Marseilles. Then they had spent a fortnight under canvas in Corsica: near Bastia a scorpion had been on the girl's blanket one morning when she awoke. They had three weeks to get back to Hamburg through Sardinia and Rome and Milan. They had no money to eat in restaurants, but bought bread and olives and ham where they could.

Corsica now was the further island, a mere thickening of clouds rimmed by cream along their base, and ahead the tilting shadow of Sardinia hardened into mountains flowing down in a variety of gradients to the sea. I remembered my first sight of Elba three years earlier: forbidding rock, covered in sparse scrub and seeming to turn its back on the sea at each angle of approach. Capri, Ischia, Crete, Cyprus, Majorca, invite; others put out a kind of feminine screen, coldly repulsing the intruder at each contour. Then, as at the entry to the harbour of Portoferraio, the grim exterior, tired of appraisal, seems suddenly to give in, and within the arms of the bay, invisible even at a short distance, everything is green and fair. Circling Elba, whose outer coasts enfold golden sands and sweeping hills almost without equal, I had wondered what on earth I had come for. Perhaps it was really as the guide-books, most conspiratorial of advisers, had described it: a small, smoky island, without beauty, kept alive and disfigured by factories and smokestacks. Few islands can have such a brutal circumference; yet in fact, as I discovered, some of the charm of Portoferraio itself, though its uneconomic ironworks no longer wave their sooty pennants over the dark-green bay, comes precisely from its concealment. One comes upon it with the joy of personal discovery, a reward for perseverance. Turning into the wide harbour, with houses set over shelving rock like seats in an amphitheatre and beyond it ridge after ridge of richly cultivated hillside intersecting on a thin base of sand, was like entering the early nineteenth century. If there were no longer British squadrons, with the frigates *Flora*, *Inconstant* and *Southampton*, of engraved record, lying off the lighthouse watering, there were water-front houses and fishing-boats that had barely changed. Napoleon's house high up a deep valley, sandstone garrison buildings, palm-trees, bastions and palazzos glow in honey-coloured light, and nothing is visible a hundred yards out to sea, so enclosed is it all.

I wondered whether Sardinia, as unkindly treated by most reference books, disregarded for centuries in its malarial beauty sleep, would, under its seemingly barren exterior, offer the same rewards. Lawrence, approaching it from Sicily, and in the winter, had not seemed to enjoy his few hurried days. Then, he had gone out of pure restlessness and in a bad temper.

I, however, was already prejudiced in favour of Sardinia, by a tragic little story I had been told in Italy the year before. The Sardinians, great lovers of poetry, hold an annual festival at which shepherds declaim in verse composed by themselves the happenings in their own part of the island. At a recent gathering—

and these poetic contests take place at a different village each year—one of the contestants, telling his story last, could see by the polite applause of his fellow shepherds that his verse had fallen below the expected standard. Ashamed at his lack of prowess, and a believer in the heroic tradition, he did the only thing a romantic could do: he walked out of sight and decently shot himself.

We began to alter course, turning in past small outlying islands, little more than rocks, and, sheltered now by the western headlands, slipped into the quiet harbour of Santa Teresa.

From the sea only a green curve of bay is evident, broken up on the west by a wooden jetty with a few whitewashed buildings at the back of it. The village itself, where we were to spend our last night before we left the island, is over the steep brow of a hill which completely seals off the inlet. We could now see only the red tops of a few tiled roofs and a campanile as indications that there was any point in stopping here at all. Two fishing-boats were anchored off the far shore, black-painted, with flared bows and yellow bowsprits, whose colour was continued a foot or so below the gunwale right round them.

A small knot of people were waiting on the quay when we tied up. The water, as our screws ceased turning, was almost ink-black. The inlet, out of the wind, was otherwise deserted: on its slopes a goat or two were grazing, shaking out their bells as they scrambled over the granite surface, jumping from rock to rock for dry stalks and rubbery-looking tufts of shrub.

A minute or two later, with no one having got off or on the boat, we cast off again, going slowly astern into the open channel and turning eastward.

For two hours we steamed along the northern coastline, keeping about a mile out to sea, while the sky thundered ominously in the distance and the archipelagos off our bows seemed to huddle together. At intervals flying-fish dived through the curl of waves, cutting from trough to trough like silver penknives. The land began to close in on all sides, island after island hedging off the sea at different angles, running it to ground in a series of bays, inlets and wide basins. Sardinia curled round in a bare, black sweep to starboard; in front of us, blocking the east, the island of Santo Stefano rose out of the water forcing us to turn to port, and, hemming us in as we did so, lay another cluster of oval-shaped islands, Spargi, Santa Maria, Budelli. Long green capes slid down from narrow shoulders of rock, rippling along from island to island. Each turn we made I expected to see La Maddalena, where we had decided to spend the night, but instead empty unbroken skylines clamped slowly round us. A house here, a shepherd's hut there, glimmering palely in the darkness, and set on viridian ledges of coarse hill; but, though the fishing-boats began to grow more frequent, sinking into heavy oncoming seas till only a matchstick of mast remained visible, we had to battle on for another hour. At last, rounding a bend, the flat, low-lying buildings of the port came into view.

Although it was only six o'clock, lights were already on in many of the houses along the quay. Rows of boats in a neat rectangular port were half-lit by overhanging lamps, and the hills that sloped down on all sides, so that we seemed to be in a Scottish loch, were pricked with light.

A crowd of fierce, gesticulating people crowded round the barriers as we came ashore. Unshaven porters, with terrifying faces, clutched at our luggage. Large, single raindrops had begun to fall, and as we eventually detached the least blood-thirsty and congenitally demented porter from the rest, instructing him to take us to the hotel, streaks of vivid lightning flamed across the sky. In a minute the cobbled roadways were running with water. Thunder ricocheted round the bay, and rain came rattling down on corrugated-iron roofs. Looking back at the ship, which was going on to Palau, a quarter of an hour's journey away on the mainland, I could see the two *Wandervögel*, their luggage littered round them, waving from portholes in the saloon. A steady stream of water was pouring off the stone quays into the sea.

We waited for a few minutes while rain dripped off our clothes: cinema posters were flapping in the wind, torn into shreds. On the opposite side of the street the colours of an advertisement for a film called *Vendetta Sarda* had run, and a series of *fauve* paintings succeeded one another like lantern slides. I could hear the rattle and click of bead curtains as scurrying figures pushed through them. Beyond the *Gallura*, the notes of whose siren came mournfully through the metallic clatter of rain, the sky was a strange electric green. It was still thundering round about, with paler flashes of lightning occasionally playing to the south, but gradually the tense greenish patch of sky began to push the blackness away behind one floating skyline after another. Greyer, clearer clouds detached themselves from the falling plaster-clouds at the storm's centre, and though the hail and rain went beating on for twenty minutes, the heavy closeness, which seemed to be strangling and suffocating one between these intersecting hills, was being squeezed out of the air. A delicious freshness, skimming the sweetness from the hills, began to refresh us. On all sides there were, I knew, lavender and myrtle, pine, rock-rose, cistus and asphodel, as well as orchid and tamarisk, and now the gentlest, most subtle of smells slowly sprayed over the harbour. By the time the rain had stopped, the *Gallura* already nosing back into a quietened sea, everything was bright and glistening. Black coastlines were now green, the port a cluster of neat white cubes, lined with palms and planted with oleander. Half a dozen yachts, tall-masted, and riding gently at their moorings, sieved the bare hillsides behind them through their rigging.

We walked through the wet streets which sloped upwards between rows of pinkwashed houses with green shutters. Streams of swiftly pouring water raced down the gutters, gurgling away into drains and carrying a floating scum of fruit peel and refuse. At the lower end of each street a band of green sea lay between Maddalena and Santo Stefano, and Maddalena and the mainland. The islands, under a torn, jagged sky, full of quickly moving pale clouds, now looked nearer to one another, and the looming depressiveness of our first sight of them had given way to a comforting feeling of intimacy. These were inner harbours from which the sea had been excluded, or rather tamed into placidity: however much the wind roared in the Straits, which it was almost continually doing, it would always be calm within these protective promontories.

The hotel, when we got to it, turned out to be not properly a hotel at all. A large, but almost obliterated sign in the Piazza Garibaldi, the first square we came to, certainly said *Hotel Ilvese*. But when we climbed behind our grunting porter, who now occasionally flashed a black-toothed smile, as if to reassure us as we mounted a winding iron staircase over an unswept, evil-smelling stone entrance, a woman, who had poked her head, but nothing else, from a doorway, pointed still higher up, muttering agreeably but dubiously under her breath. It did not look promising, especially as we had been told this was the only hotel on the island; and probably if the *Gallura* had not already left we should have been tempted to go on with it. However, on the third floor, in darkness like the others, a swarthy little peasant woman, her grey hair in a straggly bun, was hanging over the banisters, chewing. As we approached she wiped her lips with a napkin, said *scusi* demurely, and grinned.

I asked her if she had a room. Yes, she said, grinning still more, but would we mind waiting a little. She had not, she went on, expected anyone and as a matter of fact she herself had been sleeping in the bed with her daughter.

She now squeaked with laughter, pointing out that hardly anyone ever came to the hotel as they preferred to sleep on the mainland. La Maddalena was so small that commercial travellers got their business done in a morning and left the same afternoon. *Stranieri* had never come before, not for many years anyway, and the sailors had their own barracks on the east side of the island.

Meanwhile, I paid off the porter, who took off his sodden cap, and gave a most charming low bow, before clattering away down the dark stairs.

The woman hurried into her room a moment, muttered something and re-emerged smiling. Wiping her hands on her flowered apron, she led us into a small, spotless room overlooking the piazza. If we didn't mind resting here for about five minutes, her daughter Maria would prepare the better room. We protested that this looked very nice and that we should not like to put her to any trouble. No, she said, she would like us to have the better room, and, beaming through her spectacles, she backed out of the door and shuffled away.

She was, in fact, the first of the long line of hotel-keepers with whom we came in contact and who, without exception, were unfailingly kind and helpful to us. Not once, in a score of hotels, some small and unprepossessing to look at, did we come across any room that was not spotless or meet any service that was not attentive and meticulous.

A smell of *pasta* and lentils began to seep across the landing. There were few people in the streets outside, though it was no longer raining. I could make out a church tower that looked as if it had been bombed, a barber's shop and a tailor's, in whose illuminated opening a man was being measured. Rows of lights, leading in all directions up from the quays, marked the different levels of roads and I could see where they petered out at the top, just below the skyline, under overhanging olive-trees and prickly pear.

In a few moments the woman was back, and, leading us through a candle-lit salon, which gave on to a kitchen, opened a door at the far end. Breasting the enticing aromas that came from the bubbling stove on our right, we found ourselves in a handsome bedroom, with polished marble floor, furniture that seemed partly to be Empire and partly to have come from Heal's, and with a large double-bed shining under a black shot-silk counterpane. A wash-basin stood in a corner, religious paintings looked down on the bed from the walls, and on the light-coloured dressing-table family photographs were interspersed with brightly painted postcards of romantically posed lovers. *Insieme in eterno*, they said, *mio unico grande amore* and *sempre uniti per tutta la vita*. There were large windows on either side of the dressing-table, looking over the piazza immediately below us and across the harbour at Santo Stefano. Darkness had now pressed through behind the clouds, and from every direction lights spilled over the waters of the bay. Fishing-boats were stationary blobs of orange to seaward, and along the quays masts swung gently in orderly rows, the decks under them half-illuminated by onshore lamps.

The only restaurant in La Maddalena was the *Toscano*, and there, after a hurried wash, we went for dinner. It turned out to be a fly-blown little room just round the corner. Nevertheless, they had, we had been told, a reputation for local specialities: *Zuppa di pesce* and *aragoste* especially, for the lobsters of La Maddalena are among the best in the world.

It contained five or six wooden tables in a square room: two of these had been pushed together for a French family, mother, father and six pale, sticky children, who had come over from Corsica for the week-end. Otherwise there were only men, sitting alone, absorbed in the food in front of them.

The fish soup, when it arrived, was quite different from *bouillabaisse* or any French variety. There is, in fact, little liquid, only a rich, oily spoonful or two that is more like a sauce for the heap of fish bones, pieces of octopus, squid and small mullet that lie in it. The lobster, served cold with round beans and saffron rice, was, however, excellent, and so was the wine. It was here that we had our first experience of Sardinian prices, and it was an agreeable one, for both then and for the rest of our trip they worked out roughly at half what we had expected. That is to say, meals cost on the whole the same in lire as they did in francs in Corsica. The rate of exchange was then something like 950 francs and 1700 lire to the pound. In Sardinia it was possible to live, staying in the best hotel and eating in the best restaurant, on thirty shillings a day.

By the time we had finished, it had begun to rain again. The cinema crowds were just coming out, carrying black umbrellas over garish open-necked shirts and cotton dresses, and looking quite absurd with them. An old man, dressed in velvet corduroy, went by on a donkey, holding a clumsily folded umbrella at a slant on his shoulder as though it were a rifle. The streets were filled with sailors, elegant in white drill suits, the officers wearing white suède boots with considerable heels.

It was possible now, for the first time, to feel that one was in Italy. The steep, narrow streets, curving like bridges over the angle of hill on which the town is built, were all brilliantly lit from the shop windows along them. Pine and incense mingled with the smell of coffee and barbers' shops. *Espresso* machines steamed in cafés, girls were walking three or four abreast eating ices the colour of their dresses, hairdressers' scissors snipped away in rooms full of mirrors that carried endlessly repeated rows of glossy heads. Illustrated magazines and picture postcards hung outside doorways on boards and, over the curve of shops and down by the water-front, billiard saloons, the green baize tables and polished balls gleaming under overhead lights, clicked to rows of onlookers.

Billiards, played as often as not with the hand instead of a cue, is one of the great Sardinian occupations. I have vivid memories of these glowing saloon interiors throwing their patches of light over otherwise darkened streets. In town after town one would come across then, at street level, late at night, when nothing else seemed alive except this constant nervous click of billiard balls, going on far into the morning. The saloons, with four or five tables each, would be lined with spectators, the smoke from their cigarettes curling under the arc-lights, while they themselves sat in darkness and the arms of the players, cut off at the shoulder, took control. Occasionally a face or torso swam up out of the shadows into the aquarium light of the baize, the arm made its stroke, then faded away into the background of smoke and sweat-stained shirts.

The harbour was deserted now, palm-trees and masts alone vertical against the silver splashes of moonlight trailing between headland and boat, lying along the rippling curves of surrounding hill.

On our way back to the hotel all the lights failed, the whole island suddenly put out as though under an anaesthetic. We walked through darkened streets, past people sitting in doorways. The saloons alone bothered to keep going, and much later on, in the middle of the night, I got up, unable to sleep, and looked out from my window. The balls were still moving over the green baize, making their skeletal kiss under flanking oil-lamps, like so many polished skulls, long after I had heard the clock above the granite column bearing the sculptured head of Garibaldi striking three.

* * *

The next day, though the weather still looked unsettled, was better. There was a blue, rather watery sky, and the light had a rinsed clarity about it. The port now seemed lively and prosperous, with launches chugging through the bay. The trawlers and larger fishing-boats in the basin were being scrubbed and loaded, mostly it seemed with long brushwood brooms. Nets lay spread along the Via Nelson, drying off in the fresh salty air, while men squatted on them sewing and tightening. Stalls were up in the piazza, fruit and fish on one side, clothes on the other. Melons, the size of rugger balls, lemons in green crinkly paper, peaches stacked high under striped awnings, and down the sides of each stall, like ear-rings, grapes hanging in smoky clusters. Near them, fish slithered on brass scales, flashing in the sun as they were poured into baskets; silvery *alice* and *dentice*, sardines and octopus and lobsters, crabs and mullet.

We had decided, the night before, to go over early to Caprera, for there was little of La Maddalena that we had not already seen. Maddalena, for all its prettiness, is a picture-postcard town and its real interest is due to accidents of history. Few places anywhere, of comparative size and remoteness, can boast such 'plums' as this small archipelago; for here Nelson, flying his flag in the *Victory*, made his headquarters from October 1803 to January 1805 during the long blockade of the French fleet at Toulon, and here, too, a bare ten years earlier, Napoleon, in his first taste of battle, had all but been captured. Caprera, linked to Maddalena by a stone causeway, was of course Garibaldi's home long before, and after, the invasion by the Thousand of Sicily, and it occupies a curious sentimental position in the development of modern Italy.

But I had always, since reading Nelson's despatches and correspondence in the seven mauve volumes edited by Sir Nicholas Nicholas, been especially fascinated by the idea of Maddalena. I was at sea myself at the time, sailing in monotonous convoy from Iceland to Russia in 1942-3, when I first came upon Nelson's letters in a destroyer's wardroom. Isolated for what, at that moment, seemed to be for ever in the greyness of the Arctic and North Seas, the Mediterranean anchorages of Nelson's ships had for me a haunting magic. Messina, Stromboli, Capri, Monte Cristo; Elba, Cape Corse, Monaco, Toulon; Maddalena Islands, Gulf of Palma, Algiers, Tetuan. I had gone lovingly over them on the map, and, since then, I had contrived to go to most of them. The Maddalena Islands had been the only name quite unfamiliar to me, and I remember, at anchor off Seydis Fiord on a freezing winter night, particularly looking them up. In Volumes V and VI the address '*Victory*, Maddelena Islands, Sardinia', appears more and more often, and during the year 1804, when Nelson was C-in-C, Mediterranean, there are few letters that do not bear it. I had, also, another personal interest in them; for, in the pages dealing with Maddalena, amongst portraits of Nelson's contemporaries in Clarke and McArthur's *Life of Nelson*, read in that same destroyer wardroom, was one of Admiral Alan Gardner, later Lord Gardner. When, after the war, I was married, I found the original of that portrait, a painting by Sir William Beechey, hanging in the library of my wife's parents at Oare. My wife, I discovered, was a direct descendant of Lord Gardner, described rather formidably by Nelson as 'one of the most perfect masters of discipline', and it was not until I again got out the *Life* for this book that I realized where I had first seen a reproduction of the portrait.

The whole Maddalena period of Nelson's life, a period of watchful, frustrating anxiety, has a clear-cut unity about it. Before it, he was at Merton on half-pay; afterwards, he left in hot pursuit of the French for the West Indies, a pursuit that was to culminate in Trafalgar. But from October 31st 1803, when he arrived at Maddalena, to January 19th 1805, the date of his sudden departure on receiving a signal that the French fleet had put to sea, he was concerned solely with waiting for the French Admiral to break out of Toulon.

Nelson's first reference to his intention of going to the Maddalena Islands was in a letter to Captain Ross Donnelly, in the *Narcissus*, dated October 24th 1803, 'I am going with the Squadron to the Maddelena Islands to water, and shall return to the Rendezvous as soon as possible.' On October 25th he wrote in his private journal: 'Saw Corsica and Cape Longo Sardo; from noon to daylight next morning, we had a heavy swell with squally weather.' The next three days there were constant storms and his ships split many sails. But on October 29th Nelson wrote: 'We found ourselves about five leagues leeward of the place we left last night. At daylight, made sail under close-reefed topsails and reefed courses, with a very strong current against us; but the Fleet being absolutely in distress for water, I am determined to persevere, notwithstanding all the difficulties. At 1 pm fetched Castel Sardo, a small town in Sardinia, rounded in stays 3 miles from the shore; beating alongshore all night about 3 miles from the coast.' On October 31st: 'Not being able to clear the Levisena

Islands, stood towards Shark's Mouth, tacked, and fetched the Northernmost of Martha Islands. N.B. The Straits of Bonifacio lie between the Martha and Levisena Islands, the last of which belong to Corsica. When near the southernmost, Martha Island, we opened the little one to the Westward of the Island Spanioti, close to the ledge of rocks, and weathered them about a mile; we then tacked under Sardinia, and stood into a beautiful little bay, or rather harbour. After various tacks . . . the whole Squadron anchored by six o'clock in the evening, without any accident in Agincourt Sound, under the Sardinian shore.'

The fleet soon settled down at La Maddalena. Nelson's letters over this next period have a double fascination. They contain, on the one hand, constant reminders to the Admiralty about the superb harbours of northern Sardinia and their vital strategic importance; and, on the other, the variously revealing details about the problems of keeping a fleet in running order. There are scores of letters of both kinds. On November 1st he wrote to Mr Richard Bromeley, Purser, HMS *Belleisle*: '. . . You are, hereby, required and directed to purchase as many live bullocks and onions as you can procure for the use of the said Squadron (*Victory, Kent, Canopus, Superb, Belleisle, Triumph, Renown, Stately, Cameleon*), together with 200 head of sheep for the use of the sick on board the different Ships, as I find from the Governor of Maddelena that it will be very difficult to procure the number of bullocks wanted for the ships on so short notice; and as the sheep at this place are very small, meagre, and inferior in quality, you are to supply them as beef, and a Memorandum will be given directing the different Pursers to charge themselves with the produce as fresh beef, and issue them to the sick, accordingly.' Lord Hobart received a letter, dated December 22nd, containing this passage: 'God knows, if we could possess one Island, Sardinia, we should want neither Malta, nor any other: this which is the finest Island in the Mediterranean, possesses Harbours fit for Arsenals, and of a capacity to hold our Navy, within 24 hours' sail of Toulon. Bays to ride our Fleets in, and to watch both Italy and Toulon, no fleet could pass to the Eastward between Sicily and the Coast of Barbary, nor through the Faro of Messina: Malta, in point of position, is not to be named the same year with

Sardinia.... And, my Lord, I venture to predict, that if we do not —from delicacy, or commiseration of the lot of the unfortunate King of Sardinia—the French will, get possession of the island. Sardinia is very little known. It was the policy of Piedmont to keep it in the background, and whoever it has belonged to, it seems to have been their maxim to rule the inhabitants with severity, in loading its produce with such duties as prevented the growth.... The country is fruitful beyond idea, and abounds in cattle and sheep—and would in corn, wine and oil. In the hands of a liberal Government, and freed from the dread of the Barbary States, there is no telling what its produce would not amount to. It is worth any money to obtain, and I pledge my existence it could be held for as little as Malta in its establishment, and produce a large revenue.'

In a memorandum to the captains of his ships, there is again evidence of the Commander-in-Chief's meticulous attention to detail: 'Whereas, Doctor Snipe, Physician to the Fleet, under my command, has represented to me by letter of this date, the very great danger attending the health of the Seamen sent in wooding and watering parties, either on the Island of Sardinia or the Maddelena Islands, which abound with marshes; and as a preventive against the effects of disease the men are subject to on these occasions, at the places above-mentioned, has recommended that a dose of Peruvian-bark, in a preparation of good sound wine or spirits, be given to each man in the morning, previous to his going on shore on either of the above services, and the same in the evening after his return on board, and has, at the same time, stated that two gills of wine, or one gill of spirits mixed with an equal quantity of water, in addition to the usual allowance, is all that is necessary: . . . You are, therefore, hereby required and directed, whenever His Majesty's Ship under Your Command, goes into either the island of Sardinia, or the Maddelena Islands, to order the Purser to supply the surgeon with two gills of wine, or one gill of spirits per day, for each of the men sent on shore on wooding or watering parties, to be mixed with Peruvian-bark, and given to the men in the manner before-mentioned.' But, momentarily freed from the laborious household chores of Squadron Administration, Nelson wrote a series of important letters early in 1804 to Lord Minto, Mr Jackson, the Minister at Turin, Lord Hobart and Lord Hawkesbury, each letter urging action about Sardinia. 'If I lose Sardinia,' he wrote to Lord Minto, 'I lose the French fleet.' To Mr Jackson he argued: 'Should Russia go to war with France, from that moment I consider the mask as being thrown off, with respect to any neutrality of his Sardinian Majesty. Therefore, if that should be the case, would the King consent to two or three hundred British troops taking post upon Maddelena ... there is only this choice, to lose the whole of Sardinia, or allow a small body of friendly troops to hold a part at the northern end of the island. We may prevent, but cannot retake. Sardinia is the most important post in the Mediterranean.'

To Lord Hobart and Lord Hawkesbury, Nelson spoke in similar terms. Yet no action seems to have been taken, and in any event Nelson's fears were not realized. He was at this point almost equally at sea and at Maddalena. An occasional letter to the Admiralty reports a skirmish with a French ship, or the capture of a frigate. But for the most part his despatches deal with straightforward administrative matter, courts-martial, the sending of vessels out on survey, the price of fleet wine, sailing instructions to private ships, and so on. At the same time, letters poured out from the *Victory*, whether at sea or in Agincourt Sound (Nelson's own name for the roads between Maddalena and Sardinia), sometimes a dozen a day, all of them expressing a sick man's longing to get to grips with the enemy before he should die. During this stretch of nearly two years Nelson set foot outside the *Victory* only three times, on each occasion for less than an hour: the weather was unusually rough, and he had to perform several extraordinary feats of navigation in the Straits of Bonifacio, when gales came near to destroying his whole squadron on the islands and rocks that project all along it.

His correspondence, however, shows the extraordinary way in which Nelson combined statesmanship with conscientious fulfilment of an admiral's duties. It is zealous on behalf of his crews and junior officers, taking up every kind of problem, from promotion to compassionate leave, with the Admiralty; it shows over and over again his preoccupation with the fate of Sardinia; and, most moving of all, his letters to Lord Gardner and Sir

Edward Pellew reveal his losing struggle against illness: 'My services are very nearly at an end', he wrote to Pellew. 'For in addition to other infirmities, I am nearly blind: however, I hope to fight one more battle.' And to his own doctor he wrote: 'The health of this fleet cannot be exceeded, and I really believe that my shattered carcase is in the worst plight of the whole of them. I have had a sort of rheumatic fever, they tell me. I have felt the blood gushing up the left side of my head, and the moment it covers the brain, I am fast asleep: I am now better of that, with violent pain in my side, and night-sweats. . . .'

It is impossible, re-reading Nelson's account of this year of waiting at Maddalena, not to feel the mounting tension and excitement, the odds lengthening in the cat-and-mouse struggle between the British and French fleets—though in this case the mouse was bigger than the cat. So that there is a wonderful feeling of release, an authentic thrill, when one comes across the diary entry for January 19th: 'Hard gales NW. At 3 pm the *Active* and *Seahorse* arrived at Maddelena with information that the French Fleet put to sea from Toulon yesterday.' The *Victory*'s log for that date reads: 'At 4.30 weighed and made sail out of Agincourt Sound, through the Biche Channel. At 6.20 passed through the Biche Channel, Squadron following.'

What resulted was, I suppose, something of an anti-climax. The French ships, less hardy than the British, were soon crippled in the violent gales and returned to Toulon. Nelson, beating southwards in the *Victory*, made the successive signals 'Prepare for Battle', 'Form the established order of sailing in two columns' and 'Keep in Close Order', certain that he must meet the enemy near the island of Toro, off the south-west corner of Sardinia. For weeks he waited, acutely disappointed, in various Sardinian harbours, thinking that the French must be making for Egypt. 'Those gentlemen', he wrote to Lord Melville when he learnt the truth, 'are not accustomed to a Gulf of Lyons gale, which we have buffeted for twenty-one months, and not carried away on a spar. I most sincerely hope they will soon be in a state to put to sea again.'

When he finally left Sardinia, where he had taken a great fancy to the Gulf of Palma between the island of San Pietro and the coast of Sardinia, it was to take his squadron to the West Indies, on the long hunt that ended at Trafalgar. Nelson had waited for the French until late April, until, in fact, it became certain that they must have left the Mediterranean. His letters at the time, even the more personal ones to Lady Hamilton, show his refusal to leave Sardinia while the French could still attack it.

It is not surprising, therefore, that the name of Nelson is a magic one to the Sardinians. Before leaving Maddalena, Nelson, in recognition of the kindness shown to his crews, had given to the church there two silver candlesticks and a crucifix, and these, together with his treasured signature, can still be seen on a triangular pedestal engraved with his own arms.

John Warre Tyndale, author of the excellent three-volume history of Sardinia published in 1849, met in Maddalena several people who had been alive when Nelson's squadron was based there. One of these told him that on the night of January 19th, when the signal about the French fleet's departure was received, rehearsals were going on for one of the many theatrical shows and dances that were constantly arranged for the sailors' amusement. 'The scene of excitement and confusion from the precipitous departure and interruption of their festivities was most graphically narrated,' Tyndale wrote. 'It was a dark wintry evening and the quickness of the order was equalled by the skill and courage with which it was executed. The passage is so narrow that only one ship could pass at a time, and each was guided by the stern lights of the preceding vessel.'

Tyndale relates a piece of gossip, then current at La Maddalena, and which he himself saw in print, about the supposed relationship between Emma Liona, the beauty of the island, and Nelson. According to these rumours their love-affair, despite Lady Hamilton, 'became a matter of notoriety', and it was supposed to be at Emma Liona's instigation that Nelson gave the candlesticks to the church, as an offering towards their mutual safety. Charming fancy though this is, there is unfortunately overwhelming evidence that Nelson never once set foot ashore during his whole time at Maddalena. Tyndale is quick to refute the story, though it was, it must be said, by no means necessary in Nelson's time for an admiral, or indeed any sailor, to go ashore to find a lady. Nelson, however, even when invited to visit the Sardinian royal family, who had fled from Piedmont to the protection of the British at Cagliari, excused himself on grounds that he could not leave the *Victory*. When in fact he landed at Gibraltar, on July 20th 1805, he wrote in his diary: 'I went ashore for the first time since June 16th 1803, and from having my foot out of the *Victory* two years, wanting ten days.'

Driving out to Caprera, in a hired car, I had been again reminded of Nelson and of the circumstances in which I had first read his letters and seen the name of the Maddalena Islands. As we bumped over the rain-filled potholes in the road that circles the island, with sailors from the naval base drilling in a palm-lined parade ground to our left and, on the side of the sea, naval launches gleaming white against the low green hills, I felt that in some satisfactory manner two quite distinct periods of my life had been linked together.

Everyone, I suppose, loses sections of his past, forgetting completely what they were like, until, perhaps decades later, chance circumstances bring them back almost intact, with names, faces, feelings, even whole pieces of dialogue. While they surface, like volcanic islands, out of our subconscious, other, nearer periods submerge to make room for them.

I could remember now in detail, while my eyes took in the mauve, rocky skyline above, the pink oleanders following the curve of the coast, the last day we spent in Iceland, on December 24th 1942. I had sailed in a destroyer, the *Onslow*, from Scapa Flow three days earlier, and after a terrific buffeting, during which we shipped green seas almost consistently at over twenty-five knots, we had reached Seydis Fiord late in the evening. We went alongside a tanker and oiled in the icy darkness. The inlet was brightly lit, and they were the first lights I had seen for three years. The next day, with a cool sun turning the snow-jagged headlands into pink icing, I had gone ashore for an hour or two. It was Christmas Eve and we had turkey for lunch, and a double rum ration. We knew we were sailing that night. Later in the day the Captain spoke over the ship's intercommunication, and I remember his words as if it had been a week, instead of ten years, ago: 'We have fourteen ships to escort, and as you have probably guessed, our destination is Murmansk. We have a good chance of getting through. . . .'

We got under way at midnight, sliding out between the winking lights that marked the mineswept channel, to where the convoy was waiting. The destroyers with us were *Oribi*, *Offa* and *Ashanti* amongst others.

A week later, on December 31st, we sighted unknown major units of the German fleet. They turned out to be five destroyers, and the pocket battleships *Hipper* and *Lützow*. I remembered clearly reading those mauve tomes of Nelson's letters on the journey up, and, after the battle which took place in the blizzards of that morning, looking for my books in vain amongst the blood and wreckage of our listing ship. We did not lose a single merchantman in the convoy; but *Ashanti* was sunk, patiently laying a smoke-screen behind us as we engaged the *Hipper*. The *Bramble*, a minesweeper, had disappeared the night before, and we ourselves had many casualties. The Germans lost two destroyers and the *Hipper* was put out of action. I remembered, when the news came through on the radio that the Captain, R. St. V. Sherbrooke, had received the VC, hearing the First Lord of the Admiralty describe the battle as a 'tactical victory unsurpassed since the death of Nelson'. Sherbrooke, too, lost an eye; and I suppose I hadn't thought of that cold, gale-swept encounter so clearly or with a sense of such neat symmetry, at any time since, until we drove down the Via Nelson and along the sheltered bay that had once borne the name of Agincourt Sound.

La Maddalena, with eleven thousand inhabitants, has a surface area of about twelve square miles; Caprera, only about ten square miles, is almost completely uninhabited. Both islands, originally occupied by nomadic shepherds moving freely between Corsica and Sardinia, are formed of granite rock, for the most part impossible to cultivate. La Maddalena, in its four shallow valleys, has maize and a few vines, but both are essentially fishing islands, whose population lives mainly off the Italian naval base.

We drove now across the long stone bridge that links the two islands. A military permit, which we had got earlier in the day, is needed, and at both ends armed sentries, with the habitual listless look of their trade, wandered up and down outside their boxes, smoking, or throwing stones into the sea.

The road to Garibaldi's tomb, the only road on the island, swings in a wide curve, so that at the top of its climb not only all of Caprera, but the whole archipelago can be clearly seen. The weather had grown dull again, and, whichever way one looked, there were patches of craggy rock, knee-high cistus, and occasional slopes of newly planted pines. The sea barely penetrated between all these grey-green shoals, whose beaches and deserted inlets, so rippling in their curves, made them seem to be swinging round, and whose colour, in this light, made them appear only intensifications of the leaden sea and sky which they separated.

As we approached the house the road dropped through bare overhanging rock and swung into a pebbled drive. At the end of this, gleaming whitewashed buildings formed a rectangular courtyard. Huge palms threw their green arms against long, low houses, splashed at intervals with geraniums, and pine-trees edged the lower end of a gravel square.

A smiling, handsome youth, dressed in Italian naval uniform, but barefooted, opened the gates to us, clanking a large bunch of keys. He was, I learned, from Genoa, and caretaking formed part of his naval duties. The naval base, he said, was responsible for the upkeep of the museum and gardens.

They did their job well, it was evident, for everything, from the rooms themselves to the rocky gardens and winding paths, was perfectly kept. The effect, however, was more like the modern summer villa of a prosperous business man than the empty museum of a legendary hero. It was not, in fact, quite empty, for our guide, the first of many exiles we met sighing for Genoa or Rome or Naples and condemned to three or more years' service as sailors or *carabinieri* in Sardinian outposts, encouraged us to call on Garibaldi's daughter who, aged eighty-five, still lived in part of the original house. She was, however, not very well and in bed, and despite the caretaker's exuberant desire that we should just 'see' her, as though she were some rare animal, we managed to dissuade him. But he was, I'm afraid, seriously offended that such an opportunity should not be taken.

The sun emerged for a few moments as we wandered round

the garden, and the smell of cistus wafted up from the steep hillside to mix with the scent of the flowers planted in neat rows between rocks. The open sea lay green to the east, and below the dazzling white cubes of Garibaldi's house, rough moors sloped more gently to the south end of the island. All round us were the crude walls built by Garibaldi himself to keep off the pigs and goats of his English neighbour, Mr Collins.

'In the great years 1859 and 1860', Trevelyan wrote in his *Garibaldi and the Thousand*, 'Caprera proved an institution of no small value to Italy. And even after 1860, when during the last twenty years of his life he regarded himself overmuch as a privileged being, endowed with the right of levying war on his own account, Caprera saved him from making more numerous and worse mistakes.'

When Garibaldi first came to settle in Caprera in 1855 he was forty-eight. The death of his brother Felice had left him enough money to buy a small property, and with this in mind he sailed for northern Sardinia, aiming at Santa Teresa. He had once spent a month at La Maddalena, in 1849, during one of his frequent periods of banishment from Italy; and pausing there this time to look up old friends, he was persuaded to look for somewhere nearer to them. The northern half of Caprera was for sale and Garibaldi bought it for about £360.

The vagabondage of his early life, set in motion twenty years earlier when he was condemned to death for his part in Mazzini's 'Young Italy' movement, seemed now at last to be over. The long years as a guerrilla leader in South America, the changes of occupation from shipbroker to sailor, drover to schoolmaster, the four-year stretch when he fought for the Monte-Videans against Rosas, the tyrant of Buenos Aires, and the eighteen-month exile as alternately candle-maker in New York and captain of a merchant ship in the Pacific, were behind him; so also was the death of his beautiful creole wife, who perished in Garibaldi's arms in the marshes near Ravenna during his retreat from Rome.

Trevelyan is brought, in his account of the closing scenes of what he calls 'the European Tragedy', to some of his most eloquent passages. 'The idealists, patriots and demagogues who had for a few weeks borne rule in half the capitals of Europe were crowded into prisons, or huddled into nameless graves, while in little towns overlooking the waters of Swiss lakes, and on board steamers bound for America or England, groups of emaciated and ill-clad men, their faces scarred with misery, could be seen dividing among themselves scanty sums of money with more than fraternal affection, and imparting in whispers some new tale of disaster and death.'

Thus, when he arrived at Caprera with his son Menotti, the eldest of his three children, Garibaldi already bore the residue of many wounds, both physical and spiritual. His famous exploits in South America and his brilliant battles against the Austrians, when he and his volunteers took over the fight after the defeat of the Sardinian army, were offset by cold refusals of his services from Pope Pius IX and Carlo Alberto of Sardinia. After he had fought noble rear-guard actions, weak armistices had been concluded behind his back. He had been bandied from one country to another, seeking refuge. He had lost faith in the series of rash revolutionary enterprises instigated by Mazzini. He would wait patiently now for the movement for Italian liberation to gain a natural momentum; if the Bourbon tyranny was to be broken in Sicily, it could only be done with the active help of the Sicilians themselves.

It was in this frame of mind that Garibaldi, whose alternative to political and military action was to live the open-air life of a peasant, began his first spell of retirement in Caprera. Vecchi, one of Garibaldi's closest friends, has described his life here in detail in his book *Garibaldi at Caprera*, and Trevelyan, preparing his reader for the great attack on Sicily, has written some beautiful paragraphs.

Between them they give a moving picture of Garibaldi and Menotti, first of all living under canvas, then building a wooden penthouse for Garibaldi's daughter Teresita, and, finally, the present flat-roofed white mansion in the South American style. They cultivated the rocky soil on which we were now standing, planting olives and corn and potatoes. They imported goats from Malta and cows which Garibaldi called by name. Garibaldi's latent pantheism now acquired practical roots and he wrote emotional descriptions, quoted by Trevelyan, of his communion with plants and animals. They lived simply, but entertained a lot, and friends were constantly coming over to help with building and gardening. Vecchi describes how Garibaldi, when in good spirits, would light a cigar and modestly describe the great feats of arms his men had accomplished in South America, or Lombardy; and when he was sad 'he rises immediately from table, and walks out; for he constantly suffered from the feeling of desolation, re-peopling in thought the battlefield with fallen friends, and those who died for the noble cause for which he has ever drawn his sword'.

By some typical chance an eccentric, apparently surly Englishman called Collins was sharing the island before Garibaldi's arrival with the descendants of a bandit, a refugee during the Marlborough wars, called Ferraciolo. For a hundred and fifty years Ferraciolo's family had continued to live alone, through generation after generation, until Mr Collins, with the help of a rich wife, purchased a large part of Caprera from the Piedmontese Government. Relations between Collins and Garibaldi became strained, for their respective cattle strayed into each other's property, and Garibaldi eventually built a wall across—the wall at which we were looking as alternate bars of sunlight and cloud rolled over the crumbling overgrown stone.

Garibaldi's own rooms, over which we were now taken, with our sailor-guide sighing nostalgically for the *continente*, in between pointing out revered objects, are kept just as he left them. The shutters were wide open and the scent of the cistus poured in. Everything is preserved with touching faithfulness and all around were affecting reminders of his greatest days. There was the red shirt he wore in the assault on Sicily, the saddle of his thirty-year-old horse Marsala, named after the landing place of the Thousand, the green cutter in which he had set out. There was the large solid double-bed where he had slept for sixteen years, finally with the nurse of his grandchildren, whom he had married in 1880, and in a room above it the small, narrow bed in which he had asked to be carried to a window overlooking the sea a few days before he died. Hanging on the wall of this room was a faded calendar bearing the date June 2nd 1882, the day of his death.

The last twenty years of Garibaldi's life, when he retired to

Caprera after Vittorio Emanuele had been elected sovereign in a plebiscite, were something of a gradual, restless decline. The historical romances he wrote are of little interest, the various expeditions on which he led his Red Shirts from time to time, against the papal troops or on behalf of the French Republic, were not successful. The manifestos he poured out had no effect. Yet his declining years on the island, when he was often ill and crippled with rheumatism, did not see his fame lessen. He was always, and has remained, a legendary hero, through whom, with Mazzini and Cavour, Italy gained in the magic year of 1860 national independence and political union.

We went through a succession of rooms and outhouses. In some there were oddments of clothing; those, for example, which the engraving in the British Museum of Garibaldi at Caprera shows him to be wearing, narrow trousers, blouse and neckerchief; in others there were oars, an exquisite bust of Garibaldi as a boy, wax flowers, and hundreds of ship tallies from the hats of sailors from all over the world. I noticed, amongst the names of Italian ships like *Pegaso* and *Fiume*, the *Royal Oak*. Here the President of the Italian Republic, with three liners of pilgrims, comes from Rome on June 2nd every year. They make a tour of the familiar rooms, moving off across the neat gravel drive to where, under olive-trees and amongst rich clusters of geraniums, Garibaldi's granite tombstone lies flanked by those of his wife and children.

The atmosphere of Caprera, 'the noblest of all monuments of the Italian Risorgimento' Trevelyan has called it, is quite remarkably peaceful. It has, as an island estate, great charm and dignity, and wherever you are on it the noise of the sea comes gently surfing up. It is agreeable, particularly, because it is still lived on and because people continually come to visit it. Yet nothing has been spoiled, nothing built. You cannot even buy a picture postcard. The island, which English friends bought in its entirety for Garibaldi before he died, now belongs to the state, and the simple devotion of admirers, who come over daily from Maddalena with flowers, has kept about the buildings a warm, natural informality, with none of the normal mustiness and depression of a museum.

The trees spray their shadows and scent over the flat roofs and walls, and the whole island seems to bear the living impress of Garibaldi's personality. 'Such another nature', Trevelyan wrote, 'will never be bred in cities ... it had been nurtured in the solitudes of the sera and of the Pampas, and was preserved intact by the life of Caprera.'

We said good-bye to the sailor, his great melancholy eyes still smiling, and drove back through the tangled undergrowth, past the heavier green of the wind-twisted pines, and down to sea-level. The saw-edged skyline of Corsica slid gradually down behind Maddalena, and by the time we had bumped our way back over the bridge, it was again raining. I looked back at Garibaldi's *Casa Bianca*, but the intervening trees, through which heavy drops now fell, had shut it off.

★ ★ ★

The day we left Maddalena, taking the trawler that runs twice daily to Palau on the Sardinian mainland, the weather started to improve. I remember the small port chiefly now for its smells: the fish being sold on the quayside, the lentils and garlic wafting through into our bedroom, the rain-sweetened cistus, the smell of freshly ground coffee and of brilliantine. Maddalena is an elegant place, with a perpetually scrubbed look that comes, I suppose, from its being a naval base. It not only provides Italy with anchorages but with the majority of her Navy. Nearly everyone in the island is connected with supplying or working on the ships, and the naval base, far from being an imposition, simply gives the greatest number a chance of going home for the night after their day's training.

We moved out into the mid-afternoon heat, edging through a boat traffic that seemed to be going all ways on the glassy water. As we began to get a little way out, the port buildings shrank again to a huddle of white cubes amongst the forest of masts along the water-front. Lighthouses and silver pylons, barracks and customs offices remained after the rest had become only a blur in the dazzle of sun and sea. We passed motor-boats laden with flour-sacks, dogs standing up on their prows, three-masted schooners, training-ships for the Italian Navy, with sailors working on their rigging, and an elegant steam-yacht from Genoa with people lying out on deck sunbathing.

Sitting next to me along the gunwale of the trawler was a sailor, going home on leave to a small village outside Cagliari. He had been in the Navy six years, four of which he had spent in Maddalena. I asked him if he liked it up here. 'It's all right,' he said, 'for a month or two. Only one cinema though. And the beaches are not much. Cagliari, you wait till you get there. A great city. The beaches of Poetto, there's something for you. Miles and miles of sand, big shops.' He said he had a month's leave a year; now he was going off, for a fortnight. I enquired if he went to sea much. 'No,' he said, 'once we used to; now we don't have any ships, only a few launches, and torpedo-boats.' 'Suits me all right,' he went on, 'I like being a land-sailor. That's the safest sort.' I asked him what he did with his time. 'Billiards,' he said. 'Billiards in the evening, football in the afternoon. Only we have to play amongst ourselves usually, there's no one to play against.'

We were half an hour getting across, the sea now a rippling, chipped blue. Palau is little more than a stone jetty, built, with a few police buildings at the end of it, off a small bleak bay. A narrow street, with dilapidated, peeling houses, runs for a few hundred yards, tapering off into open country, and the village had that look of listless boredom, more frequent in Corsica, common to places that are at the end of a line or are a springboard for somewhere else. People come to Palau on their way either to La Maddalena or to Olbia. When a bus comes in, there is a momentary eddy of spurious life, an intense staring curiosity. Women in dirty black dresses came and pressed their noses to the windows of the bus that was awaiting our boat, while a *carabiniere* watched with detached indifference the mad rush for places in it. Immediately the bus left, everyone, one felt, would sink back into apathy. Dust lay thick over windows and the leaves of stunted vegetation, and the sea in the bay hardly seemed to move at all. The policeman to whom I talked while we waited had been in Palau for four years. His only duties consisted in watching the various small boats that arrived and giving a cursory look at their passengers. The customs formalities took place at Santa Teresa or Bonifacio, so his job had really no point at all. There was no cinema, he said, and he had got bored with bathing. 'I shall soon be like them,' he smiled deprecatingly and nodded towards the staring women, 'or like them,' and he looked towards where four old men lay asleep on stone seats under withered palm-trees.

Palau is the kind of place in which one begins to fidget after only a few minutes. The deadness and stagnation creep across like a poisonous vapour. Perhaps, one thinks, the bus won't go for some reason or other, or there will be a sudden breakdown. There are no trains, and there is no hotel. One imagines precious hours and days going by, with nothing to do but watch the muzzled dogs padding up and down the street and the ravaged women screaming at one another as they go to the water-pump.

As soon as the bus was packed like a tin of sardines, the driver, who had been standing idly smoking, decided he had better things to do and hurried away in purposeful fashion. I got out and walked along the quayside in the hot sun. From Palau the Straits of Bonifacio look like an oblong lake, bounded by steep coastlines and with smaller islands floating in it. Only in the extreme west, cut off from view by various headlands, does it seem as if there might be open sea.

The nearest island, the one at which I was now looking, was Santo Stefano: rocky, uncultivated, with a few paths running erratically across bare scrub. A few people from La Maddalena, we were told, row or sail to a small sandy beach to bathe, and I could see the rough white line of the path that led up from the beach to the ruined fortress that Napoleon had captured in his assault on the island.

La Maddalena and Caprera have reasons to be proud of their respective associations with Nelson and Garibaldi. Napoleon's few days on Santo Stefano, however, were a mixture of disturbing melodrama and low comedy, neither, it must be admitted, in any sense his fault.

When, in 1793, the French decided, during their war against the King of Sardinia, to launch an attack on Cagliari, they sent a small diversionary force to take La Maddalena. Napoleon, who was on leave from the French Army and in Corsica at the time, accompanied his battalion as second in command of a company.

Sixteen small ships, with the commanding officer, Colonel Colonna-Cesari, a nephew of Paoli, the great Corsican leader, in an escorting corvette, sailed, in the appalling weather common to these straits, from Bonifacio, eventually arriving off Santo Stefano. Corsica was then at the most crucial period of her relationship with France, and her future status was still not clear. Napoleon was undecided whether his best course lay as a Frenchman or a Corsican, also whether Corsica would be better off as an integral part of France or as an independent country. He was still juggling with the various alternatives open to him, having been coldly received by Paoli on his return to Ajaccio, when the expedition against Sardinia was planned.

Paoli, ignoring Napoleon's vital part in the decision made by the National Assembly to ask all Corsican leaders to return as French citizens, had treated him in a pointedly offhand manner. While Napoleon began for the first time to see Corsica's future in terms of gradual independence within France, Paoli, becoming over-confident in his reassumption of power, was already looking round for allies to help him to break completely free. He had cast his eye on Sardinia and consequently did his best to prevent the expedition. Similarly, he distrusted the younger Corsican revolutionaries like Napoleon, who had demanded the incorporation of Corsica with France while its status had been that of a subjugated country.

Both expeditions were complete failures. The one against Cagliari was easily repulsed owing to the poor quality of the Marseillais troops who had formed the French force. The one in which Napoleon took part failed for different reasons.

After troops had been landed on Santo Stefano, Napoleon took the small Sardinian fort and from it began a bombardment of La Maddalena. An attack was ordered by Colonna-Cesari for the next day, and it was arranged that troops should be ferried across. During the night, however, Colonna-Cesari sailed quietly away in his corvette leaving only written cancellation of the attack. The troops had to be hurriedly embarked during the day and Napoleon, firing with his battery of artillery in an isolated position, knew nothing about the retreat till nightfall. He had only just time to scramble ignominiously aboard ship himself after bringing down his guns, which he had to leave on the quayside. Despite Colonna-Cesari's statement that the sailors on the corvette had mutinied, forcing him at pistol point to change his plans, Napoleon believed it was a put-up job, designed both to make the expedition fail and to get rid of him. When he got back, he wrote in those terms to Paris.

Tyndale, in his account of the event, describes how a force of four hundred Sardinians sailed from the bay of Palau and attacked Santo Stefano, causing Buonaparte to make a sudden withdrawal 'leaving two hundred prisoners, with all their stores, baggage and artillery'. Tyndale, a gullible enthusiast for eye-witness accounts from octogenarians, reported that one old veteran had seen Buonaparte watching the effects of his bombardment of Maddalena through a telescope, and, seeing people going to mass, had immediately said: 'I should like to fire at the church just to frighten the women.' He began to do so and a bomb went through the church window but failed to explode. The pious inhabitants were greatly impressed by this divine forbearance and preserved the bomb for a long time, selling it eventually for 150 francs, according to Tyndale, to a gentleman who at once sent it to Scotland.

Tyndale, a meticulous writer on many aspects of Sardinia, is full of similar inconsequential details. His veteran eye-witness added, however, that all the shells were filled with sand and that so great was the anger of Napoleon and his men that they at once left their posts to get at Colonna-Cesari, presuming him to be responsible. The latter managed to escape them and was hidden by his faithful servant near the powder-magazine on board his corvette. When he was found there, the servant pointed a pistol at the powder and declared that if anyone approached and tried to harm his master he would blow up the ship.

Napoleon, in his memoirs, describes it all a shade more formally. 'In January and February 1793 I was entrusted with a counter-attack on the North of Sardinia, whilst Admiral Trugvet was operating against Cagliari. The expedition not having succeeded, I brought my troops safely back to Bonifacio. This was my first military achievement and obtained me testimonials of the attachment of the soldiers and a local reputation.' Thus do the cool sentences of the exiled Emperor draw decency from the subaltern's hot, vexing baptism in fire.

After a calculated interval the bus-driver reappeared. Many of the passengers, a number of whom seemed to be officials returning from La Maddalena, the rest peasants making for the country, had by this time also got out and were strolling about. The driver, giving every indication now of being in a tearing hurry, sounded his horn loudly several times in quick succession and started off a few yards down the street. The scattered passengers came running in alarm, like hens at the approach of their feeder, and, panting heavily, struggled to get into the moving vehicle. When they had done so, the grinning driver got out and lit a cigarette. A minute later another dust-coated bus entered the village, a sack of mail was transferred, and, with a grinding of gears, we were off.

The *carabiniere*, his resigned spaniel eyes smiling, saluted in farewell and, as we thumped down the sloping main street, I saw him sit down under a great, stiff-leaved palm, bring out a tin and start rolling a cigarette. The day's activity was over.

We drove now, in the stuffy ebbing of the afternoon glare, along steep, winding roads, drawing a cloud of dust behind us and thickening the cactus and olive-trees that lined the road. In the distance blue mountains sealed off the skyline, running like jagged scars from the sea to converge in the centre of a triangular plain.

It was about an hour and a half's run to Olbia, where we had decided to spend the first night in Sardinia proper. The complete absence of up-to-date guide-books made it impossible to make arrangements in advance, so we had to take each town more or less on trust. We had bargained, also, on extreme heat, and consequently, though there was so far little need for it, we planned to spend as much time as possible on the coast, making only brief sorties to the mountains and to selected places in the centre of the island.

We climbed through small, swelling hills of rough scrub, the bare rock showing through in grey, bald-looking patches, with dry, pale-green cistus carpeting the lower slopes. On the mountains to the west I could see oak and cork forests, like dark upturned hairbrushes, while in front of us only solitary twisted trees rose up from sand-coloured plains as flat as the sea-bed. We passed men asleep in the shade of dusty olives, handfuls of goats or cows grazing in arid scrub around them, and the cool tinkle of bells coming up through the heat.

At intervals passengers got out, setting off on their laden walk to rough stone houses lying in isolated groups on the hillsides. We stopped at occasional villages, driving up their main streets and then reversing where the road came to a full stop in a narrow piazza. Here there would be old men in black velvet sitting together on benches, perhaps a water-pump, a few plane-trees, a peeling stucco church with glinting dome. We would drop a passenger, pick up a sack of mail, and then swing out again in a swirl of dust.

We climbed steadily for nearly an hour, sometimes past neat rows of vines, a dribble of green stubble reaching down from bare crags to a dried-up river-bed, now and then nosing through clumps of ilex and sudden islands of cork, the trunks of the cork-trees painted with red-brown preservative where the bark had been stripped.

Then, breasting a ridge of steep hills to the east, I found we had suddenly broken through the first blue skyline dimly seen from Palau. The road now twisted gently down in wide curves to a plain, a rich and fertile-looking nest of green, entirely hemmed in by intersecting mountains. These flashed away in the distance, where the sun silvered their upper slopes, but nearer us they bulged in blue shadow, with trees dotted over marzipan-coloured earth. At the eastern edge of the plain a strip of white buildings glittered along the shores of a nearly circular bay, blocked at its entrance by a table-shaped hump of rock.

Nothing could have looked more desirable than Olbia as we swung through the blue gap and saw the coloured blur of houses from one angle after another. I could see a steamer with black-and-orange funnels lying off a tremendously long stone jetty, salt-white against the blue of the bay. Cranes groped stiffly off the quayside and small insect-like men carried sacks over a gang-way to the ship. Now there were other boats, steam-trawlers, dinghies, lying like a coloured poster against the harbour wall.

An engine shunted along the railway track that ran to the end of the jetty, pushing out black coils of smoke, behind which, on the furthest edge of the headland, I could see strips of white beach.

We free-wheeled down to sea-level, and there were the mountains moving in all round behind us, a smoke-blue ridge of wax spilling between the plains.

We bumped up a street, dirty sections of unfired-brick houses on either side, dust-laden stunted palms flapping their limp shadows on cracked plaster walls. The dazzling town seen from the top seemed to have been a mirage reserved for those who never approached. Small children, looking like Arabs, chased one another barefoot round oleanders and in and out of mud-built huts. Flies were circling in a halo round a mountainous old woman dozing behind a cone-shaped pile of water-melons, tomatoes, grapes and peaches. Discarded rusty rims of bicycle wheels were being used as hoops by two shaven-headed urchins who bowled across inches from the front of the bus and drew blasphemous mutters from the driver.

I asked the conductor whereabouts the centre of the town was and he grinned and said, 'This is the main street.' Presently we stopped in the middle of the steep curve, off which rows of houses tilted on either side. A rough road ran down past half-finished buildings to the left and continuing to the right ended in a narrow piazza with a paper-kiosk and a few benches set under a double row of trees. Depressing-looking grey buildings formed three sides.

As we got out of the bus, deflated in spirit after the promise of our first glimpse, a minute figure, unshaven, with a ravaged ferrety face, and tattered clothes, seized hold of the suitcases, croaked something and started marching off.

I asked him where he was going. '*Io sono autorizzato,*' he said, '*Uomo di fiducia,*' and he touched his stained greasy cap as if it bore some mark of authority. Then, seeing my look of distrust, he went on in scarcely comprehensible dialect: 'I am official porter to the railway, the Number One porter of Olbia. You want best hotel, Albergo Italia, Via Porto Romano?'

'All right,' I said. 'We'll have a look.' He at once humped the suitcases on his back, staggered dizzily, and set off at a shambling run as though in a sack race.

This curious gnome-like creature, who turned out to be a mixture of roguish inefficiency and touching charm, hardly left us during our stay in Olbia. He was certainly the most positive thing about the stagnant-looking town through which we now followed him. It was already late afternoon, but, for the first time since we had left England, it was really hot. A damp, sticky heat that made one sweat and feel listless. The few people sitting in the dusty, refuse-littered streets looked at us indifferently for a moment or two, then went on with whatever they were doing. A waiter was idly flicking flies off café tables; two fat men were fanning themselves with panama hats and taking noisy sips at their coffee.

I could imagine now what the malaria had been like in this low-lying bay, only recently drained and reclaimed. For centuries, not only here but throughout the whole of Sardinia, malaria had worked its way through generations of Sardinians, leaving them sick and inert. Up till 1945, in fact, sixty per cent of the population suffered in some form or other. Then American doctors, subsidized by the Rockefeller Foundation, set to work: anti-malarial research was carried out over a long period, and, with the help of Sardinian field teams, they travelled systematically through the island, completely clearing it in 1952. Their D D T stamp was like a vaccination on every house we passed, wherever we went. The scrawled black letters seemed a joyful attestation of immunity. Although, in the older people we saw, the residue of the disease was still heavy, this general freedom from malaria has given Sardinia a new chance. We could ourselves see what it meant as we went from place to place, and from Sardinians we learnt more. It was evident that, whatever else the Americans may have to answer for in Europe, their achievement here has been solid and constructive.

Eventually the man of faith arrived at the *Italia*, a seedy-looking hotel, with an unimposing stone entrance, set back off a sloping side-street. A heap of granite lay in the road, which terminated a few yards further down; opposite the hotel stretched a row of dingy outhouses that seemed to belong to the factory beyond them. Hens ran squawking through the tangled grey scrub that lay on the ochre hillside below. Like a stadium around us rose the mountains whose blue, lined peaks had glittered faintly all afternoon.

The hotel foyer was deserted, but our authorized porter, who had disappeared for some moments, returned with a key, saying the manager was asleep, and that he, personally, would show us to our room. We followed him obediently up two flights of stone stairs and eventually he threw open the doors of a large room, bowed low and hopped in after us with the bags.

'I hope you will be comfortable,' he said. 'Very *pulito* here. Good view.' He pushed back the shutters. The afternoon sun lay golden on the flanks of the mountains. There were olive-trees outside the window and a pergola of vines sheltered a stone floor with tables round it. I could hear the falsetto buzzing of cicadas and the louder croak of frogs, and in the distance the shunt of trucks along the jetty.

The man of faith gave me a scrap of paper with a telephone number on it. 'You can get me here, it's the number of the railway buffet,' he pointed out. 'Any time I'm available. I'm the only authorized one, you see. I've got eight children.'

He spoke fiercely, his small filthy face and beady eyes making him look a caricature of untrustworthiness. But he looked equally as though he expected to be clouted at any moment, and this fear in his dark eyes, simultaneous with the tough, hoarse whisper in which he imparted information, gave him a touching, absurd character.

'I've had two serious operations,' he croaked angrily, pulling up his shirt to reveal a thin white body. 'Here, look.' He undid his belt and demonstrated the unnecessary width of his trousers. 'Too big. My children eat everything.'

He darted out a sharp glance, fastening his belt and again making a formal bow when I gave him his tip. 'I'll get in touch with you,' I said.

He backed out of the door, still bowing ceremoniously, but the moment he was out of sight I heard him running away down the corridor as fast as his rubber shoes could carry him.

PART TWO

Olbia—Cagliari

THE *Italia* turned out to be an empty, but clean and agreeable hotel, with a charming proprietor who also did the cooking. In any case, it was all we wanted, for we intended to stay there only a day or two, then work our way down to Cagliari.

Olbia, though one of the most ancient towns in Sardinia, is without real interest. Perhaps the climate is largely to blame, but it has a forsaken, apathetic appearance, as though its inhabitants only bothered to keep it going for the people passing through. There seemed to be no attempt to make life enjoyable for its own sake. The town was simply a commercial port, the point of arrival from, and departure for, the *continente*. During the time we were there I was constantly reminded of those curious transit camps of the war, small makeshift centres through which thousands of people passed but which had no character except a depressing atmosphere of impermanence and futility.

It appears to have been always so. Tyndale, discussing the Greek origin of the word Olbia, meaning 'happy', makes his usual dry, barrister's comment: 'A more perfect misnomer, in the present condition of the town, could not be found.'

That was a hundred years ago, when the town, then called Terranova, was at a low ebb. 'The whole district suffers severely from intemperie. The wretched approach across these marshes is worthy of the town itself. The houses, none of which have an elegant or neat appearance, are built mostly of granite, and are whitewashed, as if to give a greater contrast to the filth and dirt within and around them.'

But there had been better days. For example, Lucius Cornelius Scipio made his famous act of magnanimity here in 259 B.C. He was then engaged in removing the Carthaginians from Sardinia, and during the siege of Olbia Hanno, the great Carthaginian general, was killed. Scipio had him taken to his own tent and buried with full honours, himself leading the mourners.

Olbia became an important port under the Romans, though thousands of Sards were taken back to Rome as prisoners. The walls built by the Romans existed until comparatively recently, but now, though the inner and outer lines can still be traced, the stone archways and most of the brickwork have been systematically removed by nearby workers for their own houses.

Its importance as a port varied. At different periods during the Roman occupation it is mentioned as a prosperous grain centre and as an insignificant village. It was several times completely destroyed, in the fifth, twelfth and sixteenth centuries, with the result that the churches, towers and walls rising up over the salt-marshes and along the blue waters of the bay seem parts of a mosaic whose patterns never quite fit together. In 1198, for example, the Pisans, who had fought the Genoese over the original site, completely rebuilt the town, calling it Terranova. Then it was damaged by Moorish corsairs, and in 1553 burned to the ground by the Turkish admiral Dragute, during the combined attack by the French and Turks on Charles V. The wretched Sards, many of whom were at mass, were once again carried off in chains.

The bay seems to have been a happy hunting-ground for marauding fleets, for twice in six years, between 1711 and 1717, it was entered by foreign admirals. Admiral Norris, cruising off Sardinia to intercept the Spanish fleet in 1711, sent ashore a thousand men and captured the town. Six years later the Austrians landed four hundred and fifty men, believing the Sards to be friendly towards them. A priest, however, decoyed them into a narrow pass on the way to Alghero. Here they were attacked, disarmed by a waiting Sardinian band, and marched back to Terranova.

From all these various invasions bits and pieces remain, sticking up through the squalid buildings of the modern town like submarine wrecks at low tide: a Pisan church, a crumbling Roman wall, parts of the original aqueduct, the ruins of a square medieval tower. In addition, vases, rings and buckles of the early Roman period, found in great numbers during the excavations made in the nineteenth century, still survive in private collections.

★ ★ ★

I was awoken in the middle of the night by the buzzing of mosquitoes. It was hot and sultry, and I was covered in sweat. I got up and went to the window. The mountains, splashed with moonlight, shone like wet black mackintosh. The sky seemed lit by concealed tubular lighting. Cicadas and frogs were noisily eloquent, lisping and croaking ceaselessly in the fallow, disused ground that stretched between gulf and mountains. There were about thirty square miles of this flat, desert-like scrub, with thin patches of stubbly green on soil that was mostly a coagulated red-brown until it reached the shadows of the foothills. Moonlight was spilling on the great cones of salt that glittered like blue ice on the long jetty. I could hear cranes moving and a dog barking and somewhere in the distance a man singing softly, a tune without beginning or end, over and over again. The scent of cistus floated up to the window with the pressure of an anaesthetic, and from where it came a cemetery of tin cans flashed like broken glass against pale, dusty earth.

I listened to the singing, the natural melody muffled, as if the man singing was lying on his back. I could see the pale outline of a row of houses, and a campanile rising up over them in the milky light. The dull glow from a single bulb neatly illuminated one square of window. I wondered if it was in there that the perhaps love-contented singer lay. While I watched, a woman came to the open window, leaning out for a second, and as she swung away her naked breasts were like the sudden glimpse of a waterfall.

We had walked over, earlier in the day, to the ancient church of S. Simplicio, founded in the seventh century, and rebuilt by the Pisans four hundred years later. I could see from where I now stood the empty patch of ground, with tiles glinting in the moonlight, that surrounds it. Like most of the churches in Sardinia it has a romantic isolation that makes the interior seem of little account in comparison. All over the island, on lonely crags, we came across these superb Pisan-romanesque buildings, their black and white horizontal strips of granite battered by winds, their towers set square against colourless skies.

S. Simplicio stands on a raised piece of ground just outside the town. You have to cross over the railway line and pass the cork-factory, the biggest concern in Olbia, to reach it. Then, at the end of a mean little street, Via S. Simplicio, full of dung and the smell of goats' cheese, you come suddenly on it: a forbidding, oblong construction of grey granite, without windows, and seeming to face deliberately away from the town. As you come up to the main entrance, the surrounding mountains swing into view. The town is hidden by the railway and by the slope down to the sea, and the peaks of Monte Pinto and S. Tomeo, the massive jagged outline of the Limbara range in the south-west, lie across the horizon like an encircling, blue crust. The bare pale stubble of the plain is broken only by boulders and occasional cows or goats, clear in the glassy distance.

The door was locked when we tried to open it, and I went back to where a pretty, dark-haired girl was sitting outside one of the dirty hovels that form the adjacent area. Her finely-shaped, bare legs were dirt-stained over their fuzz of hair, and she wore a black cotton dress, buttoning up the front but undone except for the two middle buttons.

She was cutting her nails, and, apologizing for disturbing her, I asked where I might find the key to the church. She looked up at me with huge dark eyes and then silently got up, nodding for me to follow. We went down a narrow alleyway and into a small courtyard that was shaded by a vine pergola on top of which tomatoes were ripening in rows. A huge key hung on a rusty nail and the girl, slipping the string over her arm, smiled and turned back up the alley again, still clipping her nails.

The interior of the church is austerely simple and dignified. Four granite columns reach up from an uncovered stone floor and blind arcades run down the sides, with sharply cut arches bridging the nave. No light comes in except through the door, and the cold fustiness of the air makes it like a cellar.

I wandered round the empty building, where only a row of wooden stools were set out in front of the altar, peering in the sour-sweet gloom at the granite pilasters and faded draperies. The girl, when I turned to come out, was standing in a honey-coloured patch of sun near the doorway cutting the hair in her armpits.

The church, she said, was used only on rare occasions, for example for the Festa of S. Simplicio, on May 15th. S. Simplicio, one of the most famous Sardinian saints, was martyred under the Diocletian persecution in the fourth century, and, in celebration of this, special masses are held each year, with horse-racing and dancing taking place in the town.

For the rest of the time this gaunt church, the oldest romanesque building in Sardinia, is locked up with its burden of darkness, the sun beating all day on the blue mountains that give it beauty.

We meandered back to the hotel through straggling streets with mud walls, life seeming to have been sucked out of the pale people sitting on their dark thresholds. Cork lay neatly stacked in yards, waiting to be shipped, the bundles of bark drying out and looking from a distance like alligator skins. Down the main streets, the Corso Umberto and Via Cagliari, shutters were being opened, faces heavy with sleep appearing at them and looking blearily out at the thickening traffic. The sun was losing its heat a little, the shadows of couples beginning their evening *corso* grotesquely lengthened on the dust, like silhouettes of the carnival giants at Tarragona. Dogs in muzzles sniffed about the refuse in the gutters, and at the bottom end of the street a handful of fishing-boats thrust their masts against a square patch of blue sea. The steamer for Civitavecchia was loading up, the great flat hump of the island of Tavolara behind it blocking the bay and turning it into a lagoon.

While we were climbing the hill to the *Italia* lorries trundled past us, laying the dust with trailed water-sprinklers.

The streets were lively for an hour in the evening, the Corso Umberto solid with freshly dressed families strolling down to the sea and back, the cafés selling coffees and sticky drinks the colours of chemists' bottles, and a relaxed quiet, broken only by the hoot of lorries, spread through the green twilight.

At the hotel *uomo di fiducia* was standing in the foyer, still dressed the same, but shaved and hair slicked down. Cap in hand he bowed and formally placed himself once again at our disposal. Were we pleased with our room? Yes, I said, it was *molto pulito*. He nodded deferentially, as though it was only to be expected. *Pulito* is the magic password to grace, and without repeated affirmation of the cleanliness of one's room, a thing Sardinians justly take pride in, one is deemed to have failed in courtesy. Had we exhausted the delights of Olbia? He cocked his head on one side, keeping his heels close together, like a sparrow at attention. Yes, I thought we had. Would we be requiring his assistance to the station, that is, if we were planning to depart? I said we would catch the early morning express to Cagliari, getting off at Macomer. 'Excellent,' he replied. 'I shall present myself at six-forty-five.' The train was due to leave at seven-twenty-five but it had to wait for the boat to come in from Civitavecchia, and sometimes it was late. He would warn us, he said, if such a contingency should arise. Bowing, he backed out down the stone steps.

We had dined alone in the hotel, except for a plump grizzled commercial traveller at the next table. Commercial travellers, in fact, were about the only people from the *continente* we ever met with any frequency and we saw the same groups of faces, beaming, busy, agreeable, in place after place. Some of them travelled in twos and threes, and whenever we came across them in small outlying places, like the island of San Pietro for instance, they would sit round after dinner in the one hotel and tell stories in turn, like the Canterbury Pilgrims. The bottles of wine would be set out, and, formally, with everyone else attentive, each would act out his episode, some simple commercial traveller's tale of cuckolds, with beautiful young wives, old impotent husbands or sexy widows for main characters. But so expressive was the telling, so subtle and disarming the detail, and so evident the narrator's pleasure in the *genre*, that one was instantly transported back to Chaucer or Boccaccio. There were three, especially, with whom we made friends, and one night at Carloforte, with four or five others, including the owner of the local tunny factory and his wife, they went on telling their elaborate anecdotes from ten till after midnight: the eldest, fat and bald, his head like a shiny billiard ball which he mopped with a green silk handkerchief, the middle one rather handsome, with amused dark eyes, and a hoarse voice, the youngest laughing through his rimless glasses, slapping his thigh and running his hand delightedly through his black crimped curls. But each became composed when his turn came to go on, '*Allora io continuo*', waiting for complete silence before the traditional scene was set. These three all travelled in wines and spirits, representing firms in Genoa, Rome and Milan, and came every summer for two months to Sardinia. They would come in to dinner clothed as hunters or fishermen, bearing game or fish for the hotel, grinning with satisfaction, as pleased as children to be dressed up. 'Here come the mighty hunters,' the fat one said one evening, bringing in a brace of skinny pheasant. The phrase reminded me of a day in Basra when I was setting out on a wild-duck shoot up the Tigris. I had arranged to meet one of the Prince Regent's beaters, an Iraqi known as Mighty Hunter and supposed to be the best shot in the country, at one of the small mud villages built among the reeds. When I arrived in my boat he was not there, but a different man was standing on the pontoon landing-stage with a note. Inside was written, by one of the Embassy officials, 'The Mighty Hunter is ill. This is to introduce the Assistant Mighty Hunter. This is his proper title, so please address him by it.'

The commercial traveller in the *Italia* was more silent than most of his colleagues, except in the actual process of eating which he carried out with a sucking vibrancy, each spoonful of *pasta* going off in the quiet room with the startling force of a series of belches in church. However, when he had got through, and untucked his napkin, he made some dignified conversation, recommending wines, advising hotels, and telling us the route along which he would take his glassware. His advice was invaluable, but when we told him we planned to go to Nuoro, he shook his head thoughtfully and said No, he was himself giving it a miss this time, there were too many bandits. I did not pay much attention to his remark, believing bandits to be a largely Sicilian phenomenon, not to be taken very seriously at that. But, in fact, on nearly every day we spent in Sardinia, fresh cases of banditry were reported and it became evident that successful robbery on a large scale was being practised.

We drank a glass of *Villacidro*, a green Sardinian liqueur rather like a mixture of *crème de menthe* and *anis*, with our traveller, and then he excused himself, saying he had an early bus to catch. Later, I learned from the waiter, he was seen being rowed out to the local brothel, a corrugated-iron shack, presided over by four ladies, on a small islet a few hundred yards into the bay. A prudish mayor had succeeded in driving the whores out of Olbia itself, and they were forced to set up on the present site. Business, however, had deteriorated, for the route to the island was in full view, and crowds of onlookers, out for easy entertainment, would be waiting for those who visited the ladies as they landed self-consciously at the quay.

The light had gone off in the house opposite. The man was no longer singing his song of satisfaction. Used to the semi-darkness I could now see the whole sloping road with its peeling houses and bulging ironwork balconies. White scrolls of surf were unrolling gently at the end of it, and a cock began to crow in the yard of the cork-factory. I went back to bed and tried to sleep.

★ ★ ★

There was a knock at the door. I woke up to find it light, the sun rising beyond the gulf somewhere and the air fresh and cool. Cars were hooting in the street, and I could hear carts bumping along and the cries of the drivers as they cracked their whips. I looked at my watch, which said a quarter past six. While I was shaving there was another knock, and the hoarse voice of the *uomo di fiducia* muttered something in the corridor. I opened the door to him. He was hopping from foot to foot outside, cap in hand, unshaved and looking particularly dirty.

'I have come to inform you that the train will leave forty minutes late,' he said punctiliously, standing awkwardly to attention. 'The sea is rough,' he went on, looking furtively down, as though it was in some way his fault. 'The boat is not expected for another hour.'

I told him to return at half-past seven. He snapped his rubber shoes together and turned about, like an elderly recruit on his first day in the Army, stumbling a little.

By the time he came back I had packed and drunk some coffee. The sun was warmer now, but there was a lot of cloud about, white fleets skimming the mauve peaks of the Limbara, and the weather still did not look settled. I had hoped for, and expected, solid unbroken sunshine, but the whole way across France and Corsica the countryside had been green. The plains to the south, which I had seen the day before from outside the church of S. Simplicio, certainly had an arid African look, with their flat, dusty soil, broken only by granite boulders and dwarf shrubs, stretching away to the rim of mountains. But there was no feeling of inevitability about the weather. The wind smelled a little of rain, and the sun was masked so frequently by cloud that each time it came out for any length of time one was slightly surprised.

A small group of people, peasant families with the listless air of those who expected to spend long periods in waiting, and a sprinkling of business men in linen suits and open-neck shirts, carrying brief-cases, were already at the station when we arrived.

There was no sign of the train. At the end of an hour there was still no sign. Every so often a goods train shunted up a side-track, blocking out a section of mountain, or an engine chugged through on its own, clouds of black smoke uncurling vertically upwards and thickening the soot on the dried-up oleanders that stretched along the track. *Uomo di fiducia* sat miserably hunched up at a strategic point of rail from where he could see Isola Bianca, the jetty terminus. At intervals he scampered across to say that the train was just about to start, then he dashed back to his point of vantage, sinking his head into his hands, only a peaked cap protruding from his sharply drawn-up knees.

Apathy gradually settled over the station. Nobody seemed to know even if the boat was in. The station-master, who looked like a Czech general in a magnificent scarlet *képi*, kept saying 'Ten minutes' with a fatuous disbelieving grin. A child was sick in the waiting-room. Two nuns fluttered up to the bookstall and purchased religious journals. A man drove his bullock-cart across the track, followed by a wake of small, shaven-headed urchins. From the station platform I could see the huge letters of the word SUGHEROFACIO outlined on a wall above the grey stacks of cork. The clack of billiard balls had begun in the Corso Umberto behind the station buffet, and the smell of goats' cheese surged over to mix with that of the soot of the railway yard.

We had just about given up hope when suddenly, without any warning at all, a couple of khaki-coloured coaches, shaped like those in the London underground, moved quickly and quietly into the station. At once there was a mad rush for the doors, a few people got out, and within a minute the platform was empty. *Uomo di fiducia*, of whom I had, except for the one job of finding us seats in this rush, really no need, now was nowhere to be seen. With the help of the guard I put the luggage through one of the windows and dashed aboard with the train already beginning to move. We had gone only a few yards, however, when we jerked to a stop. *Uomo di fiducia* came running through the oleanders, looking for the luggage. He glanced up and saw me at the window. I was now hot and sweating with the effort of loading the cases in such a hurry, also very displeased with him, especially as I had already overpaid him. 'Where's the luggage?' I shouted down sternly at him. He suddenly looked panic-stricken, his fears confirmed, and darted away like a rugby scrum-half in and out of doors, asking people and searching wildly about the platform. The whistle blew and we started to move off. He raced alongside the open window, offering extraordinary explanations in between breaths, cursing in a bewildered way. I could see the crucifix round his filthy neck swinging on its string, beneath it a pale white ring on his flesh. Suddenly he caught sight of the suitcase above my head and his eyes immediately softened. He still kept on running, the look of a wounded doe now on his face, and my last sight was of a diminishing figure against the dust, feet together, bowing a little, cap in hand. I felt rather sad and ashamed.

Sardinian trains are small and fast, and they sway on their narrow tracks like ships in a steady gale. They rarely consist of more than two or three carriages, one for each class, divided down the centre. They are too noisy for conversation, and extremely dusty.

This was the first of many journeys we made in them, opening up the landscape in straight diagonals, always moving through flat country with mountains on the horizon.

The landscape, in its contrast to Corsica, was fascinating. Corsica is a series of intersecting mountain switchbacks, thickly wooded and nearly always following the coast. After each curve there is a flash of blue sea, a margin of sand, before the plunge down and up green, rocky valleys and round the sides of mountains. This pattern is infinitely repeated, without rest. The towns are always built on steep slopes, theatrically set into romantic skylines, the island sweeping below them in curves of vine, olive, eucalyptus and pine to the sea. Green, dark green, grey-green, silver; and under the surf of vegetation the grey of bare rock.

The country we were passing through was quite different: empty plains flat as breadboards, a thin yellow stubble on them, broken up only by crude shepherds' huts and low stone walls marking the boundaries of farms. At each loop of the line a fresh range of mountains swung into view, but we never came nearer to them. They remained a blue-veined backcloth to the glassy, sandy landscape, framing it and dividing the sky at exactly the right height.

It was like moving through a series of contiguous arenas, each slightly different from the one before, but essentially the same. There was an extraordinary sense of space. The air bubbled like soda over desert-like soil, pitted here and there with dusty green shrubs and boulders, but stretching away, flat as a billiard table, to the inner rim of mountains. Things a long way off stood out absolutely clear: a cone-shaped hut with yellow thatch, a man in black velvet trousers and waistcoat, red sash and white shirt, riding an orange bicycle, a blue corrugated-iron shed, herds of black cattle on the foothills. The colours came through sharp and definite, as if seen through binoculars.

The track curved first through umbrella-pines and cork-trees, through low rocky hills covered in lentisc and cistus, then straightened out to bisect the plain. Dwarf shrubs, contorted by wind, sprouted singly like vegetation on the sea-bed. Occasionally we stopped for a few seconds at small stations, little more than handfuls of whitewashed houses surrounded by palms. Monti; Oschiri; rows of men in black doublets sitting on benches and gazing at the train, neat oleanders in front of square, painted houses, cemeteries in eucalyptus groves set a few hundred yards away from the station. Yellow maize-stubble came up like a sea round these coloured islands. The sugary peaks of Monte Acuto were now flashing east of us, and on slight swellings on either side of the railway lonely villages were almost lost against their blue shadows.

Tyndale, hoping to recover his health by walking, visited these various villages on foot. The two larger of them are Ozieri and Ardara, the former hidden to the left of the railway in a steep rocky valley, and Ardara spilling its few houses under the marbled peak of Monte Santo to the west. The main street of Ozieri, Tyndale wrote, was the cleanest in Sardinia, 'being washed by a stream flowing down the centre. The fountain from whence it flows is a building of good architectural design, and so arranged that the water for the houses is taken from the first compartment; horses and cattle have the use of the second; and the third is appropriated to washerwomen, like that of Arethusa, in Sicily, where the soap-sud nymphs similarly desecrate the scene.'

Tyndale was consistently allergic to feminine charm. He was prepared in his book to devote pages to the price of wheat, the selling of fish, the conditions of the salt workers, taxes, furniture, family toilets; every detail under the sun, in fact, including accounts of teachery, exploitation and cruelty, is described with urbanity; but each time he mentions Sardinian women he contrives some dry disparagement of their habits or beauty or even existence. Women and the clergy alone incurred Tyndale's displeasure. The Capuchin monastery at Ozieri contained, he noted, 'twenty-eight well-fed and fattened frati', while in the preface to the first of his three volumes he felt bound to state, in qualification of his numerous assaults on priests, 'In endeavouring to expose the abuses by exemplifying the dangerous powers of the law functionaries and priesthood, any prejudiced view or intentionally injurious reflection on individuals is most distinctly disavowed ... but as the palpable frauds, blind superstition, and that mental subjugation by which alone a people can be kept in a benighted state, are such prominent characteristics of the Sard nation, many ecclesiastical legends, anecdotes, and statistics—otherwise absurd and valueless—are inserted.' He goes on to say, describing his visit to Ozieri, 'An antithetical case of veneration was a scene I witnessed in one of the churches, where a mother, kneeling at an altar, employed her fingers alternately in the rosary and in that operation on her child's head which can be well understood, without being mentioned.' The inhabitants of Ozieri, mostly farmers and shepherds, Tyndale found rich and lazy; out of eight thousand 'only twenty-five were paupers at the last census'.

The eleventh-century church at Ardara, whose campanile I could see, gave him great pleasure as well as the chance for one of those circumstantial details in which he so delighted. 'There is evidently a crypt, but no means of descending; and the people have never ventured to try since a couple of dogs were sent down as pioneers to explore, and were never heard of afterwards.' He found the screen of the high altar covered with portraits of apostles, saints and martyrs: 'many of them are exquisitely finished, with all the fineness and detail of an Albert Dürer and Holbein, and will vie with the best specimens of the early masters in the gallery of Dresden, or the Pinakotheke at Munich'.

I was not able to return to either of these places, two out of the hundreds of perched clusters of houses one could see, glittering in the hills, miles from anywhere, on one's way somewhere else.

No other Mediterranean island has villages to compare with them, backward haunts of demons and ringed with *nuraghi*, the neolithic stone forts, three thousand of which are dotted over Sardinia. Their appearance of mirage, as they swing high above the curve of road or railway, lends them an air of fragile invulnerability. The rough tracks from the plains peter out at the end of their narrow street, there is usually a church whose square stone tower dominates the valley below, and in the crude *piazzas* rows of men in black velvet and full white shirts sit gossiping round a fountain. Sweet corns lie in the sun at the doors of houses, peppers ripen on their roofs. They remain aloof from change, untouched except by long shadows dipping from the muzzled peaks above them. From these villages, sites of historic vendettas, of ancient battles, of past splendour even, the trains and cars that follow the old Roman roads far beneath them seem remote and insignificant as toys.

We swayed on again, past Chilivani where the track divides and another line branches off to Sassari, the university town in the north-west. Here, shortly after we had left Sardinia, one of the biggest raids by the *banditi* took place. Half-way between Chilivani and Ozieri there is a sudden blind corner and behind this the bandits set up a road block. Five coaches of Italian tourists were held up within two hours, the inmates were robbed of their possessions (the value of which was set at over three thousand pounds), and then made to walk away singly in different directions. There were ten bandits, all masked and all armed except their leader, who wore black and carried only a riding-whip. A sub-machine-gun covered them from the top of a rock and the only man to protest at his treatment had his trousers removed as punishment. Most of the acts of banditry that took place while we were in Sardinia were done without violence. Clothes were nearly always removed and the wretched victims often had to walk miles in naked groups before they could get help. As they had usually lost both their money and their luggage, this, in the poorer districts, was a more serious problem than it might at first seem.

It had grown stifling in the carriage, every seat taken, and dust piling up so thick on the windows that it was impossible to open them. Around me nuns looked demurely from their Bibles to cast fleeting glances at the landscape speeding by: it was, with its pale desert flatness, its great white boulders, its thin occasional fringes of olive-trees, eucalyptus or cork, a biblical landscape. This was how Israel must have looked, the wilderness and Gethsemane. They returned meditatively to the leather-covered books on their laps. One of them discreetly put her hand to her mouth and, holding it there, lurched to the lavatory. An unshaven priest, his small plump fingers spread across his stomach, snored; every now and again he awoke with a dissimulatory look, mopped his brow with a red silk handkerchief, and went straight to sleep again. Business men in Palm Beach suits, inscrutable behind dark glasses, read newspapers or fiddled with files in despatch-cases. Flies lay like currants on a loaf of bread in someone's basket.

We began to pass through greyer country, trachytic, pitted rocks rearing up all round like volcanic animals in a lunar zoo. The train rattled through them in a wide curve, the village of Bonorva, half-falling down a hill, shuttling into view on our left. Sardinian historians describe the inhabitants as aggressive and vindictive, substantiating their opinions by quoting the story of Don Pietrino Prunas, a local landowner, who was assassinated on the day he acquired his hundredth flock of sheep, and for no other reason than that.

Nuraghi were more frequent now, nearly every rise in the ground bearing its crumbling cone of large white stones, its broken platform and low dilapidated circular wall. Most of them were overgrown with weed and briar, and grasses sprouted from their fallen towers; looking back at them, strung in groups across the dune-like land, they seemed indistinguishable from the crude modern shepherds' huts that lay amongst them.

We began to climb heavily-wooded slopes, oak-trees, cork and ilexes littering the volcanic hills, and the erratic skyline above us dazzled in the sun like sheet-metal. As we wound through the different layers of rock, striped like a cake with several fillings, the dusty plains below seemed to be rolling gently away to the west, ribbed like a beach at low tide. The light was like a mirror, the sun African in the burning impress that, with sudden desert winds and northern *maestrale*, left the dun landscape empty of vegetation except for single, twisted trees little higher than a man. Seeing them from above was like looking down on a sandy cove through transparent water hit obliquely by strong sun. The trees turned into gorgonia and tubicolous annelids, and shrubs, looking against the pale dust like sponges or caryophyllias, seemed through the heat haze to be emblazoned on watered silk. The plains themselves were abstract paintings, cut into rectangular shapes by the stone boundaries of properties; but always there was an austere harmony of colour, brown and grey, a deliberate flatness, shaded off by sky and the thin clumps of vegetation.

The air seemed crisper now, for we had climbed considerably. At the top of a loaf-shaped hill the line flattened out and we slowed down gradually into Macomer station. We alone got out, no one entered, and in a few seconds the khaki coaches had slid out of sight. The deserted railway yards were thick with smoke and soot, and the wide blue hills on all sides were cut off half-way down the edge of the plateau on which we stood.

* * *

Macomer and Nuoro are the two main towns, or rather hill-villages, in the waist of Sardinia. Equidistant from the west and east coasts respectively, they face one another, at a height of two thousand feet, across a low-lying, partly wooded plain, formerly one of the most malarial districts in the island. Macomer, primarily a railway centre and the principal dairy-farming town of Sardinia, lies among some of the best-preserved *nuraghi*, and near by, at Tamuli, there are a number of other curious remains. The town itself, with its railway station set fair and square on the flat top of the plateau, dribbles gradually down the long winding street to the plain. It is a messy, untidy town, with no apparent centre and no amenities of any kind. Torn political posters flap in the gritty air, the noise of shunting engines rarely stops, the main street is stained with oil from the various garages that line it, and the whole place reeks of goats' cheese. It is a junction pure and simple, though round it a few chemical industries, and some food processing and canning, have recently developed. Wool, too, is produced in some quantity, and these various activities have sprawled over what was originally a beautiful village, obscuring it to the extent that only the accretions now exist. The small houses stand under smoking factories, and the six thousand inhabitants have lost their free peasant status without any of the urban compensations enjoyed by workers in a large town.

I decided to stay here rather than at Nuoro. My main reason was that, as it is on the main line to Cagliari, I should manage to catch the express from Olbia without having to waste a day. Sardinian express trains tend to leave at six in the morning, so, if you miss them, you have to resign yourself to travelling all day, in a kind of Kafka uncertainty and uncomfortable conditions. It is, therefore, impossible to catch them the same morning if you come from an outlying village, for most buses from these villages run only once daily, never in time to make a connection. My plan was to stay two days in Macomer, go from there to Nuoro, and return to Macomer the night before I wanted to catch the early express to Cagliari.

The *Stazione* hotel, a grey, begrimed building adjoining the shunting-yard, boasted tired palms splayed out round its entrance, and could hardly have looked more forbidding. It was, in fact, built during Queen Victoria's reign as the private residence of an English engineer called Piercy, a name much respected in Sardinia, for he laid out the first railways. When I entered there was nobody about in the dark corridors that slanted at all angles from the foot of a winding stone staircase. Eventually a magically pretty, dark girl came in holding a pail. She greeted me, apologizing for not being present, and explained that it was her job to clean the station lavatories, as well as to serve in the platform buffet before a train was due. She tried to do both on the same journey.

The hotel possessed twenty large rooms, none of which, as far as I could see, was occupied. They rarely had visitors, the girl told me, an occasional business man for the night, a few commercial travellers, at infrequent intervals an archaeologist or two. Otherwise the three storeys of echoing passages remained untouched throughout the year.

It was unusually pleasant, however, walking in the hot sun. Once clear of the gritty station air, the beautiful transparent light lent a radiance to the surrounding dirty dilapidation. I wandered up and down the dusty Via Statale, the palm-trees along it seeming to be splitting under their own weight. Cobblers were hammering in small, cave-like shops, children sat oily and dirt-stained outside them. Bullock-carts rumbled over the pitted road whose houses were chipped and peeling. Some internal decay seemed to have reached the surface and begun to spread through the village, making repairs useless. Yet this was, I suppose, a fairly prosperous town, no longer dependent on the grudging yield of the soil. There were factories and warehouses and lorries being loaded down every road I went. Rows of shops flashed their bales of striped materials, fruit and vegetables hung like coloured lamps outside cool dark recesses in the pink brick. Raw stinks of wine drowned the smell of cheese and waves of horrible sulphurous chemicals obliterated both. I had the feeling that everything possible was being reduced to its money equivalent and that, in the way in which the life of the aerodrome destroyed the life of the adjacent village in Rex Warner's novel, the factories here had suppressed the kind of existence that went on before they had been built. This high circle of flat rock had been chosen because it was remote and out of sight. Its ugliness would be unnoticed and in any case you had only to walk half a mile in any direction to come to its frontiers. Below you the plains stretched away to the great curtaining mountains on the horizon and, from below, the factory plateau on which you stood was hidden by the jagged rocks that encircled it.

I had a warm *aranciata* at a dusty café table under a plane-tree. Two *carabinieri* were laughing and joking with a sluttish-looking woman whose partly-buttoned flowered dress split over her great breasts. A beautiful silver-blue racing-car suddenly whined at great speed through the street, sending up clouds of dust. I asked the waiter whose it was, and he said, the son of the factory-owner. He could do the forty miles to Nuoro in under half an hour, he went on, shaking his head from side to side. A screen of dust hung between us and the primitive outline of the church of S. Pantaleo on the other side of the road. In front of this sixteenth-century Aragonese building, its gothic tower the one symbol of permanence in the town, two Roman milestones, found along the ancient Roman road, gave the distances from Macomer to Torres, fifty-five and fifty-six miles.

It was at Macomer that I read most of D. H. Lawrence's *Sea and Sardinia*. It seemed to me then a jerky, often irritating piece of work. Lawrence in fact spent only six days in Sardinia, February 4th–10th 1921, and out of the three hundred pages of his book very nearly half deal with the journey there and back from Sicily. 'Comes over one an absolute necessity to move', he wrote in the first sentence, and the restlessness that took him away from Sicily pursued him through Sardinia. The trip was something of a disappointment, though he preferred the Sardinians to the Sicilians and he obviously got a great deal of pleasure from the landscape. But the grittiness in him, his inability to relax, never gave the expedition a fair chance. He had to keep moving the whole time to keep himself at bay. Sardinia was the first fluttering of wings, the first halting step on the journey out of the soft cultures of Europe to Ceylon and Australia and Mexico. It was the half-way house to Africa. Yet it failed to solve the problem, he felt all the time that some kind of allegiance was being demanded of him and that every hotel he stayed in, every train he took, was a surrendering of his independence. He hurried back to Palermo, loquaciously examining himself to see if his soul was still intact.

Yet, like almost all Lawrence's writing, it is a rewarding book. It needs, certainly, more than one reading. The first time one is struck by the tiresome grammatical inversions, the boring squabbles, the strident generalizations about cultural and sexual antagonisms. The natural writer, the poet of wide horizons and pure feeling, is being perpetually thrown out of humour by the suspicious, prejudiced traveller, darting glances to left and right to see if he is being laughed at or swindled. His thrusting moral indignation at prices or dirt or people's manners blinds him for whole stretches of time to anything else. Lawrence travelled laden with knapsacks and kitchen stoves, in the humblest way, always taking the cheapest ticket, but his querulousness over the conditions of the journey, the haggling over reservations and with petty officials, conducted in the most peremptory manner, made it seem even worse.

A second time through, these defects seem less apparent. The rhapsodical descriptions of scenery and customs, the powerful, untidy, passionate poetry of the writing, push these personal details into footnotes. One takes them for granted or skips them. What remains is a series of beautiful landscapes, Lawrence's prose appropriating to itself the physical qualities of what it describes. He went through places like an intelligent dog, nosing into the soil, sniffing, growling, occasionally rolling over with pleasure. The result is never formal, clearly constructed writing: formal prose was never vivid or immediate enough for Lawrence, and he was, in any case, too impatient to write it. But the passages of prose poetry in *Sea and Sardinia*, besides being wonderfully evocative, have a nervous force that makes them illuminating in a much wider context. Without any kind of pantheistic overtones Lawrence provides, by the sheer imaginative accuracy of his descriptions, the country through which he travels with a human significance. When dealing with people he seems to have countless antennae that jump up like water-diviner's twigs when he comes on something unexpected or vital.

When he arrived at Cagliari Lawrence was most struck by two things: how like Eskimoes one kind of Sardinian looked and the resemblance Sardinia bore to Malta, 'lost between Europe and Africa and belonging to nowhere'. All through the book Lawrence throws off curious comparative comments. Many of them seemed to me, when I first read them, wild and far-fetched; then suddenly, often in a place Lawrence had not been to, I saw a face, or an angle of hill, or simply felt a particular kind of atmosphere, that reminded me immediately of something he had written.

Most of the time Lawrence spent in Sardinia it was extremely cold. In Sicily it had been mild and rainy, but with lovely days too. 'The sunny Ionian Sea, the changing jewel of Calabria, like a fire-opal moved in the light; Italy and the panorama of Christmas clouds, night with the dog-star laying a long luminous gleam across the sea, as if baying at us, Orion marching above.' In Cagliari he wrote: 'The air is cold, blowing bleak and bitter, the sky is all curd.' Here Lawrence saw his first Sardinian peasant in costume and at once the dominant theme of his book emerges, the masculinity of the Sardinians compared to the soft Italians of Sicily. 'How handsome he is, and so beautifully male. He walks with his hands loose behind his back, slowly, upright, and aloof. The lovely unapproachableness, indomitable. And the flash of the black and white, the slow stride of the full white drawers, the black gaiters and black cuirass with the bolero, then the great white sleeves and white breast again, and once more the black cap—what marvellous massing of the contrast, marvellous, and superb, as on a magpie.—How beautiful maleness is, if it finds its right expression. . . . One realizes, with horror, that the race of man is almost extinct in Europe. Only Christ-like heroes and woman-worshipping Don Juans, and rabid equality-mongrels. The old, hardy indomitable male is gone. His fierce singleness is quenched. The last sparks are dying out in Sardinia and Spain.'

Lawrence was fascinated by the fruit-market in Cagliari. 'The green and vivid-coloured world of fruit-gleams I have never seen in such splendour as under the market roof at Cagliari: so raw and gorgeous.' Some of his best descriptive passages are lyric accounts of the food shops, grocery stores and bakeries which they came upon as he trailed after Frieda Lawrence while she bustled through the cork-screw streets in search of bargains. The technique of Lawrence's writing in this book is interesting on its own account. Richard Aldington says that Lawrence took no notes at all and on his return to Sicily wrote the book straight off in six weeks. If this is true, then *Sea and Sardinia* is a remarkable piece of reconstruction. Lawrence has written the whole book in the present tense, so that it is a kind of detailed running commentary, with the reader at Lawrence's elbow as he talks into the microphone. In a sense, too, the book is talk rather than writing. A formless monologue, full of brilliant and beautiful improvisations, but with the dull trivialities and repetitions that come from the commentator's need to keep on talking at all costs. Yet so great was Lawrence's gift, so imaginative and immediate his vision, that one follows the flat bits carefully, never able to disregard them for the sudden gem-like sentence that may be just round the corner. The best things Lawrence found in Cagliari were the eyes of the inhabitants and their saddle-bags. 'Those great dark unlighted eyes', Lawrence called them. Sicilian eyes, he said, were the eyes of old Greece. 'But here one sees eyes of soft, blank darkness, all velvet, with no imp looking out of them. And they strike a stranger, older note: before the soul became self-conscious: before the mentality of Greece appeared in the world.'

The Lawrences came across crowds of children exquisitely dressed for a fancy-dress ball; and then, suddenly and typically deciding to leave at once, they found themselves amongst a great crowd of peasants at the station. Most of the men were carrying saddle-bags, slung over their shoulders, so that a great coarsely woven pocket, banded with thick black and white horizontal stripes, hung in front of and behind them. 'These striped zebra bags, some wonderful, gay with flowery colours on their stripes, some weird with fantastic, griffin-like animals, are a whole landscape in themselves.'

From Cagliari the Lawrences went straight up the centre of the island, stopping at the small villages of Mandas and Sorgono, finally changing into a bus to get to Nuoro. Lawrence's journeys, carried out as they were in the greatest discomfort, brought out his best and worst. Reading the whole central section of this book you get a vivid picture of him, narrow-chested, dark, and disapproving, scowling on his wooden seat between vast, smelling men in velvet corduroys, while they climbed and twisted through cork forests and circled the grey slopes of mountains. All the time he is cataloguing the good and bad points of the people in the carriage. He is pleased by the old peasants, proud and erect, with their guns leaning against their tight madder-brown breeches. 'And how they smell! of sheep's wool and of men and goat.' He likes the way they wear their stocking-caps 'as a lizard wears his crest at mating time'. Then he gets irritated because one of them looks possessively at the sexy young woman next to him, or because another looks complacent. But he is reassured again by the hairiness and coarseness of the others, by their centripetal life, their animal disregard for anything outside their immediate circle of interest. And in between his strange prophetic ruminations about national characteristics and Europe's changing spheres of influence, in between the usual comic melodramas that accompany any Lawrence journey, tickets being lost, people getting left behind on wayside platforms, Lawrence picks up each successive change in the landscape. When he feels that no real sympathy can be established between him and the peasants around him—'there is a gulf between oneself and them. They have no inkling of our crucifixion, our universal consciousness'—he returns his attention to the country. Lawrence's responsiveness never fails him. By refusing to select, he avoids the dangers of running dry, of sterility. Sooner or later he warms up and the rich impressions begin to find their striking prose equivalents. What is incredible is that it was done without notes, because Lawrence describes landscapes like a painter working from a subject in front of him. His observations are not general ones, but precise evocations of particular things. Perhaps, in fact, the accuracy Lawrence aimed at was not of a literal sort. These scenes which he describes as only someone could do who was constantly taking notes, may be composite, true in essence, but imaginatively recreated. Unfortunately, his route was the only one in Sardinia I never took, so it was impossible to tell how much Lawrence's landscape differed from the real one. But whatever the degree of latitude which Lawrence allowed himself, the result is one of the best examples of a purely intuitive way of writing.

At Tonara they were lucky enough to come across another procession, which, after a terrible row at the inn at Sorgono, helped to put Lawrence back into humour. The alchemy worked again, the poetic juices began to flow.

In *Sea and Sardinia*, however, Lawrence was experiencing one of his periodic reactions from culture in any form. 'There is nothing to see in Nuoro,' he wrote, 'which, to tell the truth, is always a relief. Sights are an irritating bore. . . . I am sick of gaping at *things*, even Peruginos. I have had my thrills from Carpaccio and Botticelli. But now I've had enough.'

There is, therefore, little in Lawrence's book about the architectural beauties of Sardinia, no mention of the great Pisan cathedrals, the *nuraghi*, or any of the numerous cryptic monuments of the ancient past. In compensation for this Lawrence produced page after page of prose-poetry: 'Almond trees were in flower beneath grey Orosei, almond trees came near the road, and we could see the hot eyes of the individual blossoms. . . . Oh, wonderful Orosei, with your almonds and your reedy river, throbbing with light and the sea's nearness, and all so lost, in a world long gone by, lingering as legends linger on.'

In these incantatory passages Lawrence comes nearest to realizing his true gifts. His winter Sardinia of cold sparkling air and trees in blossom was barely recognizable in the burned-out, dry landscapes through which I travelled. He had no interest in facts of any kind, in relating what he saw to its history or wider geographical context. Thus, his journey through Sardinia was the equivalent in England of a straight trip from Portsmouth to Newcastle, with two stops for the night in Midland villages. Most writers would have felt obliged to show a token interest, at least, in the rest of the island, in its history and customs. There is no evidence that Lawrence read a word about Sardinia, either before or after he went there. The truth was what he saw, it was his own experience that set up the magnetic impulses which sustained him as a writer.

Yet, for all its inadequacy as a book about Sardinia, Lawrence's enlargement of a six-day visit into something that genuinely survives as part of its subject's literature, is a remarkable achievement. This blowing-up process of cursory observations, which in other hands would have seemed shallow, takes on, in Lawrence's writing, vivid truth. There is no padding in *Sea and Sardinia*, no inflation of language. It is simply that Lawrence was able to be interested in very nearly everything. There were no blind colours for him in the pattern of life, and where more selective writers saw only what their training conditioned them to see, Lawrence, without training, had no reservations. The smallest detail, the least triviality of his journey went down as he relived it all back in

Sicily. Each pedestrian occurrence called forth an imaginative response from him, it indicated something about the Sardinian character or about life or about its author. He always managed to work himself free of mere utility. His defects as a travel writer are those of a novelist rather than of a journalist. A novelist draws an arbitrary circle round his characters, within which everything has meaning. He does not concern himself with what goes on outside, for the sample of life he has chosen to illuminate should, and does for him, suggest the totality. The journalist tries to give an accurate picture of the whole and in doing so tends to lose concentration. Lawrence never wrote out of obligation. The arbitrary circle, somewhat erratic in its contours, was always firmly established and there was never lack of life within it.

The last stage of the journey, a bus drive from Nuoro down to Olbia (called, when Lawrence visited it, Terranova), was full of typical incidents. The bus broke down, there was an altercation at a post office, Lawrence had his customary row with the urchin who carried his knapsack (Frieda Lawrence had to carry the 'kitchenino') and finally, in a steamer loaded with cattle and convicts, they were obliged to share inside cabins with the usual sea-sick Italians.

* * *

Though it had grown hot, the day I decided to go to Nuoro was the first really cloudless one. The bus left at half-past eleven from outside the station. By the time we set off it was crammed with peasant women in black dresses, baskets like babies all round them, business men, a party of sportsmen carrying guns, and two nuns. We hadn't gone far when one of the old women and both of the nuns were sick. Several of the remaining passengers sat by open windows, eyes tight shut the whole way, beads of perspiration on their vomit-green foreheads. We might have been going over the edge of the earth.

Armed *carabinieri* on motor-bicycles, though I did not know it at the time, escorted us a certain distance behind. We were now approaching the foothills from which the bandits had been making their recent assaults. They would have a poor haul, I thought, looking round, if they succeeded in holding this lot up. Though one could never tell. Twice, in a bank, I saw the most humbly dressed peasants pull fantastic wads of money out of their patched jackets, dumping them expressionlessly on the counter as if they did that kind of thing every day.

Above the driver's head, a spray of pink paper roses shivered against the windscreen. We began the steep descent from the basaltic box of Macomer to the flat, yellow plain below. A forest lay like an island in its heat-made, watery light. On the rough, higher ridges to our left *nuraghi* protruded in clusters of two and three out of rocky crags overgrown with brambles.

We curved with a great wake of dust through small villages built on steep slopes, at each stopping for a moment in the main street; usually a small piazza overhung by trees jutted out like a ship's bridge over the plain, and on benches in the shade the inevitable rows of old men in black velvet sat close together, as if they were travelling somewhere and the concentration of the journey made speech impossible.

These villages, about a thousand feet above sea-level, each having around two thousand inhabitants, were always bisected by the grey asphalt road that could be seen, with the single-track railway curving in and out beside it, running through the peaks to the north-east. Bortigali was a flutter of pink, brown and grey houses in a small hollow; further on, Silanus glittered white in the sunshine, women swaying through the tree-lined street with baskets on their heads, their faces covered by scarves, like Arabs. The black stocking-hats of the men made them look like crows perched on the white walls of the piazza. Outside the thirteenth-century church, marbled inside from the local quarries, screeching boys, half-naked, kicked prickly pears about in wild games of football. Two small, dirt-ravished girls, pink ribbons in their hair, held a skipping-rope for a third, each circle of the rope enclosing the ragged peaks of the Gennargentu in a glazed oval frame.

We drove on through sloping hedges of dusty cactus, oleanders leaning against the overhanging rocks, before straightening out in the flat thirty-mile plain that separates the two towns. The grey volcanic rocks gave way again to empty yellow fields, listless cows or an occasional foal perfectly outlined in the clear light.

One was still conscious of the damp, exhausting atmosphere of swamp, but there were now no mosquitoes, only a few flies buzzing round the white coifs of the nuns. One of these was lying back, her pale face supported by a thin white hand, as if already obeisance and humility were stiffening her waxen features into the idealized form of a death mask. Now and again a pallid hand, groping out of a painting by Millais or Holman Hunt, settled the starch coif and sent the flies up like helicopters as they waited to make fresh landings.

The heat was intense, the afternoon turning gold round us and the plain at our back stretching out like a marzipan-coloured model, odd trees stuck in here and there, some token cattle, a copse or two. But essentially it was dead ground, overlooked by serrated mountains, leaning back in tiers as though part of some gigantic football stadium. At four- or five-mile intervals, square tomato-red buildings broke up the flatness like toy bricks. These *Case Cantoniere*, each set neatly in circles of palm and oleander, were dotted along the main routes for use of the maintenance workers responsible for their upkeep. Lawrence observed how the modern Italians, the Sardinians particularly, had the real Roman instinct for roads. The roads in Sardinia are, almost without exception, superb, and though the smaller ones are often in a bad state of disrepair, the main linking roads between the towns are like polished asphalt rulers laid over the map. The *Case Cantoniere* have other uses, too, in these deserted stretches of country. They are invaluable in case of breakdown or emergency, they break up the monotony of the journey like oases in the desert, and though their plaster is a hideous colour, they mellow otherwise arid and vulnerable areas.

The grey-green scrub on either side of the road thickened now, and we wound through outlying fringes of cork-woods. The stripped trunks glowed a luminous, deep iodine under the snakeskin grey of the upper branches, and, beneath the rough grasses in between, protruding stones glittered like glass. The fascination of the Sardinian landscape comes from this toughness, the feeling that everything has had to fight its way through rock to get to the sun, and even when it has got there the heat dries up rather than gives life. Yet despite the choked, drained look of trees and shrubs a stronger quality of antique tenaciousness sustains them. The spectacular, the luxuriant, the dramatic, have been eschewed for austere, more classical virtues: economy, discipline, the best use of space. In these spread, baked plains the least embellishment acquires singular force, the slightest changes of colour achieve miraculous lyric contrasts. It is beautifully bred country, undemonstrative, hinting at nobility, always offering plenty of elbow room. Mediterranean landscapes tend to be obviously and self-consciously romantic; Sardinia is a series of lucid statements leading up to an inevitable, but perfectly prepared, climax.

The cork-trees were isolated now amongst chestnuts and silver birch, the woods grew richer and thicker as we climbed. We had come face to face with the mountains, the peaks that always had been flowing along the skyline suddenly were upon us. In a semi-circle to the right of us lay the villages of Orosei, Oliena, Orgosolo, and Orani, where the bandit wars of the next few months were to be fought out. Later, back in England, hardly a week went by without some reference in *The Times* to one or other of these villages. Perhaps a column, perhaps only a few lines, but each describing some fresh act of banditry, some occasion of dedication on the part of a community determined to defend itself. On January 4th, for example, the following paragraph, from its Rome correspondent, appeared in *The Times*:

FIFTY SARDINIANS DEFY DEATH
Oath to Fight Bandits

ORGOSOLO, SARDINIA, Saturday.
Women sobbed here tonight as fifty of their menfolk made the sign of the Cross and took this solemn oath: 'I swear by all my children to fight until death the bandits among us and do all in my power to ensure that the law will be enforced.'

The people of Orgosolo recognized that the fifty men had virtually invited sudden death, for in the local cemetery are thirteen graves of people who had 'displeased' the bandits who have terrorized the area for two years. Names of the victims appeared on a 'public execution' list painted by unknown hands in the town square. They were believed to be people who had helped the police.

This was followed the next day by a more detailed report:

ROME, JAN 5

Fifty heads of local families assembled in the square of the small town of Orgosolo, eastern Sardinia, on Saturday and solemnly swore in the name of the population that the long and sanguinary tradition of family vendettas, lawlessness, and banditry, for which the district has gained an unenviable notoriety, should be broken for ever by the observance henceforth of a new code of behaviour which pledges the inhabitants to become law-abiding.

Orgosolo, with its unhappy history of bloodshed, lies in the heart of a desolate, rugged, thickly wooded zone of Sardinia, where the poor soil provides only a miserable livelihood for its inhabitants and is one factor which has inclined its sons towards crime. Of late years the region had, as a centre of Sardinian banditry, often been compared with the notorious Montelepre district near Palermo where the Sicilian bandit Giuliano established his headquarters. A graphic description of Orgosolo, its extreme poverty and its fierce vendettas, was given by Sardinia's novelist Grazia Deledda in her book *Doves and Hawks*, in which she also described an effort made nearly sixty years ago to pacify local enmities, similar in some ways to that which was celebrated this week-end.

The hope now is that this ceremony will really mark the beginning of an era of lawfulness and peace in the district. Organized by an influential non-political committee and blessed by the Pope in a special telegram, it was attended by more than two thousand people, including Sardinian senators and deputies.

After the fifty heads of families, placing their right hands on a wooden cross lying on a table in the square, had sworn, amid a solemn silence, 'to work well and faithfully in order to guarantee the observance of what is established by the statute of our association for the well-being of the district', the Bishop of Nuoro, the prefect, and a senator made short speeches, and the gathering then attended a *Te Deum* of thanks in the local church, upon the walls of which, only two years ago, were scrawled the names of those 'condemned' to death in family vendettas and some of whom were actually assassinated. A memorable day ended with what is described as a gargantuan banquet of the population, for which more than a hundred lambs and dozens of pigs were killed and many casks of wine were broached.

Serious commentators make the point, however, that the good intentions of the Orgosolese will bear fruit only if the Government gives adequate economic and financial aid to the district.

This banquet was in the spirit of the medieval *Paci*, the formal renewals of friendship that used to take place after severe local vendettas by neighouring villages or families. The rival factions, brought together by priests or elders acting as mediators, met in church, were harangued from the pulpit on brotherly love, and finally shared a gigantic feast. Guns were fired in the air, marriages arranged, and the *Danza di Sangue*, a ritual dance of blood pledging responsibility for his village, was performed by the head of the respective sides. If the people concerned did not take kindly to religious arbitration *Ragionatori*, or umpires, were appointed, and the differences were thrashed out by these respected men in some secluded meeting-place. These were, in fact, courts of law based on common sense rather than on legal principles, and it became a matter of honour to agree to the findings. The *Ragionatori* received no payment for their work, which frequently involved a great deal of time spent in collecting evidence, as well as numerous discussions, but they acquired increasingly important positions in public esteem, and, according to their dialectical skill and integrity, great local fame.

The outbreaks of banditry that were now taking place, however, seemed less matters of honour and family feuds than straightforward acts of robbery. The man next to me in the bus, a thin sallow fellow in velvet, with crooked nose and a stubble of white hairs round his sunken mouth, shifted the gun between his knees when we passed a notice, pasted on a wall on the outskirts of Nuoro, offering a reward for some particular bandit. He replied, when I asked him what was causing this renewal of banditry, 'American films. They're babies. They see films about gangsters, and they imitate them. If they live in primitive villages they can't become gangsters, so they become bandits. Before the American films came here there were no bandits. Once, long ago, in the seventeenth or eighteenth century, real bandits inspired literature. They made these books into films and now, since the war, young men who had never read a book learn how to be bandits from films.'

He shook his long terrier-like face as we drove up the steep main street of Nuoro, muttering to himself about how ridiculously everyone behaved nowadays. 'They don't know what they're doing, they're children,' he said. 'Lazy. They'll do anything to avoid earning money the proper way. I know, I have to teach them. I'd burn the cinemas if I had my way.'

He had mounted the bus only a few miles back, having walked down from his village in the hills. I asked him if he came in often. 'Once a week,' he answered, 'to do some shopping, pay a visit, and,' he laughed the dry sardonic laugh to which Sardinia gave its name, 'to go to the cinema.' I noticed, as we began to slow down in a wide tree-lined square, that huge posters were showing a snarling Humphrey Bogart, a revolver pointing from his hip and a girl with bared breast shrinking sexily away.

* * *

Lawrence was quite right, of course; there is nothing to see in Nuoro—except Nuoro itself. The existence of the town is a more spectacular achievement than anything that could be found in an art gallery. Each view out has a calculated theatrical splendour: dramatic peaks white under blue sky, grey falling ridges with dark patches of forest like birthmarks on them, valleys twisting round the base of mountains, and the fawn, bare plain running away to the tower of Macomer in the west. In this obvious sense, Nuoro is not typical of Sardinia. Nature, so discreet elsewhere, has played all her cards here. The peaks and crags of the Gennargentu, dazzling in their equal nearness and remoteness, have the picture-postcard beauty of the Swiss Alps. The air is sweet and cool. Ortobene, the granitic mountain towering above Nuoro to the north-east, has a statue of Christ the Redeemer near its summit. Expeditions and pilgrimages are made there, in the hot weather it is a favourite place for picnics. This, in fact, is tourist country that has not received its tourists, that is saved by inaccessibility.

Grazia Deledda's novels have made this part of Sardinia familiar to Italians. Though she won the Nobel Prize in 1926, her books have not, I think, been read much outside Italy. Yet when she died, aged sixty-one, in 1936, she had done for Sardinia much of what Mérimée and Dumas *père*, in their different ways, did for Corsica. She had given Sardinia a place in literature. Mérimée's *Colomba* was a work of conscious literary art beyond the range of

Grazia Deledda, but although her novels have some of the flamboyance of Dumas's *Les Frères Corses*, they are much more intimately related to their subject. Certainly *L'Erdera*, recently made into a film, has none of Dumas's histrionic and romantic excess. Grazia Deledda, who was born in Nuoro, happened to have at hand a store of unusual anecdote as well as much untapped and fascinating local history. With this she interwove fictional romance in the style of the nineteenth century. Nuoro, with its mountains and hidden valleys, its traditional costumes and traditional bandits, its priests and prisons, in a sense wrote her novels for her. What in another writer would have seemed the artificial result of historical research, an exploiting of the picturesque, was for her simply an act of memory. The novels of Grazia Deledda are realistic in the way that Silone's or Verga's are: that is to say, they deal in detail with contemporary issues in backward local settings. It is this backwardness that gives them a period flavour. 'Contemporary' however is a word that takes on a different meaning when applied to Nuoro, for Nuoro, even now when it has sharp political problems, a Communist party, modern flats in the German style of the 'thirties, is an eighteenth- or nineteenth-century town.

Here, more than anywhere in Sardinia, traditional costumes flourish. Usually, traditional costumes in Europe look artificial and affected, their wearers self-conscious, with the air of those on their way to some amateur theatrical. The Nuorese wear their costumes simply, like functional clothes. The black stocking-caps, smocks, waistcoats and gaiters of the men are shiny with use, the velvet rubbed away. They are workers' clothes, not fancy dress. It is only the full white sleeves and white breeches, dazzling in the sun, that create an effect of economical elegance. The short, stocky men with white, neat beards are transformed from peasants into romantic outlaws. And the women, too, in brocade jackets over white blouses, in full embroidered skirts made out of two solid-coloured materials, the front and the back different, dress to their surroundings. Banks, garages, cinemas, fun-fairs spill down the hill, but the great lemon-and-white mountains form the real arena, and it is from them that Nuoro takes its character; in keeping with them its people create their own drama.

Nuoro is the capital of Barbagia, the province singled out by both Ovid and Dante for the indecent dress of the women, and is also the seat of a bishop. It is a constantly developing agricultural town, the modern extensions spreading out from the old enclosed centre and seeming to press it thinner as new buildings reach higher up the hill and deeper into the valley. The angle at which the town clings to the rock gives nearly every house a clear view of the plain below. Most of the recent additions are white rectangles, so that from a distance Nuoro looks like a Picasso painting of the cubist period. From this mass of regular, intersecting and similar-sized blocks ambitious public buildings break up the horizontal symmetry. The prison, for example, the dominating feature of the town, is circular, and might be taken from the outside for a casino or luxurious nursing-home. Its round, flat roof swells out like a huge stone mushroom, vultures and eagles swooping under its therapeutic dominion. The biscuit-coloured post office completely overawes the centre of the town, thrusting itself into the blue air like a palace. The magnificence of Sardinian post offices and banks is a public-works compensation for the lack of fine private houses. It is in these imposing sandstone monuments that the transference of power from the individual to the state can be seen at its most emphatic. Less impressive than these two emblems of civic pride are the cathedral and the new *Albergo Ortobene*, the only other buildings to distract the eye from the shapely arrangement of town and mountain. The cathedral, built in the neo-classic style, was begun in 1836 and completed seventeen years later. It still looks unfinished, however, and considerable activity seemed to be taking place when I visited it. A priest, who was supervising workmen as I entered, and of whom I asked a few questions, insisted on writing the answers down in my notebook lest I should forget them. He then signed his name with a flourish and gave me full permission, amounting almost to instructions, to mention him in connection with anything I might write about the cathedral. The *bravura* of his signature unfortunately broke the pencil and the completion of his name with mere indentations of the paper did not survive the passage of time. I must offer this as explanation of my failure to take advantage of his generosity. The cathedral, like Nuoro itself, is more beautiful in situation than composition. Large, gloomy, somewhat cold in feeling, it stands at the top of a long flight of stone steps and seems altogether too pretentious for its purpose. In some new industrial town of northern Italy it might have looked all right. Here, on this superb promontory open to wind and sky, something simpler and more solid was needed. Elsewhere in Sardinia I noted with admiration how wonderfully the Pisans, with their black and white striped basilicas, built on remote crags, had made use of the romantic wildness of the landscape. Only the primary virtues of strength and simplicity of conception, a design that created clear, unfussed outlines, could have survived in this towering, elaborate scenery.

The *Albergo Ortobene*, on the other hand, is a modern building, several storeys high, with the cool, blind look of much contemporary architecture. In the upper part of Nuoro the houses are compromises between varying styles of European building, the drab, olive stone and plaster creating the effect of a German suburb. These villas lie virtually on the backs of the eighteenth- and early nineteenth-century houses that run in parallel streets beneath them. Walking uphill at right angles from the Corso Garibaldi, the main street, you move in spurts of a century at each intersection. The higher you get the more haphazard and colourless the town becomes. The vitality lies with the past in the centre. On the outer rings of Nuoro heaps of stone, scaffoldings, and dumps of various kinds mark the latest efforts to get a grip on the granite. The roads are so steep, however, that everything now being built has a temporary, makeshift air. A push, one feels, and the edges of Nuoro would crash into the valley, leaving behind only the narrow cobbled circus, with streets splaying off it like the spokes of a wheel, at the eastern end.

★ ★ ★

I lunched in the restaurant of the *Ortobene*, a green-shuttered room like a water-tank. Waiters glided through the sea-bed light silently as fishes. Some stood motionless in the shadows, observing the affluent eaters with inward eyes, others flicked at flies with white napkins. There were more waiters than clients. Paper flowers leaned, pink, cinnamon and turquoise, out of long thin vases, and a radio played softly from behind the bar outside. A dozen brief-cases hung from pegs along the wall.

Out in the hot street I could hear children shouting to one another. A hoop bowled down the pavement, followed by thin bare legs cut off at the knee by the shutters. The white-coated waiter at my elbow, an elegant handsome young man with a slinky walk, slid away my salad plate, brought a bowl of plump grapes, and asked deferentially if I could sell him some Senior Service cigarettes. I offered him one from the packet I had left on the table, but he declined. 'My desire for them is so great,' he said, 'I should only be provoked by smoking an odd one.'

It was rather comforting to find such a passion for an English cigarette. I asked him how he had acquired it. 'During the war,' he grinned. 'One got many new tastes. A British naval officer in Cagliari gave me some as a tip. I did some small services for him, and he sent me some for a little while afterwards. Then he stopped.' He smiled reprovingly.

I said they were hard to get in England, too. He inclined his head and, bowing, walked briskly away.

The room was festooned now with blue cigar-smoke. Cups and glasses clinked under whirling fans. I began to regret the huge plate of *riso bianco al burro* I had eaten before the *vitello tonnato*. Perhaps a cognac might keep sleep at bay a little longer. I summoned the waiter back, ordered some coffee and brandy to be brought to me in the lounge, and went to look for an armchair.

A few fat men in crumpled alpaca suits sat round a table talking. Business men, I thought, commercial travellers or perhaps civil servants. The waiter appeared with coffee and a tray of liqueurs. He poured the cognac, looked disarmingly at the Senior Service packet in my hand and turned to go away. I called him and gave him the cigarettes. He flashed his teeth, thanked me and disappeared. The men who had been sitting at the window table left. When the waiter reappeared he held a red flower in his hand. He came up and laid this by my cup, with the stalk pointing towards me like a knife.

'If you will excuse me, sir, the bill,' he said, putting a piece of paper deprecatingly in front of me. 'You will be my last customer, for today I am leaving the hotel.'

He smirked. I looked at him more carefully. He was well built and had black wavy hair. 'I am to be a singing-boxer,' he said, 'on the music halls. Those gentlemen who just left are in the boxing game and I am to return with them. On Saturday there is a championship fight between an Italian boxer and the Sardinian middle-weight at Cagliari. I am to fight exhibition fights with the winner all round Italy. Then I shall sing at the microphone.' He thought for a moment—'Or perhaps I shall sing first. Yes, that might be better.'

I had seen posters up for Saturday's fight at Cagliari. I asked whether he had done much boxing and singing already. In the Army, he replied, he had been champion of his regiment, but he did not care for real fights. Exhibition bouts were more in his line; that was science, not just strength. He had sung, too, with a local band. Last year at the Festival of the Redeemer in Nuoro he had been 'discovered' by the promoters, who came each year for a shooting holiday in the Gennargentu.

I wished him good luck. He said perhaps he would come back here when he was older, it was a good hotel. A Singing-Boxer's life was short, even an Exhibition Singing-Boxer's. At the same time it was important to get away and make some money when the chance came. I suggested that, when his boxing days were over, he could continue as the Singing-Waiter. They were very fond of them in Hollywood, he might get a job there. Surprisingly, he did not like the idea. The Americans were not artistic, he said, he liked life to be artistic. In any case he did not expect to get an offer. The Americans only made offers to girls. I agreed with him, paid the bill, and said I hoped he would send me the programme of one of his performances. He took my address solemnly and said he would, of course. But so far, over a year later, it has not come.

I emerged into the afternoon sunshine. The singing-boxer had taken away my desire to sleep. Or perhaps it was the cognac. Two cars had drawn up on the sloping street outside the hotel. People were beginning to arrive for the *festa* in three days' time, the same *festa* at which the singing-boxer had been discovered. There would be people from nearly every village in Sardinia, dressed in costume. The hotel was completely booked up, I learned from the manager who was standing in the entrance, but he could fit me in if I wanted to stay. I said how sorry I was to have to go, but I hoped to attend the *festa* at Oristano in a few weeks' time. There was always another year, anyway. Yes, he concurred, putting his pale round head on one side, there was always another year.

Children were still bowling their hoops down the Via Attilio Deffenu. A few men were working on the first stages of a new building, their picks ringing out on large white stones. Cars lined the street down one side, mostly Lancias and Fiats, with American-type bodies and some of them protected from the sun with pyjama-striped materials fitted over them, so that they looked like pets—great aluminium dogs asleep in the heat. An old man came slowly down the hill on a donkey, the animal's legs stretched out stiffly to resist the slope. The man's chessboard colouring was split by a scarlet sash round the waist, and at each step his black stocking-cap bobbed like a tassel. A child ran his hoop screeching past the donkey and was overtaken in turn by a stuttering Vespa. The old man wiped his face with the hanging end of his cap and beat the donkey across the buttocks.

I went down the Via Papandrea and along in the shadow of the huge sand-coloured post office. The bright light lay like water on the cobbles of the Piazza Crispi. Rows of old men lay in the shade, their black, gaitered legs stretched across the pavement, idly swishing at flies with their whips. Several stalls were up on the lower side of the piazza. Large women sat on stools in the fierce sun, seeming to have split open with ripeness like the fruit around them. Folded cloths lay like saucepan-lids on their heads, and melons, oranges, red peppers, tomatoes, grapes, figs and artichokes, some built up in pyramids, others cosseted in green *crêpe* paper, reposed under their patient custodianship.

The town, asleep on its feet, was alive only in its planes and diagonals: sun on brass scales and windscreens, pavements hit by light at oblique angles and hard with glare, tilted red roofs blotting up heat. The grey rock that ringed the town filled in the angles of houses and streets like cement.

I strolled under an avenue of dust-laden trees and turned up the Corso Garibaldi towards the old quarter. A smell of wine and cheese came through the bead curtain of a restaurant. The pencil line of the mountains bisected the sky. Most of the shops were shut. The Corso opened out at the top into two piazzas, the Piazza Plebiscito and the Piazza San Giovanni. The main building in the former was the headquarters of the local Communist party, while the Piazza San Giovanni was covered in monarchist posters. Groups of men were sitting on walls under the protective security of the respective slogans. Between the two groups, like a stolid but respected umpire, stood a church. Birds strutted about amongst muzzled dogs on the dusty squares, and at the bottom of wide white steps I could see some soldiers falling in on the parade ground of a barracks. Beyond, where the mountains began to rise again in a series of razor-edged gradients, a man was walking beside his donkey on the path that twisted between the wooded foothills. Every moving object attracted the eye like a magnet in the clear air, so that the tilt of his gun, easily discernible even though he was nearly two miles away, merely emphasized the dwindling, sharp perspective of the mountains racing above him in their diagonals to a distant blue smudge.

Above the cathedral the Via Aspromonte leads out to Orosei, and then the town peters out in narrow tracks as the hill slopes down to the south. Small box-like houses, with rough chicken-runs off them, stand amongst refuse and débris on roads that have never been made. The town suddenly comes to an end, stray, humble buildings desperately clinging to its edges before the rock begins to drop at too steep an angle.

This part of the hill was now in shadow, Nuoro itself hidden from sight. Pine-trees covered the upper slopes, circling the bald tops of buildings like a tonsure. The whitewashed villas that lay in terraces all faced inwards, away from the open switchback of the valley and the purple-blue mountains. Only back-yards and kitchens looked out on the bare, green plain through which the white road to Orosei twisted like a scar and above which, wonderfully grouped, the granite peaks flashed in the declining sun. The whole town seemed to have been deliberately built to avoid the harsh beauty of the mountains, as if somehow they constituted a threat to contentment.

Narrow roads twisted under giant boulders, flat, grey rocks

overhung blind corners. A few cork-trees were dotted amongst rough scrub; scraggy cacti marked paths cut into the undergrowth. Somewhere a solitary church bell was ringing, its melancholy echo thrown back by the surrounding crags. I could see goats moving over the green, plasticine-looking flanks of Ortobene, their tinkle like the constant shaking of ice. Reference books describe the whole of these mountains as once being covered in oak-trees, and again plans have been made for the reforestation of the whole of the Gennargentu. Now the barrenness of rock was broken only by dark patches, the glitter of a church near the summit, the dry parting of a road through thin myrtle.

I turned back into the town. Clouds were lying over the distant peaks like gunsmoke. The air had become oppressive and it began to look like thunder. On my way back I heard what sounded like a game of tennis. It seemed such an unlikely possibility that I tried to trace where the sound was coming from. I followed a path that wound uphill to some large white gates. The postman was coming up the road behind me. Inside the gates, at the top of a neat drive, on one side of which were carefully planted firs and on the other a series of flower-beds, an extraordinary chocolate-and-white house faced across the valley to the mountains. Clearly from behind the towers and crenellated façades came the regular twang of racket on ball, the carry of voices calling out the score.

While I stood looking with astonishment at this confectionery building, a mixture between Gaudí's unfinished Templo de la Sagrada Familia in Barcelona, a Surrey baronial mansion and a Swiss chalet, the postman arrived at the gate and rang a bell. A minute later a maid, dressed in black and with a white apron, trotted down the front steps to fetch the letters. The postman took a bundle of mail out of his satchel and I could see, among various Italian illustrated papers, the shiny contours of a rolled *Tatler*.

The meeting between the postman and the maid seemed to be in the nature of a tryst. I walked away in a wide detour past the barracks and the cathedral, up through the Via Mannu and into the Via Grazia Deledda. I could still see the jutting outlines of this valiant outpost of civilization nestling among its pine-trees. I met the postman hurrying downhill a few moments later and he smiled at me. He nodded up to the brown stucco tower that rose like a periscope over the trees and asked whether I admired the house. I was framing a suitable reply when he said, well, it was a fine house, very finely furnished, and there were fine servants too. I should have had a look at the gardens, and did I know there was a tennis court? Nice people, the owners, very learned. Rich too. Owned factories, lived most of the year in Rome. Some of the townspeople didn't approve, of course, the Communists for instance. Everyone couldn't be rich, he said, it was a matter of luck. He didn't grudge anyone their money. All the same, that was not everyone's view. Some people thought of everything in political terms, one had to be either a Fascist or a Communist, or, if one didn't happen to take an extreme interest in politics, they regarded one as an irresponsible weakling who ought to be suppressed. There were those in Nuoro, would you believe it, who would not do business with people of different political views, let alone meet them. He clicked his tongue in perplexity. All the same it didn't seem quite right that some should be nearly starved and others not work for their money, did it?

He broke off suddenly, pointing to a house for which he had letters, blew his whistle and waved me good-bye.

Down the Corso Garibaldi shops were reopening. The hard dazzling light had softened now to leave a syrupy glow on the walls of houses. The groups under the scrawled slogans and political posters in the Piazza Plebiscito had thickened. Girls in brightly coloured skirts, solid reds and greens, with stiff white blouses, walked in twos and threes behind the backs of the old men perched like clay pigeons on the low walls. Bare-footed women in tattered black dresses, their heads in ornately embroidered scarves, came and stood in turn to use the water-pump. I turned down past haberdashers' shops, their dark interiors lit by the hundreds of brilliant linens and cottons that lay piled like swathed mummies, past picture-postcard shops and barbers, paper-kiosks and flamboyant fruiterers.

In the public gardens, an oasis of green in the dusty Piazza Vittorio Emanuele, couples sat under palm-trees watching the fountains splash on the goldfish ponds. Children were sailing tiny boats on the nearly stagnant surface, and on the hard wooden benches along the freshly watered flower-beds more old men sat stiffly together, erect as though they were being photographed. Below the gardens, loud music came from the amplifiers in an adjacent, bright-blue fun-fair. Coloured lights marked out the area of a track for miniature racing-cars and above them swings curled up over red and gold booths. The track, as I walked up to the barriers, was empty, except for two young priests roaring round behind one another, the yellow cars occasionally colliding with a screech of brakes. Were it not for their giggles it might have seemed, as they crouched low over the wheel, rimless glasses glinting over their black cassocks, that some extraordinary expiatory rite was being enacted.

I took the evening bus back to Macomer. We drove into the sunset all the way, the sky sliding successive screens of mauve, pink and yellow over the windscreen. Men in green velvet corduroys and carrying guns got on at various places along the road, the women with them holding sacks bulging with game. Higher up the slopes of the Gennargentu huntsmen were coming in from Italy for the wild boar and moufflon, the partridges and pheasants. Here it was mostly rabbits and varieties of small birds. At intervals the bus stopped, and, as we moved on again, I could see the women clambering ahead of the men as they picked their way through narrow clearings in the undergrowth, making in the gathering dusk for the pale glimmering shapes of their isolated houses.

Fires were burning in the last electric-green light over the plain, small dots of flame on the edge of woods marking the night encampments of shepherds. Villages hung like nests of stars in the smeared velvet of the hills. By the time we had begun to climb again darkness had fallen and Macomer, on the great promontory above us, glittered like a huge illuminated church.

We stopped outside the station café, where a few *carabinieri* were drinking coffee under the plane-trees. Everyone scrambled out and disappeared down the ill-lit Corso Umberto. The grit seemed worse after Nuoro and the air still reeked of goats' cheese and chemicals. Although it was only about eight o'clock the town was dead. The only noise, which continued most of the night, was the endless shunting of trains on the railway lines that curved, glinting like a sea, round the hotel.

★ ★ ★

I did not in the end get to the various *nuraghi* and other prehistoric remains at Tamuli. The two cars in the town had long been ordered for the *festa* and there were no other means of reaching them, except by foot. Since there were so many, nearly identical, elsewhere, it hardly seemed worth staying longer in Macomer to visit these, each of which would have meant several hours' walk over rough, overgrown hillside. The one unusual feature at Tamuli, however, is a row of six conical stones ranged opposite one of the two 'giant's tombs' that are almost buried in the undergrowth. These *tombe di giganti*, of about the same period as the *nuraghi*, that is to say built some time between the end of the neolithic age and the Roman occupation, were the tombs of tribal chieftains and their families. Mostly they consisted of large flat stones, laid on top of one another to form walls round areas varying between thirty and forty feet in length and three and eight feet in breadth. Inside these cells the bodies were apparently placed sitting up. Over this rough grave more large stones were laid as a roof, and at the end of the rectangle there was a headstone, square, conical or elliptical, about twelve feet high; round this a further row of stones spread out in a kind of fan. At Tamuli there is a curious extra row of stones, nearly five feet high, three of which have stone breasts. Nobody seems to agree about their meaning.

One of the great charms of the prehistoric remains in Sardinia is their comparative mystery, for the few reference works that exist consistently contradict one another. The painstaking Tyndale, for example, laboriously goes through the opinions of various authors about *nuraghi*. 'Stephanini believes them to have been trophies of victory; Vidal, the houses of the giants; Madao, the tombs of the antediluvians; Peyron, the tombs of the ancient nomad shepherds . . .', and adds: 'It is hardly necessary to notice the utter improbability of the four first opinions, or that they were the residences of families, fortifications, watch-towers, or prisons; for their forms, constructions and localities are sufficient refutation of such suppositions.'

Tyndale's own conclusion was 'that these extraordinary monuments were probably temples of sacrifice and worship, built by the very early Canaanites, in their migration when expelled from their country; and that as such they may have been occasionally used as a depository of the idols, or remains of the immolated victims, or even of some exalted personages connected with their worship and rites'.

E. S. Bouchier, writing nearly a hundred years later, says in his *Sardinia in Ancient Times*: 'Some, probably the oldest, were placed high enough to supervise whole districts, and they give the impression of being the homes and fortresses of an invading race, pressing up from the South and West among the earlier cave and hut dwellers, but never very firmly established in the wildest mountain districts of the east midlands, or in the almost isolated mass to the north-east, now known as Gallura.'

This is the modern view, now held with some conviction, and one feels rather sorry for Tyndale, grouped by more authoritative archaeologists with those whom he had himself castigated for the 'utter improbability' of their opinions. Similarly, discussing the scattered rock-tombs known as *Domus dei Gianas*, which consist of two or more chambers, one behind the other, Tyndale works his way through eight pages of learned conjecture to arrive at another equally outmoded opinion. These 'fairy houses' or 'witches' houses', an earlier version of the *tombe di giganti*, are always found in the vicinity of *nuraghi* and it is evident now that they belonged to the owners of the *nuraghi* and were used by them as family tombs.

I was sorry to miss the female stones near Tamuli, but in the heat the baked, coal-dusted plateau of Macomer suddenly became insufferable. I made one more tour of the melancholy, dispirited-looking village in the morning, the surrounding mountains a crust of brilliant purple, and then waited in the stifling station for the Cagliari express. The idea of the sea had begun to be an obsession. At half-past ten, an hour late, the brown worm-like carriages, without head or tail, rattled into view. I settled into a seat beside a nun, her face like a paper flower in its dead crinkled fragility, and spread out a map. Within a minute we were sliding past the last of the platform oleanders, tired and drooping like sprays in a night-club, and tilting sharply down through palms and prickly-pear bushes to the white, dusty plain.

We were back now in the flat, boulder-strewn landscape that

had spread out on either side of the line from Olbia to Macomer. The train, trying to make up for its lateness, tore along, jerking sharply on its rails like a ghost train at a fun-fair. The passengers, roused from the familiar airless torpor, lurched from side to side as if undergoing therapeutic massage. Papers were folded up, unread books put away, neglected minute-sheets returned to brief-cases.

The journey, all of it made at the same hectic speed, took three hours. I looked out at mile after mile of cracked earth that seemed to be only an intensification of thickly dusted window. Behind the dead flies on the glass, huge flints pointed skyward like rockets waiting to go off. Ahead of us, on the horizon, rose the blue cluster of peaks round the town of Santu Lussurgu, the highest, Monte Urtigu, so my map told me, something over three thousand feet. Santu Lussurgu, I remembered, was one of those priest-ridden places that had so incurred Tyndale's displeasure. Though there were less than twenty at school out of a population of over four thousand, 'there were seven regular, besides other priests, twenty monks in a benedictine monastery, and two confraternite of about six members each'.

We stopped at tiny villages, each little more than a street of whitewashed houses behind the palms and bougainvillea on the station platform. We twisted through grey rock-cuttings or flashed past a eucalyptus grove. Islands of cork-trees rose at intervals out of the yellow stubble, swimming with heat, that stretched away to the foothills of Monte Ferru. About four miles away I could see the dark-green patches of the orange-trees of Milis, circling the small town like the rings of a target. In the bull's-eye the tower of the beautiful romanesque church of S. Paolo, built in the twelfth century, flashed in the sun. I had seen photographs of this church, admiring it against its superb background of orange-trees, protected from the wind by a great barrier of elms and laurels. Here, my nun companion told me, the finest oranges in the world were grown. Nearly all of the fifteen hundred inhabitants of Milis work in the orange-groves, except for the few who make the reed mats that are a traditional speciality of the region. The orange-groves, covering an area of three square miles, belong in part to the dean and chapter of the cathedral at Oristano, and the canon who superintends the property,

I learned, is allowed to count the time spent at this work as so many hours of church service. Tyndale, when I came to his account of a visit to Milis, observed drily about the priest then responsible for this task, 'Judging from what is said of the fulfilment of both duties, it would be hard to say which is the least attended to.'

For a while we hummed through stony deserts broken here and there by the white, crumbling cone of a *nuraghe*. Miles from anywhere we swayed past the dimly-marked boundaries of a football ground, a black umbrella leaning against a goalpost. Near Abbasanta the cork-trees thickened, and we swung gradually round, through sudden grey flecks of olive-trees, towards the west coast mountains. We passed to our left the gold campanile of the mosque-like church of Ollastra, a village in yellows and mauves that might have been in Africa or Iraq, before coming to an abrupt halt at Oristano. Here the nun got out, and the last I saw of her was her fluttering black figure, an attaché-case in her hand, walking up the long road to the town, while comfortable-looking men rode by in carriages and two magnificently bearded and costumed figures overtook her on horse-back.

We had reached the northern edge of the Campidano, the fertile agricultural strip running diagonally south-east to Cagliari. Vast drainage and reclamation schemes have made this rectangle, seventy miles by about twelve, the most richly productive part of Sardinia. It was the third stage in a landscape that had begun in the north with wild rocky hills and thick forests, had then dropped suddenly to baked yellow plains devoid of vegetation, and now had become an orderly pattern of green vines and neat small-holdings.

We might, were it not for the extreme flatness, have been in Provence. Olive-trees twisted above houses made from red unfired brick, the vines stretched out symmetrically in every direction to the mountains. We lurched through this green sea, wonderfully refreshing after the burnt glinting aridity of the last few days, with the wake of vines seeming to close in over the track behind us. Looking back, as we climbed slightly coming up to Marrubiu, there was only this rippling silky tide islanding the tiled roofs of villages as it flowed to the horizon.

The tree-edged lagoons that stretch southwards for nearly ten miles from Oristano flowed past the window. Nets sagged from cork floats and rowing-boats were being slowly paddled over the ashen water. Under trees men were sleeping or eating lunch, though somewhere a group of fishermen had waded into midstream.

We stopped again at Uras and San Gavino, the latter a red-tiled village completely hedged in by cactus; the thick pink fruit formed a kind of circular buffer to the white houses within it. These were agricultural centres, idyllically set amongst almond-trees and figs, with saffron meadows flooding between the houses. At San Gavino a fourteenth-century church, flanked by a monastery founded two hundred years later, looks out over luminous orchards reaching to the railway line. Factories of various kinds have recently been built, and a lead foundry, whose two great chimneys I could see sticking up like funnels to the east of the village, has now developed into the most productive of its kind in Italy.

We curved down past Villasor and Decimomannu, circling almond-trees and vineyards, till the houses began to thicken into suburbs and the great sandstone hump over Cagliari loomed ahead of us. Salt lagoons, the pans drying out in the sun, balanced our swerving train on their blue surfaces and finally we rattled through a last cluster of eucalyptus and Indian fig before slowing down on the outskirts of the town. We crawled through sidings bordered by cement-works and factories, tall black chimneys smoking straight into the sky like steamers run aground, and at various levels in the hill hoardings for chemical products and ceramics clamoured for attention. At the entrance to the station, so the excellent *Guida* of the Touring Club Italiano told me, the Phoenician-Roman necropolis of ancient Karalis might be glimpsed. But already we had slid into a glass-covered recess whose *graffiti* were entirely to do with refreshing drinks, the elimination of bad breath and the restoration of the monarchy.

PART THREE

Cagliari and the South-West

THE history of Cagliari is, to a large extent, the history of Sardinia. I spent my first few days in the capital lying on the wide curving beach of Poetto, attempting to get the facts and dates into some sort of order. When the last of the heat had been squeezed from the sun, I made endless tours of the town trying to relate the different quarters and buildings to their periods. It was in fact comparatively easy, for the demarcation lines between the Pisan and Aragonese influences are clear enough. In the magnificent Museum of Antiquities, founded by King Carlo Felice, scarabs and rings of various kinds, collected from all over the island, linked up the Phoenician, Carthaginian and Roman epochs, while the bronze carvings of the proto-Sards, the builders of the *nuraghi* and *Domus dei Gianas*, glittered in their glass cases to remind one that it was in its prehistoric period that Sardinia attained its greatest influence. Nothing is quite so impressive in Cagliari, not even the Torre dell' Elefante, the Pisan watch-towers that dominate the bay, as these relics of the original Sardinians. To these votive ships and warriors, animals and chieftains warring in their formal world of glass, I returned again and again. Compared to their beauty and strength, the sculptures of the Roman period seemed almost meretricious.

The earliest inhabitants of Sardinia are not in fact precisely established. A complete lack of native historians has meant that the chain of events has had to be laboriously pieced together from stray references in various classical authors, no two of whom are in complete agreement. Strabo, Diodorus, Pausanias and Justinus all give separate accounts, while the earliest genuine authority seems to have been Timaeus, the third-century historian of Sicily. However, it is apparent that the first colonists were Libyans, who crossed over under Sardus, the son of Heracles, some time during the neolithic period and established themselves in the mountains.

A second colony of Africans followed later, during the Bronze Age, and it was the feudal chiefs of this group that began the cultivation of the island and built the first *nuraghi*. These two groups of invaders, combined with the native inhabitants who are thought to have been Etruscans, have left their mark on the present race of Sardinians, who, as well as being especially dark, are also short and dolichocephalic.

About the sixth century B.C. Phoenician traders, on their way to Tarshish, the ore port of southern Spain, began to put in to the western harbours of Sardinia and during storms their ships took refuge in the sheltered roadsteads that now form the harbour of Cagliari. The Carthaginians, most aggressive of the Phoenician colonies, eventually settled in the plains, bringing with them fresh supplies of African labour to work the mines and on the land. These were the first people to undertake military occupation of Sardinia. The Sards, however, defeated the first Carthaginian expedition, made in 560 B.C. under Malchus, and it took another fifty years for the Carthaginians, this time led by Hasdrubal and Hamilcar, sons of the famous general Mago, to quell the tough native wielders of bronze swords and wearers of breastplates—the life-size originals of the scaled-down but sturdy figures thrusting bows and arrows at their glass prisons in the Museum of Antiquities. Hasdrubal was killed, but by now the Carthaginians had formed an alliance with the Etruscans, and together they drove the Greeks out of Corsica, before making their assault on Sardinia. A treaty was made with Rome and though Roman ships were permitted to enter Cagliari for trading purposes, no other foreign settlers were allowed on the island.

This was the beginning of an oppression that lasted with increasing severity for over three hundred years. Moreover, it established the pattern to which the whole of Sardinia's history, with little deviation, has conformed. The Carthaginians occupied the fertile plains and the coastal ports, while the wretched Sards retreated to the mountain ranges in the north and east. The occupiers used the Sardinian corn for their own armies, employing the natives as serfs and even conscripting them into their forces. The Sards were forbidden to work the land on their own account, and their forests and crops were cut down. Soon the Romans were refused all trading access, and Strabo reports that if foreign ships were forced to shelter in the island's roadsteads the crews were seized and drowned. Similarly, if a Carthaginian ship on its way to southern Italy was forced to put in for any reason and any foreigners were travelling, they, too, were thrown overboard. Such were the security measures that the Carthaginians adopted to keep their private mines and granaries safe from intrusion.

It was not till 259 B.C. that the Romans, heavily involved in their first war with Carthage, turned their attention to Sardinia, Scipio, the Roman Consul, landed at Olbia, but was defeated by the Punic garrison. His successor, Sulpicius, arriving the next year with a stronger force, defeated the Phoenicians, whose commander Hannibal was killed. The Sards, delighted at the chance of getting rid of the Carthaginians, now mutinied everywhere. The mercenary troops employed by the Carthaginians rose up also, and the various garrison officers were slaughtered. But the Sards, unaccustomed to independence, and longing for stability and protection, meekly offered their island to the Romans.

Sardinia, though some of the mountain tribes refused to recognize the Romans, thus became the first province of Rome. But the Romans, like the Carthaginians, were interested only in exploiting the island and devoted as little time to it as they could manage. There are, therefore, fewer signs of Roman occupation than in any other possession held by the Empire. They sent home as much corn as they could lay their hands on, they hunted the mountain tribesmen with bloodhounds, burned their villages and sold them as slaves in the markets of Rome. The Sards fought back when and where they could, and though reduced to abject poverty by the ruthless tributes they were forced to pay, never completely surrendered.

The Romans, through a series of rapidly changing praetors, held Sardinia for nearly seven hundred years. Most of the praetors were ruthless and extortionate, so that the Sards were no better off than they had been under the Carthaginians. Cato was one of the few exceptions and it was he who discovered the poet Ennius, then a centurion in the Roman Army, extricated him from his service in Sardinia and took him back to Rome. Ennius was, in fact, a Greek by birth, but he was born in Calabria and was a

Roman subject. His epic poem *Annales*, a history of Rome in dactylic hexameters, was one of the few fragments of his work to survive, but it was enough for him to be regarded as the earliest original poet of the Roman language.

Some of the Sard chiefs had already begun to regret the good old days under Carthage and constant battles now took place between Sard armies, secretly reinforced by Carthaginian troops, and the Romans. Running fights all over the island, in caves and forests, and always with tremendous bloodshed, inevitably ended in Roman victories. Licking their wounds, though never dispirited, the Sards once again retired to their mountain redoubts in the north and east.

It was the same story over again. When the Romans were finally driven out of Sardinia by the Vandals in 456, so that the Sards once again came under Carthaginian influence, there was fresh persecution and even heavier extortion. The island was flooded with deported Moors and a kind of marauding anarchy reigned. However, the occupants of the island now began to change with greater rapidity. Vandals were replaced by Byzantines; Goths, Romans and Saracens all won rounds of this ruling musical chairs and the Sards were gradually left more to their own resources. On the death of Charlemagne, in 814, they offered their allegiance to his son, Louis, who in turn gave Sardinia into the custody of the Pope. The Pope, in an effort to get rid of the Saracen princes who were still established in Sardinia, encouraged the Pisans and Genoese to invade the island, and after they had done so successfully, they were given joint authority. From this time, 1025, to 1298, when Boniface VIII invested the King of Aragon with Sardinia, the Pisans and Genoese squabbled incessantly at the expense of the Sards. One extortionate overlord had simply been replaced by two and the pattern remained the same. The island was divided into four provinces, Cagliari, Torres, Gallura and Arborea, each ruled by *giudici*, or judges, who quickly set themselves up as independent princes.

It was not till 1327 that Alphonso IV of Aragon, having reached Cagliari after defeating the Pisans in a series of battles round Iglesias, was able to exercise his rights over the island. He immediately set up a government on the lines of that of Barcelona, and almost for the first time in history the Sards were given some control over their own affairs. When Aragon and Castile were united in 1479 Sardinia was administered as, and given the privileges of, a Spanish dominion. The native princes were deprived of their independence, and Spanish Viceroys, making their headquarters at Cagliari (which had been the capital of the island since the middle of the Roman occupation), looked after the Sards with unusual concern for their interests. This Spanish-Sardinian honeymoon lasted until Sardinia, by terms of the Treaty of Utrecht, was surrendered to the Elector of Bavaria in 1714. He in turn ceded it six years later as a Kingdom to Vittorio Amadeo II, Duke of Savoy, in exchange for Sicily. In 1720 Vittorio Amadeo was proclaimed King of Sardinia at Cagliari.

The eighteenth and early nineteenth centuries, during which period the descendants of Vittorio Amadeo ruled the island, saw Sardinia alternately conciliated and neglected. Vittorio Amadeo II abdicated in 1730 and his son Carlo Emanuele III, an austere, virtuous and exacting disciplinarian, set about making the social conditions in Sardinia conform to his own high standards. He rounded up most of the professional *malviventi* and *fuorusciti*, ancestors of the present-day bandits, organized commerce and agriculture, established schools and colleges of law, and linked the island with proper communications. Had there been trains, he would doubtless have made them run on time. He did for Sardinia what Mussolini later did for Italy, and he was as illiberal. Vittorio Amadeo III, who succeeded his father in 1773, had a taste for military pomp, ceremony and tactical invention—a taste that lost him within twenty years all his money, nearly all his titles, including Duke of Savoy, and most of his territories to the French. King of Sardinia, however, he remained, though, by removing the Sards from their offices and appointing Piedmontese in their stead, he caused a discontent that came near to losing him Sardinia too. In 1794 there was a general revolution against the Piedmontese government, and the insurgents seized the castle at Cagliari, threatening to kill the Viceroy and all the Piedmontese in the island, unless they were removed at once.

Vittorio Amadeo first yielded to these demands, then went

back on his word when the danger seemed over. His son, Carlo Emanuele IV, who came to the throne in 1796, determined to make good his father's losses and increased the taxes so much that further insurrections broke out. Rather than deal with them himself, he moved to Rome, became a Jesuit, and handed over his throne to his brother. The new king, Vittorio Emanuele I, lasted precariously from 1802 to 1821, by when his despotic absolutism and Jesuit intrigues faithfully brought about the necessity for his own abdication, again in favour of a brother, Carlo Felice, who died ten years later. He and his successor, Carlo Alberto, both went some way to improve the dismal picture of the island's hundred years' rule under its own kings. Carlo Alberto abolished Sardinia's autonomy in 1847; and the elevation of his son Vittorio Emanuele II to the Italian throne in 1861 united Sardinia with Italy.

Ironically, however, it has taken yet another occupation—the Anglo-American one of 1943—to remove the malaria that had been, throughout its entire history, the main obstacle to Sardinia's development.

It is evident from even such a brief and elementary sketch as this that the Sards have had little opportunity to express themselves as a nation. Yet the unending series of oppressive occupations which they have had to endure has given them a resilience not to be found amongst other Italians. The fact that Sardinia has been treated as a bone to be snarled over by almost every Mediterranean power in turn has produced an immunity to the vacillations of fortune. They are more reserved, more dignified than most Latin races. They have cultivated a fatalistic indifference that, combined with a natural Arab laziness, has meant that most of the wealth in the island—the mines, salt-works, fishing industry, factories—belonged, until very recently at any rate, to foreigners.

Again, the variety of races that have been strained through them—Libyans, Phoenicians, Romans, Arabs, Spaniards—has tended to give them a quite different outlook from the ordinary Italian. Their resourcefulness, their pride in achieving even such local independence as the mountain tribes had managed to preserve, has made the modern Sardinian the least disrespected of all Italian soldiers. Driven inland by their invaders they have become essentially landsmen. The Sardinians are still poor fishermen, with little taste for the sea.

The constant change of administrators has had its obvious effect on architecture. Cagliari, for example, remains essentially a Pisan city. The old quarter, built on a mound of rock sloping steeply down to the harbour, still dominates the modern town that has spread out along the water-front. The castle, the public buildings and palaces, the cathedrals, are all Pisan. Yet from the fourteenth century to the eighteenth century Sardinia was under Spanish rule. There are therefore no buildings in Cagliari in the style of the Italian Renaissance, and such additions to the town as were made during this period are mostly Spanish baroque. Early in the nineteenth century the town darted westwards, with wide roads and piazzas, banks and offices, this time in the imposing pure baroque of Piedmont.

The names of streets, as one repeats the order of Sardinian kings to oneself in a kind of litany, take on meaning. The restorations of churches, the replacement of gothic by baroque as a natural style, the figures on monuments staring out to sea, become memoranda to epochs. Through the liquid eyes of people passing one can look down to the tangled sea-bed of unkind oppressions. The Roman slave, the tribal chief with his bronze weapons, sit at their café tables reading *La Nuova Sardegna*. The long-headed Libyan goes by whistling on his bicycle, the Saracen with a squint sells you a pale silk tie.

* * *

I had expected Cagliari to look something like Ajaccio; instead it reminded me of Barcelona. Much smaller of course, yet nearer to it in conception than to Ajaccio. It is essentially a citadel; also a town that works for its living.

From the station you emerge into the beating sunlight of the Via Roma; a wide, white street, with palms and bougainvillea down the middle, the sea on one side. Green, dusty trams rattle continuously along the water-front, and motor-bicycles hoot and accelerate past immaculate point-duty police in white uniforms. The ships are easy to see, for they are backed right up to the quays and almost overhang the street. Flags of Spain, Japan,

America and Sweden hang limply over the black hulls. On the thin pincer-like arms of the jetties, cranes claw up their cargoes of ore, skins, cork, cheese and cement. At intervals along the quays great mounds of salt, of a whiteness almost blue, wait to be loaded. The sea glitters beyond. On the horizon, linked by a series of lagoons, the magenta mountains of Capo Spartivento sink in mist.

The Via Roma is hot and dusty, for daily, at about eleven, a strong off-sea wind, straight from Africa, gets up and blows hard till sunset. The dust thickens, coating the oleanders, the glass windows of shops, the café tables in the arcades. During the day it is a town of glint and dazzle: tramlines, windscreens, salt, sea. The salt tented against the distant mountains, the great sandstone battlements you come suddenly upon as you turn up the broad Largo Carlo Felice, the lagoons to east and west, are what give Cagliari its particular flavour.

The town sweeps uphill from the sea, so that, looking down from the honeycomb of houses at the top, blue sea flows by the foot of each street. The Largo Carlo Felice, at right angles to the Via Roma, takes you steeply away from the accessories of commerce to the wide bastions that support church and state. Within the citadel, the university, the cathedral, the palaces (now civil service offices) are joined to each other by narrow, walled alleys which open out into squares. The effect is like a Chinese box, the outside of which is formed by Pisan battlements. The medieval town, a network of arches, gates and towers, seems to be built on stilts, its houses, once the stately residences of officials, now strung together by lines of washing. The pale, rinsed colours of shirts, skirts and sheets flap from one wrought-iron balcony to another. Ten families occupy a building that once held one. The courtyards are uncared-for and the handsome elaborations of Pisan and Aragon architects fall off gradually to lie about like amputated limbs. The buildings themselves, flanked by spiralling roads that twist in the sun like barley sugar, have sunk further and further into the rock, as if taking refuge. The sky is like a weight.

These houses at the apex of the citadel are some of them ruins, for sixty-seven per cent of the buildings of Cagliari were partially destroyed in sea bombardments during the war. The light on the terraced piazzas round the cathedral is dazzling as sea. The fourteenth-century Torre di San Pancrazio, looming over the Piazza Indipendenza, balances the twin Torre dell' Elefante rising from the southern, supporting wall.

Lower down, the bastions have been made into terraces. Palms throw their shade over benches, and children play hop-scotch on burning stone bordered by several hundred yards of low wall. As you look out from this semi-circular wall the gulf is spread like a model beneath you. Clouds seem to have been pasted on the lagoons. Cars draw the sun after them on the Via Roma, site of the ancient Roman town, where square white hotels, the twentieth-century Palazzo Comunale, its two turrets in sham Spanish gothic, and shuttered flats line up along the harbour. In the Darsena, a small fishing-basin, like the *vieux port* at Marseilles, the sailing-boats and launches are squeezed together, gunwale to gunwale.

Further east, the shoreline winds past endless lagoons, squared out by reed banks, and looking like leaded windows. The Botanical Institute and Zoological Gardens are isolated by canals, reached only by bridge and boat. Capo Sant' Elia, the centre of the gulf formed by Capo Spartivento in the west and Capo Carbonara in the east, stretches its great fawn paw seawards.

Then the beaches swing on a wide hinge of sand, seven miles of it held by headlands at either end and backed by lidos, restaurants, bathing-huts. A road follows the shape of the bay, and behind the road the salt-works cover the plain like the tents of a giant army. Nearer the citadel the red-tiled roofs of the Villanova suburb are parted here and there by gold campaniles. But mostly Cagliari has sprawled outwards through sections of yellow, cube-shaped houses, and looking eastwards from the Bastione Santa Caterina you might be looking down at a Moorish town.

* * *

Rituals of Cagliari. The station, for example; there are café tables spread out near the entrances to the platforms. People passing the station on their way to and from business look in for an *espresso*. The station has a grimy elegance: polished stone entrance, magazine-covered kiosks, silver and glass cases to house the flower-patterned biscuit called *zicchi ladu*. Foam from the *espresso* machine erupts over the bar, palms wilt in painted tubs and there are always *carabinieri* lounging about. The *Capo di Treno*, the official in charge of each train, wears an exquisite cerise and gold cap with black peak. Waiting for his coffee or beer, the unhurried civil servant or business man has time to see in action the trains he pays for. The unobtrusive brown carriages slither in from the sunlight, rattling the bones in the limestone chambers beneath them (vertical in the Punic tombs, horizontal in the Roman necropolis), and nuns, peasants in costume, soldiers, postmen and commercial travellers push their way out of the barriers.

A woman, so settled in her corner near the café that she seems to have grown through the stone, sells flowers. Her skin is the colour of the paper with which she wraps the gladioli, and as she sits framed in her bar of flowers she knits and chews.

There is a gramophone, too, that amplifies the voice of Roberto Murolo, Neapolitan tenor, now grown hoarse with the repetition of his records, the competition of trains and *espresso* steam. The bead curtains of the bar click like needles through the heat, and the music is interrupted at intervals for an announcer to state the precise lateness of each successive train. At night the station, under its green-glass exterior, has the aqueous light of a tank. People moon fishily about, drink *vernaccia* waiting for relations or lovers to arrive, and occasionally cool themselves looking at the flowers. Where the track curves northwards past the platform it follows the line of the Roman aqueduct. Under the chocolate factory and the cement-works a network of canals and reservoirs, remains of Roman skill, offer the modern engineer an opportunity to admire the workmanship of his forebears.

Arrivals and departures are events instinct with possibility: in Cagliari poetic indulgence is given to their suggestiveness.

Another ritual, the ritual of 'Poetto'. Between 11 am and 1 pm a systematic exodus takes place from town to beach. Trams leave the Via Roma at five-minute intervals, taking twenty minutes to reach the Lido, the most popular section of sand. (The seven miles of beach are divided by breakwaters, each area having more or less identical amenities but a different name.) The earlier trams are filled with young girls, mothers and children, youths and gentlemen of leisure. These are the professional sunbathers, all burnt a smooth, toffee-brown; they have acquired a second skin, surrendering the gift of nakedness. Later come shop-girls, secretaries, office employees—amateur bathers, who use the beach to cool themselves before returning to work. Vespas and cars, racing alongside the green trams, do the trip to Poetto in five minutes.

The first part of the journey is along the Via Roma. Through the arcades, women are strolling in shocking-pink, lemon-green, or fawn cotton frocks; or else in white shirts and red or green skirts clasped tight by wide black belts. Girls are well dressed, not sexily like French girls, but with a bourgeois neatness. Above the arcades (men sitting at tables reading newspapers, or just sitting) three-storeyed flats spread their green lattice shutters behind bulging stone balconies. The tram lurches in a wide loop past the *Moderno* and *Excelsior* hotels—glass and palm-trees and aseptic, box-like rooms—stops between the adjacent offices of the Monarchist and Communist parties, and then rattles on again past the Astra Super-cinema (for three-dimensional films from Mars?) and out of the main part of the town by the harbour. There is a smell of sacking and spices and rope. Warehouses and customs, tanneries and police barracks surround the congested fishing-boats. Across the bay the mountains are a faint purple, the water deep lilac in between. The Viale Armando Diaz is a street of garages, laundries and cobbles. Then the tram swings clear of the suburbs, and now, on one side, the villas begin—spruce pink, yellow or white stucco squares, each behind iron gates, their gardens thick with palms, geraniums, bougainvillea and almond-trees. The sea breeze rustles across reed banks and lagoons. To the left there are in quick succession the cemetery, a dentist's and the football stadium. Open country now, with Cagliari sturdily carved into its hill behind you, a perfect model fortress. The tram seems to take wings, the sea air in its nostrils.

The prehistoric remains here are nearly all underground and though you may still find Greek and Roman coins if you poke about beneath the olive-trees, terraced in a series of silver ruffs round the rock, there are no longer visible signs of the original settlement or of the temple to Venus Erycina mentioned on an inscription in the Museum of Antiquities. Moreover, a new hotel, which will surely have one of the key positions in the whole Mediterranean, is shortly going to be built at the top—where the rock dips between two sharp peaks called the Sella del Diavolo (the devil's saddle).

Over the S. Bartolomeo canal, and the tramline runs in a straight line between sea and salt-works. Hills of dazzling salt, falling into blue draperies where they are in shadow, have an icy, crystal glitter in the midday sun. The tram stops at each of the bathing establishments which run along the back of the beach, completely sealing it off. Faded blue beach huts, tin advertisements for toothpaste, apéritifs and soft drinks, flags, palm-trees and white confectionery-looking buildings. *Ecco Lido!* Striped parasols line the beach, embedded in the sand like exotic marine trees, and under each a family of varying size sits in deck-chairs or spreads outwards in luxuriant fleshy foliage. The bay curves under them, the sea, ridged white by the African wind, surfing up the gently shelving shore. The early morning expanse of white sand is thick with bodies, so that the beach seems to be striped black and white. A Pisan beach in fact. Yachts ride at their moorings in the glassy lee of the near headland. White floats paddled by young men draw a wake of toffee-headed urchins. Girls shining as oil-skin carry light in the hollows of their faces. Children dive and spurt out water like dolphins. In the shade families eat grapes, raw ham, *mortadella*.

After lunch, late lunch eaten at half-past three, the beach empties. The breeze drops and the sea has a smooth bloom on it, a skin like a white grape. Between the bathing-huts, where there are water-pumps in the shadowed sand, the afternoon sleep engages those who are now pumped with sun. Girls are spread like starfish, half-moons of starfish reading paper-backed romances or knitting. Chairs bulge under matronly bottoms. Later there forms a frieze of young men playing football, the limpid sea at their backs; rows of mermaids sit on low walls, combing out their hair and watching them. Maidservants in black plait the bleached locks of their Signoras (Cagliari was always a feudal town, and the Signoras, dark-skinned as olives, have sometimes blonde hair).

Now, on the beach, shadows caricature last bathers, the plock-

plock of deck-tennis played with gourds begins and lasts out the light. Fishermen paint their boats, children collect shells. A ship's siren bleats in Cagliari and soon a steamer, well loaded, rounds the Capo Sant' Elia, Naples bound. In the Lido Bar ice is shaken, tables are set up under the palms. Cars glide in, their occupants laundered as their clothes, glowing under sunburn. Lights are strung out over the headlands, coloured bulbs wash the sand pink and peach and emerald. Drums begin to throb and whisk, a lazy accompaniment to the sea. Darkness coats the salt-hills lilac and electric-blue. Soon, with the town still stifling and silent in the distance, there is dancing on the courts where earlier the tennis players thumped their gourds.

The ritual of the markets, a cauldron of noise in the metal-blue sky, the first thing that comes truly alive. Dawn skims off the bay, the mountains suddenly rising out of the clean sea, the sun lying like a pink feather on them. And already the black fishing-boats are making for the Darsena, the sea streaming from their imaged bows in long green ripples. The African breeze has not yet arrived, the sea is flat, the streets dustless. In this oyster light the outlines of the town are clean and hard. The vertical empty streets run like canals between plane-trees; the palms and oleanders in the piazzas, and along the Via Roma, have a precise symmetry. The great bulbous mound of the citadel, its sheer battlements, its houses wedged together like overcrowded teeth, the breaking crenellations of towers, seem to have been cut out of the sky, as from a scrapbook. The trams still lie in their depots, rows of untethered green carriages cooling off, and the cranes along the quays hook at the air, the light spilling on the salt heaps behind them.

But off the Largo Carlo Felice, under awnings that now hang still, later bulge with sun, flap in wind, the markets are great zoos of noise. Women in black, carrying straw baskets with heraldic emblems on them, stream in the same direction from all over the city, like insects fastening on some sudden dropping. Water slides over concrete, bullock-carts rumble in from the country, men's voices ring out in the razor-sharp air. Great blocks of ice, a blue, Polar landscape embedded in them, lie under sacking, then are hurried to restaurants and stalls. Inside the two markets it is like a garden going up: or a beach. Striped, folded blinds, vegetables seeming to be growing through the stone floor, fruit stalls opening like coloured umbrellas. Then, in a smaller, adjoining market, seas of glistening fish shimmer in their crates. Meat spins on huge hooks, *mortadella* and *salami* and cheese are laid out, everything brightly wrapped as prizes in a fun-fair.

The larger market becomes a fragrant frenzy, women in coloured scarves and wide black skirts tied up like sacks at the waist, all bustling to make the most of the cool. Smells of fish, smells of fruit, smells of almonds, of peaches, of cheeses, collide. From this stone sea-bed rises a crepuscular vegetable mist, a dawn of melons, a sundown of oranges. Shiny twisted peppers ring their scarlet gongs, figs and grapes bruise the light as they are opened from the sleep of their boxes. Sleepwalkers might wander in voyages of dream through these exotic sandbanks, peasant women motionless on them as buoys, but in fact these fleshy fruits of the island are being rapidly stuffed into baskets, the fish wrapped and avidly seized, the cheeses carried off leaving a wake behind them.

The sun still trains only an indulgent beam of heat, the green shutters are closed like lashes over the window-eyes of hotels and peeling houses. By the time they are opened the blue-striped, apron morning is over, the market is ordinary bustle, not peasant-ferment, the banks have unlocked their palatial doors, and over the marble floors freshly-shaved clerks are wiping the sweat off their necks as they enter, brief-case (containing lunch) in hand.

Then, of course, the ritual of the *corso*. During the day the movement of people is away from the Via Roma, up the Largo Carlo Felice to the government offices in the citadel, to the university beneath the Torre dell' Elefante, to the shops in the Corso Vittorio Emanuele and Via Manno, or out to Poetto. But at night the crowds spill down the streets that surround the citadel like a halter and converge on the Via Roma. The sun drops its final mauve flare over Capo Spartivento, the pale-green sky forms like a skin over it, and then suddenly the whole town is glittering like a chandelier in the enveloping, velvet blueness of night. The streets hold the warmth of the day as though they were bowls. The hooting of traffic acquires a melancholy siren-note that seems to hang in the twilight. By dusk, when the smell of pines and shrubs drifts down to mix with the scents of the stalls full of cut flowers, the wind has dropped and the sea out in the bay has a flowing, chromium glitter.

You can see whole families taking their evening walk on the paths above the Anfiteatro Romano, the people who live in the dark stone corridors washing or eating on the edge of the arena. Pine-trees stand out hard and black, the changing saffron sky flooding the gulf below, the breeze in the botanical gardens beyond the amphitheatre like the constant rustle of silk. Along the Viale Fra Ignazio da Laconi, drenched in the scent of pine and magnolia, the inmates of the row of poor-houses walk up and down, the arena glinting in moonlight beneath them, the sound of singing coming through the open doors of the Chiesa dei Cappuccini. This is where the space in Cagliari is, on this series of white looping roads that curves round the whole town like the back of a high chair. You are high up, the sea far down a deep valley at your feet, the plain glowing at your back. The wider horizon is still mountains, for they are never lost in Sardinia. From here, the crescent of the evening *corso*, you see precisely how the city seems to dive down to the harbour. In the day it is a steep, stony staircase, at night a chute. You feel, too, the nearness of Africa: in the sunset, in the dark staring faces leaning over wrought-iron balconies, the narrow clustering streets, the round campaniles and minarets, the white cube-like suburbs, the heavy, scented air.

The early evening walk begins on this high western edge in strolling families, in leisurely moving couples: lower down, where the streets pack into one another, the crowds thicken and walk with more purpose. Then the lighted shops above one seem to hang like golden birdcages. The streets leading vertically to the water-front, the Via Ospedale, the Via Santa Restituta, the Via Napoli, the Via Barcellona, which are only four out of twenty parallel streets, are so full of descending people they might be escalators. The shops in the Via Manno (the narrow Bond Street of Cagliari) are like lighted caves, jewels sparkling in crammed glass cases, patent leather glistening, and everywhere bales of luminous cottons phosphorescent on their shelves. The streets are heavy with women's scent, with men's brilliantine, with incense pouring out of the open doors of medieval churches. The cafés down the Largo Carlo Felice, as well as along the Via Roma, are full of people drinking coffee, eating ices. There is a deceptive air of bourgeois prosperity, because in fact the women are pretty and tidy, the men astringently dressed for the heat; and then one realizes how little is required to make a show in a hot climate. A white blouse, a thick black belt, a skirt or two, some stiletto-heeled shoes: or a white shirt, a pair of linen trousers, a pair of sandals.

All the same, Cagliari is essentially a provincial town, or rather it is a capital city with a provincial population. What is imposing about Cagliari is the past dreamed into stone. Even at night there is a constant awareness of top-heavy palaces, towers, bastions, fortifications, thrusting out into the upper darkness. Everywhere there are great white steps, like waterfalls in starlight, pushing the peeling houses apart. The smaller, cobbled streets corkscrew their way along in the shadow of huge yellow buttresses. The humbler piazzas, their shoddy stalls full of bootlaces and belts, ties, toothpastes, combs, their water-pumps playing the part of Bernini fountains, are, one suddenly finds, overlooked by a thirteenth-century church in late Spanish gothic or an imposing sixteenth-century basilica in Genoese baroque. You can never escape the images of war and religion; they coexist round every corner with their silent but eloquent reminders of occupation and feudal pomp, of serfdom and ceremony.

The arcades now are stacked with chairs and tables, brushed by the two-way moving stream: girls with swinging hips, high stuttering heels, young men with jerseys slung over their shoulders. Waiters in white coats dart through, balancing sickly syrups and ices the colours of medicines, and then the streams form round them again. Suddenly, at about half-past eight, it is all over: the groups that have been going back and forth for nearly two hours have each continued their walk out of sight. It is like a coloured balloon deflating, the ephemeral, diurnal gaiety gradually subsiding to leave only cigarette stubs and piles of saucers. The public emotions and appetites have given way to private ones. The individual retreats into the family, and where, twenty minutes ago, Cagliari was a gay, noisy city it is now a dead town. Half-empty trams go rattling by, a beggar or two remain on, but the ritual is over. The crowd disperses as though leaving a football match or a bull-fight.

* * *

From my bed in the *Albergo Italia* I could look across the narrow Via Sardegna at the games of billiards going on in the saloon opposite. Sometimes, late at night, I would sit up on one elbow and follow an entire game through, its close cannons, the long definitive pots. The streets would be empty, the whole town in darkness. But immediately opposite me, also on the first floor, the red and white balls would skim across the glowing green baize, clicking together for hour after hour in the smoke-filled room. There would be, on occasions, four or five tables going, sometimes only one; and eventually, after I had put my own light out, unable to go to sleep because of the heat, the click-clack, the bang of the cue, the thump of a ball being potted, became so familiar a sequence of noises that I only noticed when it stopped. It was like having a waterfall or a dynamo out on the balcony. The players, who nearly all wore grey trousers and white singlets, hardly spoke. They played with intense concentration, eyes barely leaving the table. Arc-lights hung low over the baize, and the unsmiling seriousness of everyone was such that an operation might have been taking place. When it was all over, the players went off on motor-bicycles, and, until that moment, sleep was impossible. I waited for the roar of each exhaust, like the traditional commercial traveller who hears one shoe being thrown off on the floor above and cannot sleep until he hears the second.

Getting any sleep, in fact, was the great problem, for Cagliari must compete with Barcelona as being the noisiest port in Europe. We had tried two hotels earlier, the *Excelsior*, which I had left as an address in London, and the *Moderno*. Both these hotels are new and agreeable; unfortunately, both are off the arcades in the Via Roma and there, particularly, the noise is unbearable. It is not the kind of continuous noise, the hum of talk or consistent traffic, to which one grows used: it is a series of sharp, various screechings and accelerations that reach concussive force in the stilled air. The shunting of trucks along the quays, the grind of winches and cranes loading through the night, trams rattling from 5 am onwards, the bumping of bullock-carts as the *contadini* bring in their produce to the market, the crazy exhausts of Vespas. Sorrowfully, for the people in each were charming and efficient, we had been obliged to leave both after a few days. The *Italia* was older and less imposing, but it had large rooms, pleasant wrought-iron balconies, and was altogether quieter. We had meant to go to the *Scala di Ferro*, which is higher up and has its own garden, but a travelling opera company had installed itself there for a month. Some of the overflow from this company was in the *Italia*, and I saw them daily at Poetto. Their slim, elegant appearance marked them at once as members of the chorus.

Across the way was the hotel restaurant where we dined on alternate nights. The menus never changed, so the other nights we ate at the *Moderno*. The food in fact differed little in the half-dozen or so places we sampled, but, though it hasn't much variety, the quality is surprisingly good. It is fairly typical Italian food, the normal meal consisting of *antipasta* and melon, veal or a steak, cheese, *zabaglione* or fruit, but the veal, usually done with tunny-fish sauce, is always beautifully tender, and the steaks, too, are excellent. I have never eaten better grapes or peaches, and the lobsters are probably the best in the Mediterranean. Sardinian wines vary from place to place, the inhabitants themselves most admiring the *Vernaccia*, a strong, sweetish wine, golden in colour, but *Nuragus*, the white wine of Cagliari, is potent, dry and only too drinkable. The restaurants were never more than half-full, an indication perhaps of how small was the floating population. Nearly always there were the same familiar figures, sitting in their shirt-sleeves under whirring fans, reading newspapers. Occasionally a nun or a scruffy itinerant priest would push apart the bead curtains and bring round an alms-box. More rarely, a peasant and his wife, both in costume, would come in for lunch. They would sit, awkward but magnificent, scrubbing the *bolognese* sauce off their plates with crusts of bread, noisily but skilfully sucking up their *pasta*.

By nine in the evening the streets became quite empty. There is no night life in Cagliari, and, more surprisingly, practically no music. It was rare to find a café with juke-box or gramophone, and none of the restaurants had them. The modern Sardinians are curiously unmusical, and the haunting, native music of the island is hardly ever heard. The *launedda*, the ancient reed instrument used for accompanying the *ballo tondo*, the Sardinian national dance, is now played only by shepherds in outlying districts, or on feast days, and I heard it only twice during my stay in Sardinia. Most of the traditional songs have been recorded, however, and they have a wonderful savage melancholy, sung, as they are, like Arab or Spanish songs, in the back of the throat. But they have largely ceased to be the Sardinians' natural means of expression, and the only times I heard these records played was when I especially asked an architect, whom we later met in Tempio, to put them on for us.

The Sardinians display none of the superficial gaiety of the Italians, none of their malleability or lightness of heart. They are courteous, generous, but essentially reserved. They are also typical islanders, with the islanders' mystical belief in what they call the *continente*. There is strong family feeling in Sardinia and with it the survival of a stern code of moral conduct. The result of this, combined with the fact that very few people visit the island, is that life seems to be more or less on one level. Though many of the peasants live hard, struggling lives, there are no great extremes of wealth, on the surface anyway. Cagliari has none of the undercurrents of feeling that one associates with ports. Even the sailors who roam the streets in immaculate white, do so as though on parade. When, at the end of the daily *corso*, public life is turned off like a tap, Cagliari becomes a derelict, spectral city of towers, battlements and spires, with no animation at all. At first this sudden cessation of life at half-past eight is disconcerting. One hunts round for bars or cafés where, perhaps unknown to one, people might be meeting and enjoying themselves. Eventually I realized that they simply don't exist. The reason, of course, is fairly obvious: there is no spare money in Sardinia, not because it isn't being made, but because those who live in the island are the employees, not the employers. Few Sardinians control the rich industries like cork, mining, tunny-fishing and pottery; they are merely managers. The mark of a successful man is to live in Italy, at any rate to see his children are educated there. Thus Sardinia still bears all the attributes of a province; its economy, its entertainments, its cultural standards are provincial. The ancient feudal aristocracy, who used to live in the island on large estates, have mostly gone. The new rich are the petty bourgeoisie, the mine-owners, the post-war industrialists who have cottoned on to a good thing, but for whom Sardinia is only a stage in their development. The large estates have been broken up, and now the peasants nearly all own the land they work. In consequence, there is no leisured community in Sardinia, certainly none in the hot summer months, for then the various government officials, students and lecturers at the university, all return to Italy. Every town in Sardinia is essentially a working town, and this is equally true of Cagliari.

There are now signs that this is beginning to change. The complete eradication of malaria has suddenly opened the eyes of the Italian government (or rather its Sardinian representatives, for Sardinia was made a *Regione autonoma* in 1948) to Sardinia's tourist possibilities. Consequently, the Roman snobbish antipathy that has operated against Sardinia since the Empire is rapidly being replaced by non-altruistic interest. While the pleasure resorts of the Gulf of Naples, of the Sorrentine peninsula and the Riviera di Levante, became more and more expensive, more and more crammed, Sardinia, with the best beaches of all, the most varied natural scenery, lay deserted and undeveloped. That was a realization of some consequence. The ancient sites of the island, neglected for centuries, are now being re-excavated. The mountains are being reforested, the swamps drained. Soon, quite apart from its mineral wealth, this rising native prosperity is bound to affect, in towns at any rate, the whole texture of Sardinian life.

When the new villas are dotted more thickly over the hillsides and along the coasts of Carloforte and Alghero, and the new hotels perched on their rocky pedestals, the streets will not be so quiet at night. Nor, presumably, the prices so low.

*   *   *

The great mauve headlands of Capo Carbonara and Capo Spartivento, the white curving sand of Poetto in between, were the background for most of the three weeks I spent in Cagliari. From a purely visual point of view there are few more impressive beaches in the Mediterranean. The extreme whiteness of the sand gives the sea a pale cellophane greenness, an extraordinary clarity. The sea here is rarely blue, certainly not blue in the Ionian or Aegean sense. Much more is it Pernod-coloured, sometimes turquoise or emerald. But the beaches shelve so gently that the surface retains its milky consistency far out to sea. The liners cutting across the horizon may be passing over pure blue water, but the sand juts out from the corners of the coast like a huge starfish, and on land you see only within its fleshy circumference.

Three weeks is not too long to stay in Cagliari, for there is much to absorb as well as to look at. The evenings are dull, but even they have their compensations. For example, there is the *Grotto de Marcello*, a place of entertainment recommended to me by the proprietor of the shop where I had bought some Sardinian gramophone records.

The *Grotto de Marcello* is at the top of the Largo Carlo Felice, in the Piazza Yenne. Since it is the only place of its kind in Cagliari, it has to combine the duties of a night-club and those of a Palais de Danse. It is a place of great bourgeois respectability, where the men wear collars and ties, and where the women are in their most formal dresses. The particular points about it are that you can dance there and that it is extremely cold.

Cagliari on a summer night is hot and airless. When you enter the *Grotto* you feel as though you have walked into a refrigerator. The air-conditioned interior is white stucco formed like a grotto, with white stucco stalactites hanging down from the roof. Water tanks have been cut into the walls and goldfish flicker through streaming grasses and over beds of coral. A long bar, all silver and ice-blue, leads from the door to the chamber of the cave where a tiny dance floor is surrounded by marble tables. At the far end, under a ceiling of larger stalactites, the band, in pale-blue uniforms, play alongside splashing fountains. Through these caverns waiters glide and flit, coloured lights striping them like angel-fish. The walls seem perpetually to be dripping, so realistic is the effect, though it is merely the fountains hissing into their stucco pool.

The night we went, the *Grotto* was nearly full, However, an elderly waiter, with protuberant eyes like a barracuda, found us a table near a goldfish tank and we settled down to cool off. All round us people were eating ices or drinking coffee. A dozen couples or so were gyrating slowly in the middle of the floor, coloured rainbow lights changing over them, while the band beat out some popular tune in a Victor Sylvester manner. Some of the men dancing wore blazers and white suède shoes, and one girl was wearing white gloves. Each couple danced very decorously, concentrating on doing the steps carefully and well, and nobody talked.

The *Grotto*, it became apparent after a while, was all things to all people. To business men it was a place to discuss affairs in the cool; for families it was somewhere to show off their clothes and their solidarity, for their young people to get to know one another; for shop-girls and their escorts it was something of an occasion, a setting for dancing like a Hollywood film.

The extraordinary unreality of the place, buried just under the walls of the honeycombed citadel, was equalled only by the effect that formal clothes seemed to have on the young men and women inside. In the cold light of the dance floor all their natural golden glow was washed away, their features seemed to congeal. The men were turned suddenly from vital, laughing Mediterraneans into tailors' dummies, wearing clothes in a shop window. The girls hanging on their arms had been wheeled in from the Ladies' Department, their flesh changed to plaster, the price-tags still on their skirts.

The music stopped and started again: a waltz followed a quickstep, there was a tango, then a slow fox-trot. The band in the refracted light of the illuminated fountains seemed to be artificial, half-way between waxworks and fishes. The young couples paired and danced and then went back to their ice-creams or iced *aranciata*.

It was a ritual fascinating to watch: the south, transformed from hot dusty streets to an arctic grotto, was taking on the habits of the north. I was reminded of the strange, nightmare waltz in Gian-Carlo Menotti's *The Consul*; these couples had the same hallucinatory movement, the false compulsion of people out of their element. A gum-coloured light swept the floor and the stucco grotto looked suddenly like a dentist's impression of someone's mouth.

The tables remained full till midnight, the dancers continuing their correct routines as if they had been wound up. The ices came and went, coffee and glasses of water succeeded them. Then, with a final chord, the band, noisily packing up their instruments, intimated that they had finished.

The dancers, the families, the pale, jowled men with brief-cases, stood up and streamed out in orderly fashion. The fish flickered past them in their glassy caves and the waiters whisked away the litter. Only the fountains went hissing on, till, eventually, they too meekly subsided.

Outside, the streets were suffocating and empty. The citadel was washed in moonlight above us and, down below, the sea glinted through the palm-trees like gunmetal. The crowds were coming out of the cinemas in the Via Roma, talking in high-pitched voices and laughing. The trams were rattling along by the harbour and motor-bicycles were being started up in battalions. Round us the effigies from the *Grotto* had become real people again, mopping their brows in the hot night air, strolling away into narrow streets where drying clothes blotted out the sky between the tall stained houses. It seemed surprising that we were still in Cagliari, not walking on ice to some snow-covered hut. It was a feeling that took some getting used to: but it was also a relief.

* * *

The Museo Archeologico Nazionale is at the highest point of the citadel, in the shadow of the Torre San Pancrazio. On one side there is the Piazza Indipendenza, leading down past the governor's palace and the civil service offices to the cathedral, and on the other you look down to the red-tiled roofs of Villanova, the swimming light of the plain, the salt-lagoons and the scar of the mountains.

The museum is somewhere to get lost in, to go to when it is officially closed and there is no one else there but the bland attendant with the downward, communing eyes. Beginning easily, you mount stone winding staircases with open parapets facing the sea.

Sun drips through circular windows, delicate iron-work repeating itself in shadow on the stone. The caretaker's bicycle on the landing spins the people in the Piazza Indipendenza through the spokes of its wheel. If you do not care for the method of air-travel, if you want to reach places logically, not just arrive arbitrarily in them, then you can walk down the centuries by going upstairs first and slowly descending. The air-traveller will not go upstairs, but nosedive to the scattered well-shrines, rock-tombs and *nuraghi* of the proto-Sards. In fact, he will not miss much, for what is above is only elegant bric-à-brac, jewels, tiles, swords, medallions and small *objets d'art* belonging to periods between the fourteenth and eighteenth centuries. The walls are a panorama of Sardinian painting—that is to say, Tuscan, Genoese, Catalan, Italian Renaissance, Flemish and Spanish techniques worked out through the Sardinian temperament. Here the manners of Leonardo, Van der Weiden, Raphael and various others exist in pale reflection. Most of the best paintings were done by medieval Catalans and Genoese, though from time to time there were schools of native Sardinian painters. These pictures are all of religious subjects, conventionally pious in character, but given a certain strength by the crudity of the composition. On this upper floor, too, the sun ripples over glass cases containing Arab pottery, as well as vases and jugs made by the Vandals and found near Pula, on the way to Capo Spartivento.

These fragments do not really belong to Sardinia, they only lead one back to Italy or Spain, to the countries where painting is a continuation of the landscape, a definition of prayer or ecstasy. The Sardinian landscape does not exist in painting, nor the mental outlook of the people. Self-consciousness was not something the coastal Sardinians, the urban men, possessed in the Middle Ages; where it existed, in the north-east and in the Gennargentu, there was racial memory but no means of expression. The warriors of the neolithic age like dogs buried their bronze carvings round their *nuraghi*, and the strength of their achievements, the products of free men before the subjugations of westward-moving empires, blots out all subsequent history.

The rooms on the ground floor, spraying out from an atrium, are cooler. You walk here in a well, the light aqueous as in a sunken monastery. Roman heads turn to meet you with sightless eyes, a cemetery of aquiline noses points the way to anterior darkness. King Carlo Felice, founder of the museum, greets you from his pedestal, introduces you to Count Alberto La Marmora, nineteenth-century historian of the island, both busts posed against a model *nuraghe* made from cork.

The rooms dominate through glass and silence, haunt with a kind of lyre-music made from obsidian and granite and bronze. The sea-bed plains, the grey, glittering rocks, the boulder-strewn valleys, the skylines pitted with *nuraghi*, are dismantled here into component parts, each a synthesis of place and time. You move through rooms bearing the legends *Preistoria sarda*, *Punica*, *Punico-romana*, *Romano-cristiana*, and *Età cristiana*, and the beating light of that early sun weakens as you move from arch to arch. The stone implements used for working the obsidian, the flint arrowheads and knives, bring the Libyans out of death-dreams and put them back on the rocky hills near Olbia and Oristano, Nora, Abbasanta, Pula and Macomer. The yellow corn stubble laps round them, the blue mountains with wild boar and stags wait for their hunters. In glass cases the men of the *nuraghi*, themselves foreshortened by history, strut and pose and pray, in bronze.

Mostly these men are warriors, dour, sturdy and defiant as they arch their bows or raise their swords to hack at the light rippling round them. They wear thick sandals, tunics flattened over their thighs, and carry circular, decorated shields. Some are obviously chieftains, sternly looking out under helmets with great horn-shaped prongs, and wearing long cloaks. Some are huntsmen, wearing caps, cross-belts and game-bags, and carrying daggers or clubs. Yet, though each has an individual character, miraculously expressive features showing disdain, or fearlessness or sulkiness or veneration, they all bear the marks of a common, distinctive style. The finishing may sometimes be crude, but the conception is never primitive. These beautiful objects have cut their way pugnaciously through time, so that they now seem ahead of us in plastic accomplishment, in directness of meaning. They are short-cuts, perhaps, but they are short-cuts that isolate the essentials of their subject and remove trivialities. Picasso seems to be looking forward to them, not back. They have both energy and discipline, these swordsmen and slingers, priests, musicians and deities, the accoutrements of their world spread out around them—votive ships with stag's-head bows, musical instruments, doves and wild boars, weapons, tools, and water-cups. Religion and war are their sustaining ideologies, and in consequence they look serious, devout and determined. Women play no great part in their lives, except as mothers with child-warriors in their laps.

What is exciting about these bronzes, all of which are votive offerings made to attach or solder on to temple shelves, is the completeness with which they suggest their civilization. The cases that hold them have the effect of being stages on which some real prehistoric drama is being enacted. One has swum underwater and come upon an ancient ritual, or battle, arrested by an unknown act of fate, but preserved at its decisive, arrested moment in its entirety. No one can doubt that these are real men, going about their daily business over the sun-struck plains and granite ravines of their island. Looking at them, men under sentence of history, their gestures and prostrations do not seem futile but assertive. They witness, for our evidence, the quality of their faith, the style of their tribal authority. Oxen roam over the dusty valleys, ships rock off their southern coasts, and the chiefs stare out from the platforms of their *nuraghi* confident in their destiny, doves on their shoulders, breastplates glistening, families peacefully at work around them.

Nowhere else in these rooms is history so water-tight. The Punic remains from Karalis, Sulcis, Tharros and Nora show increased knowledge and increased doubt. Certainty is already breaking down as the sea, for so long shut, begins to open to traffic.

The Phoenician and Roman rooms, for all the beauty of some of the terracotta vases, glass vessels, scarabs and engraved rings, are less striking in effect. We are in shallower water, the relics we come across not compulsive offerings to a trusted god, but the personal embellishments of a foreign upper class. Mythological animals stalk their way through a landscape in fragments, but they do not seem to belong. The rows of Phoenician and Roman coins, except possibly for a few made in Sardinia by a Sicilian Greek craftsman, were all minted in their home capitals. The cases devoted to amulets, laces, rings and jewels, mostly found in the Phoenician tombs at Tharros, bear Egyptian symbols. Two granite sphinxes collect light under a window and opalescent glass vases from the Roman cemetery at Cornus spill over with liquid shadows. Funeral coins and terracotta jugs glow in warm, honeyed colours, and busts of imperial dignitaries, dusted of the soil of Olbia, turn noble features towards them and away from the temptations of young men's nude bodies, of boyish women with sun on their marble breasts. This is a Graeco-Roman decadent world, far from the rude simplicity of the neolithic Sards carving obsidian outside their *nuraghi*. Necessity has been succeeded by luxury, invention by art, barter in kind by commerce through money. Gold, bronze and silver coins, Phoenician, Roman, Byzantine, Arab and Spanish, string their dates together like a necklace symbolizing the encirclement of Sardinia. Money talks here with a Babel of voices, paying as little as possible for as much as it can.

Beyond all these cool rooms, noisy with memory once you start letting it work for you (alternatively you can glide unheeding through waterfalls of silent stone, indifferently nodding tribal chiefs, Roman consuls, and fertile goddesses, back into recesses of dream), the sun glints on a garden full of flowers and statues, on the inscriptions of Roman legionaries and sailors. Heat melts round Roman milestones torn from the old road from Cagliari to Porto Torres, and large terracotta containers, once used for grain, now collect the sun. Lizards skim across low walls, beneath which the sea blisters and churns with light. The inward-eyed attendant blinks like a mole in the glare, looking dazedly out at the long mauve arm of Spartivento, the white houses of Nora flecking the distance. The wind buffets you up here, and the salt-lagoons of Santa Gilla flash far below like mirrors.

* * *

We were on our way to spend a few days at Carloforte, the capital of San Pietro, a small island lying to the south-west, the other side of Spartivento. We had been told on all sides that it was a beautiful island, *molto tipico* and *caratteristico* (phrases of commendation that were used to describe anything at all), and that we should find a good hotel there run by a Dutch lady. I had remembered that Nelson, in his vain dash after the non-existent French fleet, had taken the *Vanguard* into the bay there and, in his own words to Lady Nelson, 'been refused the rights of humanity'—a churlishness that was explained by the fact that the inhabitants were Genoese colonists, not Sardinians at all.

We left Cagliari, after a hurried cup of coffee, at 5.30 am. Trains to places any distance away leave at this hour, and, except on the Cagliari–Iglesias, Cagliari–Olbia runs, there is usually only one good train a day. The early start, however, leaves room for plenty of elasticity in the time-table, and after a few such journeys one ceases to fret, thankful that one left in good time. The result is a constant feeling, shared apparently by passengers, guard, driver and engine itself, that there is an hour or two in hand, therefore almost an obligation to hang about as much as possible. Another great advantage of these early departures is, of course, that you can travel in the comparative cool.

Our train was only a couple of carriages, almost empty to begin with, though we could see mailbags being loaded and some particularly scruffy postmen getting on board. There were also the usual priest or two, a nun, and a few unshaven men in corduroys, carrying game-baskets and guns. These were the standard passengers on any branch line.

By the time we were clear of Cagliari, rattling across the lagoons, the sun was breasting Capo Carbonara behind us. The hard pearl-grey light began to soften, flushing the glinting water from gunmetal to pink. The morning was cool and windless, the mountains and forests ahead black against the sky. As we skirted the bay I watched the buff sides of fishing-boats making for harbour, the horizon line still firm before the African breeze could ruffle it. We slid now past reed hedges, reflected in the water like green silk curtains; boats, dotted over the lagoons, drifted with men fishing from them, while others with rods stood submerged up to their thighs, their legs seemingly amputated by the clean cut of the surface. We stopped at Elmas, an agreeable wayside station full of dahlias and zinnias, moving on again through eucalyptus-groves that assumed their own colours as the sun peeled its black shadow off them. Beyond were seas of vines, with women swaying and stooping like great dark insects amongst the pale, ruled lines. We were on the southern edge of the Campidano now, red-tiled houses floating above flat rich plains, crests of olive and vine rippling to mauve-ribbed mountains and occasional cypresses sticking up like the masts of wrecked ships. Then we branched off the main line at Decimomannu and turned due west, through bare plains with sheep and cows slumped down on them, to Siliqua. We changed trains here, having a leisurely black coffee in the station buffet before inspecting the white fourteenth-century parish church. It was still only seven o'clock, the sky rinsed and clear, and the mountains now looming to the south. Men were bicycling to work along the dusty roads, some to the orange-groves, some to the near-by mines. These medieval villages, apart from the thin railway lines disappearing past them, look much as they must have done when they were built, for they are simply circular clearings cut round a church, with the same pattern of meadow, vine, olive and wood coming up all round them, the pale mountains blocking the sky.

The new train was smaller and slower, parts of the two compartments open like old-fashioned trams. One of the postmen came and sat opposite me, very intrigued by the map I had spread out on my knees. After a while he asked if he might look. I handed it over to him and he began to pore over it. He took so long finding where we were that I thought perhaps he couldn't read. I pointed to Siliqua. Slowly he spelt it out to himself, then suddenly he began grinning, the dawning grin of a peasant who has just received physical proof of the existence of God. I don't believe he had really expected that Siliqua could exist in the mind of anyone who did not live there or who was not Sardinian. Yet here it was, in an English printed map. He chuckled delightedly as he came across other familiar names: Domusnovus, Santadi, Tratalias, Narcao. He called out to his friends in corduroy suits, all sitting together across the gangway, their guns between their legs. 'Michele Antonio! Alberto! Look! Santadi in English! And Barbusi! Fancy them knowing about Barbusi in England, eh! Giovanni, but they haven't marked your house, what about that, Giovanni?' He passed the map over, getting up and leaning over them to point out their villages. They could barely read, and I'm not sure that he could, but when they came across the familiar letters they repeated the names aloud, nodding wisely. The postman, if that was his title (for his only duties, he told me, were escorting the sacks of mail from one sorting-house to another, not actually delivering it), came back to his seat with the proud air of one who has enlarged the territories of knowledge. Occasionally he giggled, shaking his head in amazement. Barbusi, imagine Barbusi being minded about in England.

From Siliqua we chugged due south through a bare brown plain, rising from which, like a set by John Piper, were the ruins of the Castello di Acquafredda. The castle, built by the *Giudici* of Cagliari at the end of the thirteenth century, stands on a sharp rock, completely isolated, the sun pouring through holes in the stone. Round here Alfonso IV of Aragon, marching to Cagliari to claim his throne, fought several bloody battles against the Pisans. The great empty shell of the castle, its battlements swinging round against the light as we curved away from it, now seemed like part of the landscape, so long was it since it had any living purpose.

We began to climb now, the railway line twisting through deep ravines, bare granite glittering under sparse green scrub. The sun was warming up; it was going to be a boiling day. Here and there surprising clusters of oleanders thrust through the undergrowth, their fallen petals like pink confetti along the railway line. All round, the mountains, whose rich lead, zinc and copper deposits had, since the Phoenicians, drawn invaders to Sardinia, dipped and rose in black waves. We might have been going through one of the mining valleys of South Wales.

Occasionally we saw parties of men with guns walking along dried-out ravines which, the postman said, overflowed after the winter rains. Now there was only a thin trickle, glinting like mercury, at the foot of huge cliffs. The soil was obviously useless for agriculture, but the hills were lively with game. 'A hunter's paradise,' the postman pointed through the window, 'wild boar, stags, moufflon, rabbits, rooks', and from time to time, as if to underline his enthusiasm, shots rang out and went on echoing in the rocky gullies. The base of the hills, following the river line, was marked by a strip of deeper green, where gardens, pear and peach orchards, as well as vineyards, had been laid out. But whoever worked them must have had to come miles, for there were no houses to be seen anywhere.

Soon we were completely cut off by mountains, the bald peaks, snow-capped in winter, spilling down to the closed-in, cistus-scented valleys beneath them. Huddles of white houses above us marked the mining villages of Terrubia and Rosas; then, round a sharp bend, the landscape changed again. The mountains gave way to a holed, volcanic tableland, the sun seeming to melt it into soft rearing shapes. This in turn was followed by well-cultivated, dry river-beds, poplars and cypresses lining them, which flattened out eventually to the plain and railway junction of Santadi.

The sun was rising fast, the carriage brimming with heat. A short stop, time for the driver to cool off and smoke a cigarette, then, with only a handful of passengers left, we rumbled on again past the beautiful thirteenth-century romanesque church of Santa Maria at Tratalias and eastward to S. Giovanni and S. Antioco. Here the postman got out, shaking hands with us before dashing out into the sun to unload the mailbags. Ten minutes later, while we were still waiting in the smoky station, we saw him hauling a fresh lot of mail aboard the Cagliari train on the next track, jumping up himself, grinning and waving, just as it was moving off.

The sea was ahead of us, a dazzling flint-blue; we curved through drooping palms, their leaves heavy with coal, edging out past rows of coal-trucks, factory chimneys, and long, low warehouses. A slight breeze met us as we skirted a series of lagoons, with marshy islands moored in the reed-edged water and three-masted coal-boats loading alongside crane-hung quays. Men in pointed straw hats, bare except for turned-up cobalt trousers, stood motionless amongst the reeds holding long fishing-rods, while further out rowing boats splashed gently along the line of nets. On the horizon, as we slowed down across the dyke joining S. Antioco to the mainland, the strange rock-islets of Toro, Vitello and Vacca were nearly hidden in heat-haze.

We stopped at the port of S. Antioco, whose impressive harbour was built just before the war to hold the fleets of mineral boats that run between here and Italian ports. The whole island is covered in Carthaginian and Roman remains—coins, statues, and buildings—and during the construction of the new harbour the wreck of a Roman galley was found. The sky behind us was black with smoke, coastal villages looking dwarfed and dingy at the base of sprawling grey mountains. The idle Mediterranean had been changed here to something gritty and purposeful, the heat beating down on quays and barges and ugly squat cargo boats.

Men patrolled the train selling ice-cream and orangeades, cakes and the crushed biscuity *zicchi*. Then we were moving again, the sea on one side, the town of S. Antioco rising in tiers to our left. From the railway the town tapered up the hill to a church tower, the tower of the twelfth-century parish church which rises over vertical streets and stained white buildings. This was the site of the ancient Phoenician city of Sulcis, the industrial capital of Sardinia till the end of the Empire. Beyond the triangle of houses vineyards reached down to the little fishing village, all domes and cubes like an Arab settlement, of Calasetta. The island of San Pietro, a few miles off, seemed to have just risen from the waters. At the end of the jetty, where rows of gaudily painted boats blistered in the sun, the *Capo del Sandalo*, a sleek, white steamer, awaited us. The train pulled up on the very edge of the sea and we hurried aboard the hooting, already crowded boat. Within a minute the ropes had been cast off and we were under way.

Immediately the atmosphere appeared to change, one became conscious of a holiday spirit spreading through the ship as it nosed into the open sea. The bows lifted gently to a faint swell, and the naked fisher boys, diving off the landing-stage and slithering about in our wake, became bodiless heads floating on the glass-green water.

Groups of girls, their dark hair streaming back, stood in the fo'c'sle singing Neapolitan sailor songs, their voices drifting down-wind till they were answered by a crowd of young men leaning over the rails. It was the first spontaneous singing I had heard for weeks, a beautiful melancholy siren-music that seemed to have travelled underwater from Capri or Ischia. I realized then the essentially un-Italian flavour of Sardinia, how much it was a place that, dourly working to keep going, had no overflow of feeling.

The sense of release on the boat, as if circuits of pleasure had suddenly been reconnected, was too obvious to miss. For, no matter how far back, these people were all Genoese or mainland Italians, not Sardinians, and their natural exuberance could no longer be contained.

The mauve-green blur of San Pietro clarified, the tunny-fishing islet of Piana flashing like a marine palace off its northern tip. We passed stationary fishing-vessels, and a sailing-boat was tacking as it came out of the harbour ahead of us. Phrases from *Ritorno del Marinaio* and *Santa Lucia* floated back from the bows as we cut through the water-silk calm of the port entrance. A fleet of emerald mineral boats was anchored off the wide, palm-lined water-front. Behind the curve of salt-white buildings spreading in a half-moon up the hill, the pale noon blueness came flush to the green conical skyline. The usual crowd of *carabinieri*, port officials and loungers were collected on the quay.

★ ★ ★

San Pietro is a mountainous, trachytic island about seven miles long and five miles wide. The legend behind its name is that St. Peter, sailing to Cagliari, was blown off course and took refuge there; the island, because of its variety of hawks, was called Accipitrum under the Romans, and Hieracum by the Phoenician sailors who regularly put in there on their way to Spain. As in San Antioco, Roman and Carthaginian coins, tombs and amphoras are constantly being found, but from the end of the Empire until the eighteenth century the island appears to have been deserted. In 1736 Carlo Emanuele III allowed a colony of Genoese, established for four hundred years on the island of Tabarca, off the Tunisian coast, to settle in San Pietro, and it was they who founded the town of Carloforte. Seven years later Carlo Emanuele ransomed a further lot of Genoese Tabarcini, who had been made slaves by the Bey of Tunis on his capture of their island, and they also were landed at Carloforte. The town had hardly been built before the inhabitants were forced to burn it down to prevent its capture by the French. Soon after its reconstruction Tunisian pirates made a series of assaults on it, on one occasion sailing away with a thousand prisoners. Since then visitors have been regarded with a certain amount of suspicion, as Nelson, who arrived shortly after the first wave of Tunisians, quickly discovered. This atmosphere of suspicion still surprisingly persists, though for different reasons. During the 1914-18 war the harbour at Carloforte was used as a naval base, and a geodetic station set up; but though Carloforte has long ceased to have either military connections or importance, the old signs forbidding photographs and binoculars still remain up and zealous *carabinieri* do their best to give dignity to their profession. On our arrival, for example, we had no sooner freed ourselves of the loitering crowd on the quay, hoping to find the hotel quickly, than a *carabiniere* approached, saying that our immediate presence was requested by the Comandante. Our passports, too, were required, he added, smiling fatalistically, and he would show us the way. I declined, however, to follow him, but said I would present myself and the passports as soon as we had found a hotel. This was against all regulations, he persisted, pulling out a toothpick and distractedly scraping at a gold-crowned tooth. Later, when we arrived at the Comandante's office, we were kept waiting an hour in the corridor. Eventually a dark, handsome little cavalry officer, with flashing teeth and appealing eyes, came strutting up the stairs from the street, bowed with great flourish, and, unlocking the door of his office, apologized for his lateness. He showed us in, then, removing his cap with feminine care and adjusting his hair, sat down behind an enormous desk. He blew on his nails, smiled again, asked to be excused for a moment and began ripping open a pile of envelopes in front of him. At each he scowled or looked grave, as though receiving information about plots for the blowing up of the port. Finally, with a heavy sigh, he pushed the papers away and looked up with the air of one who was about to attend to altogether lighter matters, a self-indulgence he should not really be permitting himself. He relaxed, pretended to forget what we were there for, then suddenly appeared to recollect. 'Ah! Yes, of course. You arrived this morning, English, yes, let me see, then, you will have passports.' He went on like this for some minutes, how long were we staying, what was my profession? H'm, interesting, had we been to Rome, what was this now (flicking a page of my passport over), a visa for Moscow? No, I pointed out, only for the Russian Zone of Germany. Then what was this, he asked, and that one there. They were for Israel and Iraq, I said, and if he gave us the forms to fill in perhaps we should get on more quickly. He looked up, surprised for a moment, then, with a laugh, pushed the forms and passports over. He regretted, he said in Italian, that he was not better at English.

But he was determined on a long conversation: he came from Rome and was very fond of racing and the theatre. Here, of course, there was neither. He liked also, he went on, to ride at gymkhanas. It was very lonely here, no social life, everyone knew what everyone else was doing. With luck, though, he would be back in Rome by the spring. For him this was a kind of exile, he continued, but then it was always better that the Comandante should not be a native of the island. His smiles were now flashing out with the regularity of traffic lights. He extended a slim, jewelled hand across the desk. He hoped we would enjoy our stay. With a jump he was at the door, clicking his heels, bowing us out.

It had, after the boring wait, been an entertaining little interlude. It was rare, of course, that he had a chance for such a comic opera display. I discovered later that only six foreigners had been to the island in the last eighteen months. Any variation of routine, any opportunity to bolster up *amour-propre*, was therefore welcome. After my initial irritation, I felt more sympathy with him than anger. It must have been difficult to make a show, even keep up appearances, with such scanty materials. He was, after all, a Roman, with a taste for ceremony: and in Rome Commander of the Island of San Pietro must have sounded quite another matter. His rueful eyes, as he stood at the top of the steps saluting us, seemed to be watching the future deflating.

Today San Pietro is inhabited almost entirely by fishermen. The development of ports on the Sardinian mainland is reducing the importance of Carloforte as a mineral centre. The island is rich in various kinds of stone, especially red jasper and obsidian, and a constant shuttle of carts and lorries rattles down to the quay. There is also a salt-works, its produce used as ballast in the mineral boats. But fishing, particularly tunny, coral, sardine and lobster, is the permanent and most rewarding occupation. The harbour is packed with fishing-boats, full of the cries and shouts of the men working on them, mending nets or putting on fresh layers of the grass-coloured paint that seemed to be unique to Carloforte. (Each port in Sardinia appeared to have proprietary rights over a particular colour. The boats in Cagliari are mostly pale blue and in Alghero orange.) The Tabarcini, as they still call themselves, retain, as well as Genoese costume and dialect, the industriousness and commercial acuteness common to their race. They are, unlike the Sardinians, natural fishermen and Carloforte harbour has a spotless, scrubbed appearance of which the inhabitants are greatly proud.

The *Albergo Aurora*, to which we had seen a sign on the waterfront, was a charming villa some way inland and set back from the solitary road that bisects the town. We walked slowly past newly whitewashed houses with iron balconies, and through a large piazza with palms and a modern church. Beyond this, a long street with shops at one end tapered away into countryside. The perpendicular sun blazed off the white houses, throwing no shade. I was reminded a little of Procida, only it was cleaner here, more orderly. The skyline was a jagged, glittering grey above us, the rocky hillside barely cultivated. I could hear the tinkle of goat-bells and presently a man ambled past us on a donkey. The *Aurora* was on the edge of the country, hidden behind high white walls. We pushed open the gate, entering a garden thickly planted with orange- and lemon-trees; almond-trees and giant palms almost obliterated the villa at the end of it. The air was full of the smell of almond blossom. I had a feeling our stay here was going to be both civilized and agreeable, and I was not wrong.

The Zanottis, of whom we became very fond, had bought the villa in 1950. She had been a photographer in Amsterdam; he had run a travel agency in Paris, lived a long time in Spain, and been to most places in Europe. They had married just after the war, choosing Carloforte, out of many possibilities, to buy a villa, settle down and try and live on it. They were both cultivated, lively people, with great interest in the arts and a touching faith in their project. Signor Zanotti, who came from Milan, was an excellent cook, and quite the best food we had in Sardinia was at the *Aurora*. Unfortunately, the islanders have so far shown little flair for building up a tourist industry, and to most Italians, let alone to anyone else, Carloforte doesn't exist. As I write this fifteen months later, I have in front of me a letter from Signora Zanotti, dated December 1st. 'We have warm, sunny days, without any wind, like June in England. Daffodils, almond blossom, roses, and all kinds of wild flowers. The oranges are ripe and soon the first lambs will be born. But alas! we don't know if we will be able to hold out till next summer.' It is sad to read this, for rarely have I come across an island more suitable for a civilized holiday, or a place that combined so discreetly the advantages of a well-run hotel with the atmosphere of a private villa. San Pietro is, in essence, a private island: there is about one house to each bay, the best beaches can be reached only by boat, and there are no public amusements whatever.

My most constant memory of Signor Zanotti, a spare, dark-haired man with a sad, bright face, is watching him pore over advertisements for English fishing-tackle. Milward's *White Spider Yarn* was his especial joy. He was a great underwater-fishing enthusiast, a sport for which San Pietro is one of the best sites in the Mediterranean. Cyril Connolly once suggested that one day new maps would be made in terms of underwater resorts, with hotels specially built to cater for this new race of sportsmen. If this should ever come about, San Pietro and the *Albergo Aurora* will find their just public.

We had our first meal alone, the radio playing softly while we ate delicious lobster and roast veal. In the evenings the harbour commander, a tall, lugubrious naval lieutenant of about thirty-five, usually came in to dine. He had recently got engaged, though he frequently talked of breaking it off, on account, he said, of his bad headaches. Each night he sat alone at his table near the terrace, immaculate in white uniform, his long, yellowish head in one hand as he toyed with his *pasta*. One evening there were our familiars, the three commercial travellers; otherwise just our two tables, the radio playing dance music from Rome, and the Zanottis coming in from time to time with dishes bearing the mark of the individual artist.

I retired to bed after lunch that first day, taking with me Maugham's *Theatre*, which I had found with several Simenons and a Graham Greene in the bookcase. The lunch and the heat, however, were too much for even the younger Mr Maugham's prose, and to the occasional sound of ships' sirens wailing in the port I fell asleep.

I awoke to flies and rifle-shots. The sun, streaming through the half-closed shutters, only gently spilled over the hillside. The air smelt heavily of cistus and fig and almond. I could hear someone hosing the flowers in the garden and, getting up, I saw a small Arab-coloured boy in white shorts, a huge straw hat on the back of his head, spraying the bougainvillea. The rubber hose twisted round his bare body like a snake.

I washed, dressed quickly, and went out. The moon was already rising. I turned up the hill, taking the narrow path that twisted steeply to the central peak. Birds were chattering hysterically in the oleanders. As I climbed, men were coming down the hill, walking behind their donkeys or driving sheep. Some had been shooting. There was practically no soil on the rock, only enormous tomb-like boulders and strange fissures. At the top there was about half a mile of nearly flat ground, hidden in a slight curve, and there were two or three white houses whose only view was sky. Cows were grazing among sparse grey undergrowth, but mostly the holed, trachytic rock rippled in mauve waves to the sheer precipices that brought the island up short on all sides.

A warm wind was blowing across from Tunis. The sun, flushing the horizon, had turned the sea into sheet metal. The nearest land, looking due south, was Algeria, due west Spain. This was the narrow, untenanted sea over which Corsairs had made so many plundering dashes, and, standing now on the bleak, deserted cliffs, the light failing, one could almost feel the hereditary fear in the air, the lost, remote vulnerability of the slave-haunted islanders.

The sky over the Sardinian coast, as I turned away, began to change fron zinc to saffron, from violet and turkish pink to electric green. The sea was flooded with light, speckled here and there with white sails. Right down below, mineral boats circled gently at their moorings. The town looked like a box of salt-white bricks spilled between the long grey quays of the port, only the campanile of the church and the large cream rectangle of the school distinguishable from the rest. The air was so still that every noise from the harbour came clearly up: the hoot of a car (there were half a dozen on the island), the grind of anchors being hauled up, the sound of fishermen's voices as they called to one another from their boats, preparing them for sea. Lower down I could see the salt-heaps, the lilac twilight shadowing them and the sky leaving its ebbing colours like dregs in the lagoons.

By the time I reached the water-front, darkness had fallen. The port was now crowded, the evening *corso* taking place between the palms and the sea. Long lines of girls and youths, mostly in white, passed and re-passed in the comforting ritual, eyes always watching, but never meeting. All except the youngest men wore white, buttoned-down caps, producing a faintly surrealist effect. Small children, hand in hand, with bows in the girls' hair, darted among them. Round the floodlit statue of Carlo Emanuele III, erected in 1788, carried away by the French in 1793, and now back again with an arm broken off (from an angle it looked very like the Venus de Milo), a group of men were discussing politics. Along the quays I had noticed earlier in the day numerous hammers and sickles drawn on the walls, and there had been more on the rocks at the top of the hill. Here there were also giant slogans in black paint: EVVIVA CRISTO RE. Zanotti had told me at lunch that the mayor of Carloforte was a communist, the first efficient administrator the island had had for some years. In fact the whole southwest of Sardinia is communist; nor, considering that a series of new towns has been recently built to exploit the mines, is this surprising. Most of the workers in these towns were originally drawn from different provinces on the mainland, each area having to provide so many men. The volunteers had been restless, discontented people, others, the pressed men, political agitators and criminals, of whom their own provinces had been only too glad to be rid. Now, working under skilled technicians, they had found themselves on a good thing, with a powerful corporate identity.

Moonlight streamed through the palms, laying a thick chromium bar on the water. The harbour was nearly empty, but a few coral boats bobbed alongside the quay, riding lights on, the moon outlining their prows and the coiled ropes on deck. On one of them a boy strummed vaguely on a mandolin. Fruit-stalls had been set up in front of the boats, their water-melons, peaches and grapes glowing under hanging bulbs.

I had a Campari-soda in a café, before strolling slowly back through the town. The piazza was being marked out for a net-ball match, to take place at nine o'clock, Carloforte *v*. Cagliari. The goals were already up. Incense drifted through the open door of the church, and in the dark sloping streets old crones with black and brown hoods crouched alone outside their houses.

★ ★ ★

Next day we sailed round the island in a sardine boat. Zanotti had insisted that we see the extraordinary cliff formations on the open side of the coast and had accordingly arranged our excursion with two fisherboys. Early that morning two Swedish dentists, blond and lobster-coloured, put in to the port and somewhat reluctantly they had been pressed into accompanying us and sharing the expense. They had brought their own gleaming boat down the canals of France, had been to Corsica and were now on their way to Sicily and North Africa.

We pushed out at once into a head sea, the nose of the boat thumping into troughs of waves and showering us with spray. One of the boys busied himself with the engine, the other sat at the tiller. The Swedes and I, naked to the waist, were alternately burned and soaked as we lay back along the gunwale.

We circled the island, keeping about a quarter of a mile out to sea. We could see the *Capo del Sandalo* waiting off the Calasetta jetty for the Cagliari train. Behind it the buildings of San Antioco curved up to the centre of the island where, so I had learned at dinner, over a hundred families were living in the Roman tombs. To our right the green headlands were pitted with villas, waves breaking like soapsuds on the deeply indented cliffs. The salt marshes slid by, then low sandy bays with surf running in to empty golden beaches. At the south corner, the Punta delle Colonne, the rock has broken away to form two sturdy columns and we edged in close now, the boy at the tiller grinning as he aimed us at the base of the jagged gateway, slewing round at the last moment. We passed a cave, used in prehistoric times as a burial ground, and further on, at the top of a cliff, its modern successor, situated like Valéry's *Cimetière Marin*.

> Ce toit tranquille, où marchent les colombes,
> Entre les pins palpite, entre les tombes;
> Midi le juste y compose de feux
> La mer, la mer, toujours recommencée!

The Baia della Mezzaluna loomed up, the purple, wind-split rocks turning the coastline into a huge mansion, with waves splashing into long caves looking like hallways. Gulls screamed over us, flying off rocky battlements with shrill swoops and banking steeply to regain their gaunt towers.

Impressed, we drifted round while the Swedes dutifully got out their cameras; then, with a following sea, headed home. Half-way back we turned into the Spiaggia della Bobba, one of several otherwise inaccessible beaches, whose still, green water came up in a transparent sheet to a strip of dazzling sand. A small shepherd's house stood some way back from the beach, and in a minute the fisherboys had swum ashore, returning a few minutes later with armfuls of figs and grapes. We dived off the boat, helping them to bring the fruit on board, and then, swimming long enough to get cool, dried ourselves on the sand. We glided into the harbour a few minutes before the *Capo del Sandalo*. Waiting on the quay, the Comandante, gloves in hand, surveyed his territories through dark glasses.

Later that day we went over to have a drink with the de Plaisances, who, as well as owning the tunny fisheries at the northern end of the island, own the islet of Piana which I had first seen on our way across from Calasetta. They were friends of the Zanottis and had dropped in for a brandy late the previous night.

We hired the only taxi in the island and were soon bumping down the long avenue of palms, black now against the curdling sky. The sardine boats were going out one by one and the waterfront lay empty before the *corso*.

The houses soon gave way to rough scrub. The road became worse, the landscape bleaker and more deserted. There was now the sharp, pock-marked outline of the Guardia dei Mori, the highest point of the island, above us. We cut through flat, volcanic rock, escorted by screeching sea-birds to La Punta, the de Plaisances' house, whose low white walls reached to the cliff edge. In a few miles the whole aspect of the island had changed. A strong wind had blown up, and waves were foaming over the cracked, mauve rocks.

We walked round empty courtyards, roofed with esparto grass from Alicante in Spain, where the tunny are treated and dried before being packed, and Pierluigi de Plaisance explained to me the technicalities of the *mattanza*, the ritual killing of the fish to which visitors flock as though to a bullfight.

Pierluigi and his wife Claudia, a tall, honey-blonde with a romantic yearning for fogs, are both Genoese and live, for all except the summer months, in Genoa. During the winter this huge sprawling house, built a century ago, is shut, attended only by a guardian. But about the middle of March, when preparations for the *mattanza* begin, the first batch of Genoese arrive from the mainland. Then, for the next six weeks, they work at making and laying the *madraga*, the sectional net barrier against which the tunny will eventually be driven to the surface and killed.

This net barrier is laid in the shape of a T, the vertical stroke of which reaches out from the coast for about a mile. The top of the T consists of six adjoining 'rooms', four on one side, two on the other. These rooms are grounded on the sea-bed by anchors, and when the tunny, which appear almost to the same hour each May, hit the barrier, they turn into the rooms on either side. A passage is in fact left open, but so strong is their urge to move eastwards, following the shoreline of the Mediterranean to the Black Sea, that rather than turn back to freedom they stream in to their death. On May 3rd the *incrociatura*, the laying of the nets, takes place, with the *rais*, the captain of the whole operation, now personally supervising affairs. The nets are blessed, special barges are brought alongside the final chamber, which is called the *camera della morte*, and watch is kept for the arrival of the first batch of fish.

In recent years, Pierluigi said, the tunny have been arriving on May 8th. By that time, the whole of the area over which we were now walking would be swarming with men who dry, clean and pack the fish.

When the first shoals are sighted, a white flag is hoisted and the *rais* takes up position in his barge flanking the *camera della morte*. Leaning over the side he watches the tunny moving in from one room to the other, and when he has decided that enough have entered the *camera della morte* he orders the entrance to be shut. The *rais* then begins a series of prayers, calling on all the saints connected with fishing, praising them and asking for a generous catch. Tyndale, in his account of a visit to a *tonnara* in the north of Sardinia, adds: 'Besides the saints of such undoubted authority and interest in tunny fishery, the shrines of general as well as local celebrity were called over, and a blessing demanded for the principal towns and places in the Mediterranean which purchased the fish.'

The most exhausting part of the business is now begun: the nets on the sea-bed are gradually raised until the tunny are forced to the surface. Their circling becomes more and more desperate, and the sea is a mass of foam as they collide and flail at one another. The men round the sides hold out their *crocci*, long poles with iron spikes at the end, and as the fish break water they drive the spikes into them. The *camera della morte* is immediately filled with blood, which the frenzied creatures churn up over the fishermen until they are eventually worn out. The tunny are then hoisted into the barges and towed ashore.

Once there, they are taken out of the sun, cleaned and treated by groups of men, each trained for a particular job. The fish are quickly dissected, soaked first in salt water and then in olive oil, pressed, and finally sterilized in large barrels kept heated for two hours at a temperature of a hundred and twenty degrees.

By nightfall they have been loaded into waiting ships, and are on their way to Genoa.

This process, the actual number of *mattanzas* varying from week to week, lasts for about forty days. Sometimes bad weather can reduce the catch to almost nothing; sometimes swordfish, which often accompany the tunny but always work their way out of the nets, lead the tunny out with them.

Now, of course, it was the fag-end of the season. The *tonnara* was empty except for Pierluigi and Claudia, and the next week they too were returning to Genoa.

We walked with them round their desolate volcanic coastline. The sky had clouded over and the jagged contours of this north-eastern edge of the island, devoid of house or shrub, might well have been those of some derelict northern outpost. Claudia de Plaisance said that this was where she liked to come and sit all alone at sunset. 'I get so sick of the sun, day after day, and here I can see the sky and the rocks becoming one colour, the sea breaking up as though on the end of the world.'

When we left to drive back to the *Aurora*, she said: 'I do long for the winter, it's so lovely and sad. You cannot imagine how dull it is here, the same, week in, week out, no rain, no cloud. In Genoa I sit and drink tea and think of mists all day to make up for it.'

* * *

We sailed from Carloforte a day or two later, rested and refreshed. The de Plaisances and Zanottis were on the quay to see us off. As we were waiting for the *Capo del Sandalo* to arrive, Zanotti pointed out a shaggy, white-haired fisherman in patched, faded blue jeans, who was clambering about the sardine boats. This particular man, Zanotti said, was the richest man on the island, owning a restaurant on the harbour, several houses and a fleet of boats. Most of his life he had worked as a beggar in America, eventually making a great fortune out of it. A few years ago he had returned to Carloforte, where he had been born, had bought his various establishments and properties, and settled down to living as a great gentleman. However, he had soon tired of this and, although still extremely rich, had leased his house and taken a bare top room in his own hotel. Now he just pottered about in old clothes, sitting most of the day in the sun and drinking himself to sleep by dusk.

He was already, it was apparent, fairly drunk, though it was only four o'clock, When, half an hour later, we had got aboard, and were slowly edging out to sea, his voice, singing gently as he lurched about the quay, slapping friends on the back or shaking hands vigorously with the dispersing crowd, was the last sound we heard. The faces on the jetty shrank, and by the time we had turned towards the Sardinian coast, San Pietro was only a mauve shadow, without definition or inhabitants. Gulls circled the ship, the westering sun gilding the sea ahead of us, and as we moved back into the radius of the known world, Carloforte seemed to sink without trace.

We reached the mainland at Porto Vesme, where the de Plaisances had a third *tonnara*, continuing the journey back to Cagliari by bus. The first village we stopped at, Porto Scuso, consisted only of a stagnant-looking beach and a few warehouses. An extraordinary crowd of lunatics, degenerates and deformed men had collected together in the piazza. They gathered grinning round the bus, some squinting, others humpbacked or with no sense of equilibrium. Those in the bus shouted abuse at them, and they smirked back as if being complimented. One youth, with great jutting-out teeth, made shrill crowing noises, apparently unable to produce any other sound.

When we moved on again, he ran crowing after the bus, and as the dust cleared away, I could see him lying on the road, shaking his arms like a rag doll.

The bus had filled up with miners. The landscape was bare and hilly, the road twisting through ugly little settlements and down through smoky, mine-scarred valleys. We reached Iglesias an hour later, changing the bus for a train.

We waited some time for a connection, and what I remember most about the town was sitting drinking wine in the new piazza, darkness falling, and lorries, laden with coal, rumbling down the main street. The old town is built into the side of a hill, with steep narrow streets connecting perfect medieval piazzas. We wandered past the illuminated caves of shops, moonlight splashing on the steps of the Pisan cathedral, and lighting up the reconstructed town-walls. The castle, now a factory, hung above us, outlined against the rock. The yellow disc of the moon rose like a pumpkin above its Pisan towers.

In the huge, tree-lined square, round which the modern mining town has spread, the *corso* was in full swing, the men in black and the women in long red skirts. The whole history of the town was resumed in these lines of swishing figures; the old, poor families emerging from the crammed airless citadel and mixing with the new, richer families of engineers and technicians, all of whom had their motor-bikes and cars drawn up along the kerb.

It was a Sunday evening and miners had come in from Carbonia, the mining town built by Mussolini in 1936, a few miles south. Though every effort had been made to make the new town imposing and spacious, it was still the half-derelict old citadel that dominated the utility modern suburb straggling down the hill. Perhaps in fifty years there would be only one prosperous industrial city, but now the two existed side by side, like exhibits in a museum.

We caught the eight o'clock *rapido* to Cagliari, and an hour later I was unpacking in the *Albergo Italia*, to the welcoming click of billiard balls.

* * *

I made one more expedition from Cagliari. Fagioli, the large, jovial director of the *Ente Turismo*, drove me out one afternoon to see the ruins of Nora, the most ancient of Sardinian cities. It had begun to cloud over as we swung out of the town, and soon the lagoons and beaches of La Plaia, the sulphurous sea unfolding listlessly on empty sand, were pitted with fine rain. This western sweep of the bay of Cagliari is a humbler version of Poetto; instead of wide beaches and lidos a narrow strip of sand, used almost exclusively by peasants and local fishermen, stretches for miles. The road follows the beach for about ten miles, and now the sea was a violent bruised colour, broken only by the black sails of fishing-boats. We turned inland, driving through successive sections of olive, carob and almond trees, before reaching the rim of a yellow plain, its corn stubble stretching to where clouds were breaking up over the Iglesias mountains.

New excavations had been recently begun at Nora, Fagioli told me, and, during the four months that they had been in progress, much fresh material had come to light. Two archaeologists, one from Naples and the other from Cagliari, were in charge of operations, with forty-five men digging for them, and gradually a complete plan of the Phoenician and Roman cities was being formed. Owing to its exposed southerly position, the town had been deserted during the medieval period, and successive Arab invaders had looted all the temples, breaking up the marble columns and carrying off quantities of jewellery and gold plate.

It was, in a way, more impressive seeing the whole bay in semi-darkness, with black, crumbling clouds thundering in from the sea, and rain spattering the amputated marble of theatres and temples, baths and mosaic floors. For there is now no town at all, no houses or sign of life. Some three or four miles inland there is the tiny, pretty village of Pula, and then the road cuts in between two gaunt headlands, each with its broken tower built in the fifth century B.C. as part of the defences against the Arabs. On the foothills dropping from Pula to the sea stood the original Phoenician city, later the seat of the Imperial Roman government, but now it is only when you reach the rocky outline of the coast that there is anything to indicate that this romantic and melancholy shore was ever inhabited. As we drove down the centre of the bay, the white surf the only object of light as far as the eye could see, Fagioli pointed out the mounds of earth, wired in all round, where the excavations were taking place. We parked the car and, let into the heavily protected area by an ancient caretaker armed with a rifle, clambered up over the dykes that hid the ruins.

Once over the top, the half-exposed city, as though it were a modern building site, lay in sections about us. There was nobody around, for the excavators had retired for their summer holiday, and the rain dripped bleakly over the upturned soil. A shaft of silvery light suddenly broke through the racing cloud, lighting up the fragments of Phoenician pottery that stood piled on the edge of the mosaic floor at our feet. A small but beautifully preserved Roman theatre faced the sea, which we approached along a Roman aqueduct. It was like being in an overcrowded antique shop or in a museum undergoing reorganization: cylindrical stone water-tanks leading to tombs, the seats of the theatre flanked by tall Phoenician vases, and Roman busts stacked on the stone that was part of the ancient Tempio della Dea Tanit, the Carthaginian Venus Astarte, who had once been the object of a great cult. Nearer the sea, blocks of red Algerian marble, surrounded by superbly worked corners of pediments, lay on their side. So much glass had been found, Fagioli said, that it seemed likely the whole temple had been covered in it.

The sea was smooth now, like asphalt, and we could see the tops of columns and houses just breaking the surface. It was under the water that most of the Roman city still lay, and the sea was unnaturally calm over the ruins as though contained by some great tank. Divers had been down taking underwater films, some of which, Fagioli told me, were of extraordinary beauty. From the beach I could see the luminous glint of stone where green transparent water stretched over it like oiled silk, and here and there small whirlpools eddied round sucking concavities.

We passed on our way back to Pula the pretty romanesque church of S. Efisio, where, Fagioli explained, the most impressive *festa* in the island took place every May. Santo Efisio, the patron saint of Sardinia, was reputedly an officer in Diocletian's service who was martyred at Nora for his conversion to Christianity. In 1656 the festival of the Sagra di Santo Efisio was instituted, largely in the hope of alleviating the plague then rife in Cagliari, and, every year since, the image of the saint has been carried in procession from the Church of S. Efisio in the capital to Nora. This procession is the most gorgeously costumed of any in Sardinia: the saint is flanked by soldiers on horseback, the civil and religious leaders of the island, as well as peasants in costume from all over the Campidano. They leave Cagliari on May 1st, spend a night on the way and reach Pula the next morning. A number of services are held, fishing-boats are illuminated in the small bay of Nora, and when the procession arrives back in Cagliari on the 4th, tremendous celebrations take place. These junketings, called the *Primavera Sarda*, consist of carriage-and-pair races, horse-racing, *gimcane automobilistiche*, folk-dancing, firework displays, art and craft exhibitions, and competitions for vegetables; finally, the Lido at Poetto is officially opened.

We drove back a different way to Cagliari, turning inland and following the original Roman road (at one time all the roads in the island radiated from Nora). Darkness was falling quickly, and as we climbed through thick pine-woods and eucalyptus-groves, the dusk full of their odour, we could see the lights coming on all over the bay beneath us. The rain had stopped, and by the time we came bowling down the hill into the outskirts of Cagliari a full moon was flushing the diamond-rock with its hard lemon beam.

* * *

We spent a few more days in Cagliari, visiting churches—of which there are several dozen, many of great interest,—bathing, reading, and walking endlessly through the streets. I read two more of Grazia Deledda's novels, *La Madre* and *Cenere*, and although I began them out of a sense of duty I continued with increasing pleasure. Many of her novels were not about Sardinia at all, but were set in Rome, where she lived most of her later life. *La Madre* and *Cenere*, however, are set in the hills round Nuoro and they have a wonderful nostalgic feeling for the Sardinian landscape. They are, in a sense, old-fashioned, but only in the sense that Sardinia remains a traditional island, torn between, on the one hand, Church and progress, duty and desire, and on the other by the desperate urge of each younger generation to escape to the towns of Italy. *La Madre* is a story of possessive mother-love. A servant woman whose son has become a priest threatens to expose him for his infatuation with a rich woman. It develops two familiar themes: the destructiveness of lust in a tradition of strict chastity, and the way in which an ambitious mother, who has achieved local standing in an isolated community, will sacrifice it rather than lose her son to another woman. In *La Madre* the mother prevails over her son to stop seeing the woman while there is still time; but when, in explanation, he informs his lover of his vow, she in turn blackmails him. In a scene of great melodrama she walks to the altar rails while he is taking Mass and turns, as she had threatened, as if to scream their secret to the congregation. However, at the last moment, she drops to her knees in front of him. But so great has been the strain that the priest faints, and the mother, aware of his tension, has a heart attack in church and dies. The son and the woman are left with no material obstacle between them, but the old mother's death, coming too late, clarifies their spiritual dilemma and leaves them even more firmly bound by their consciences.

Cenere, 'Ashes', a novel of far greater scope, also describes the conflict between duty and love. A young peasant girl has an illegitimate son, Anania, is turned out by her parents, and lives almost wild in the mountains near Nuoro. Eventually she abandons the child on his father's doorstep and disappears. The boy is brought up by his father's real wife, befriended by the man's employer, and sent to study in Cagliari and Rome. He falls in love with, and gets engaged to, his patron's beautiful daughter Margherita, yet is continually haunted by his mother's possible fate. He searches the brothels of Rome for her, convinced she has become a whore. Then he discovers she has been living with a blind beggar, following him from *festa* to *festa*. He hesitates whether to tell his fiancée about her, afraid to lose her. The mother, fever-ridden and hideous, appears in the district and he goes to her. She, fearing to handicap him, takes her own life; but again it is too late, for Anania, upset by Margherita's anger at his preoccupation with his mother, has already renounced her.

The real fascination of Grazia Deledda's novels is their realism. They seem, at first sight, to be conventional elaborations of the struggle between good and evil, with fate playing a rather more capricious and revengeful part than usual. But they are, in fact, novels forced out of the Sardinian character and attitude to life. They are local in the best sense, touching off on almost every page illuminating truths about the Nuorese peasantry, their customs, ideas, ways of feeling. The wild, mountain landscape, as did the Lake district for Wordsworth, provided her with an almost intact manuscript. At any rate, it formed her style, solid, economical but capable of fine descriptive flourishes, so that her novels are the best substitute for Sardinian landscape painting. It would not be far-fetched to call Grazia Deledda, on a much smaller scale, a Sardinian Thomas Hardy. For anyone who wants the authentic flavour of Sardinia's mountain villages, their inhabitants' alternating feelings of freedom and isolation, these last two novels, as well as *L'Erdera*, could not be a better introduction. Moreover, they remain true, emotionally and visually.

In the evenings, I used to go and read on a bench overlooking the Roman amphitheatre, high up at the back of the town. I could raise my eyes and watch the sea bruising into twilight far below, the sky squeezing out its final colours and the air resinous and sweet. Families would emerge from their homes in the gapped corridors off the arena, and perform their evening ablutions. Candles flickered in the dark under the cooling stone seats, and, while a man was washing outside or walking his dog in the arena, I could see the table being laid. Every night, at the same time, someone practised his flute, and the melancholy notes, liquid among the harsh dry croakings of frogs and cicadas, seemed to belong more naturally to Grazia Deledda's world, with its triumphs of obligation over passion, than to our own.

PART FOUR

Oristano—Sassari

THE day of the *festa* at Oristano, when the annual crowning of the image of the Madonna del Rimedio would take place, was hot and cloudless. I was sorry in a way to leave Cagliari, one of those places which, when their superficial potentialities seem exhausted, renew their interest on another level. Yet the offer of another lift from Dr. Fagioli was too good to refuse. Several times we had seen him about the town, the shark *dottore* amongst a shoal of pilot-fish *dottori*, blinking at the sunlight and smiling agreeably while he told us of his various commitments: guests of the government arriving from Roma, a 'growp' of tourists from Milano (on the whole Fagioli spoke plausible English, learned in a British P.O.W. camp, but 'group' he essayed with no distinction), some students from Torino, an archaeological 'growp' from Napoli . . . and he would hurry away, sweating profusely, to inaugurate someone else to the newly discovered beauties of Sardinia.

We set off shortly after lunch, whirling at great speed up the dead-straight road that followed its Roman predecessor for well over a hundred and fifty kilometres without perceptible deviation. Grandstands were being erected for the weekend motor-race, when racing-drivers would cover the two hundred kilometres from Sassari in an hour and a half. At intervals Fagioli would take his hand off the steering-wheel to point out some feature of landscape—the corn stubble that was particularly good for *pasta*, the red mountains on the horizon, the system of small-holdings by which the flat, bare land was divided up—and each time we swayed alarmingly across the road, once narrowly missing a bullock-cart with nodding, suddenly amazed driver. For most of the way the road was flanked by prickly-pear hedges and olive-trees. Dusty fields reached away to the mountains and occasional strips of vine outlined the quiet villages through which we flashed. As it was a Sunday, streets were deserted, but there were usually tables set out in the open, with four or five men playing cards round them. Bottles of wine cooled under each chair, and every doorway framed its black-skirted, knitting occupant. They paid no attention to the *dottore's* violent honking, which went on non-stop from the first house in the village to the last. Sardinian towns and villages have often the effect of being a series of period illustrations, barely seeming to be alive; at intervals striking new compositions are formed and the moving people, at the instant of exposure, are halted against their background of brown earth and blue sky. These compositions, which bear no relation to the style of any painter, have brown, black and pale blue for their basic colours. The Sardinian landscape, its sombrely-dressed peasants working on parched soil or seated on bullock-carts that grind their way over bare plains or cypress-lined roads, has the gravity that one tends to associate with the eighteenth or early nineteenth century. The mountains, remote barriers never out of sight, seem both to cut off the island spiritually and to give it a self-absorbed intensity. The people themselves, with their beautiful, formal carriage, their sturdy grace, instinctively take up positions that a painter, Manet or Degas, for instance, might have composed. Elsewhere in the Mediterranean, peasants, while remaining close to the soil, seem more nearly contemporary. The Sardinians, partly because they wear a traditional costume, partly because they are an introspective, primitive people (most Mediterranean islanders look outwards, longing for escape into the urban world of opportunity and gadgets), appear becalmed in the past. It is, in fact, only the inland Sards who have this historical detachment, yet it means that whenever you leave the coast you enter a nerveless area, within whose boundaries the eye is charmed and refreshed as by a daguerreotype. This is the world which produced the drummer-boy hero of De Amicis' *Il Tamburino Sardo*, that sentimental story of a youth whose Sardinian origin, with its implicit pride, courage and traditional independence, singled him out for the task of getting a vital message through the enemy lines.

At Santa Giusta, two miles south of Oristano, we saw the first signs of the *festa*. The road, which had been following the reed-edged, silvery lagoons, glimpsed on the way down to Cagliari in the train, dipped under the cathedral of Santa Giusta, which stands at the top of a steep flight of steps in otherwise open country. The diocese of Santa Giusta was suppressed in 1503, but the cathedral, one of the many beautiful romanesque buildings in Sardinia, has outstayed the lay history of its position, looking now like a great galleon aground in the lagoon. All over the north-west I came across Pisan basilicas and churches, in wild rocky positions miles from anywhere, that had survived the extinction or dispersal of the communities whose centre they had been, and which housed only high winds, chickens or stray peasants. As we got out to look at the church, which was built in the twelfth century, long and low, with blind arcades, a simple façade in the Lombard manner, and a campanile at the back, the doors opened, and a procession, headed by two priests bearing the Cross, began to descend the steps. A dozen priests carrying staves were followed by a small group of women wearing brilliant head-scarves. This was the first of numerous small processions, making their way to Oristano from outlying churches, which we passed on our way in.

The interior of Santa Giusta, like that of many Pisan churches in Sardinia, is supported by columns taken from ancient sites, and here marble and granite from Tharros have been used with other materials to build the pillars separating the three naves. The Pisan-romanesque style, with its bare, austere beauty, its uncluttered narrow aisles, perfectly suits the Sardinian character, and in general few countries have an ecclesiastical architecture which blends so strikingly into the landscape. By the time we had left the church, the procession was a blur of white and black diminishing between the pines and eucalyptus that converge like an arch above the Oristano road. We caught up with men in corduroys, carrying guns and game-bags (it was the first day of the partridge season), girls in full pleated skirts, richly embroidered, riding on the pillions of motor-bikes, whole families straggling across the road. The sun was slackening now, silver on the lagoons where half-naked men, under great straw hats like West Indians, fished from their boats. We overtook the priests of Santa Giusta, red-faced and sweating. The crowning ceremony was to be performed in the Piazza Roma, but long before we reached the Via Tharros which leads into it, the crowds and buses and men on horseback—for Oristano is the great cattle-town of Sardinia—made progress impossible. We got out, thanking the *dottore*, who was now alternately hooting at the pilgrims as though they were chickens, and wondering, the car at a standstill, anxiously about the 'growps' he was due to supervise. Then we, too, were engulfed and separated in the surge of people.

It was nearly six o'clock when I reached the Piazza Roma, an attractive country market-place, lined with palms and flower-beds, and off which twin medieval towers formed a gate to the north. The streets running off it were packed with pilgrims, and in the square itself it was possible to move only by pushing aside other people. Over the heads of the crowd I could see the large red-velvet dais, with gold draperies falling from an enormous crown, where Cardinal Tedeschini, from Rome, would address the populace. Coloured light bulbs were strung along the streets, and flags hung on wires between the palm-trees.

The air was stifling. A small space, like a boxing-ring, had been cleared in front of the dais, and *carabinieri* lined the approaches to the square from the Palazzo di Giustizia and the cathedral. The dust eddied with the mixed smell of sweat and wine as swarming pilgrims fought their way through side streets to establish vantage-points. A band was playing, the brassy tunes bumping off the crowd's chatter, and the pattern in the square itself kept on changing colour, like a shaken kaleidoscope, as fresh groups of women, each in the embroidered neckerchiefs and skirts of their particular village, threaded their way through.

Enthusiasts had been there since early morning and these had made themselves comfortable, forming little islands as they sat on the ground, with bottles and bits of paper all round them. An old man in stocking cap and black-velvet waistcoat lay full length on the pavement, giggling gently to himself and making feeble attempts to catch hold of the embroidered skirt hems that flicked past his nose. In amongst self-conscious clusters of girls, bright as peacocks in their stiff brocades, tired and dusty old crones, singly or in pairs, brooded over their sticks. Men in velvet corduroy, holding bottles of wine and taking noisy mouthfuls, rinsed and spat. The houses round the piazza were nearly all flat-roofed, and rows of people in shirt-sleeves and cool dresses sat along them like spectators at Wimbledon. Some had umbrellas up, and on one house a line of nuns sat in striped deckchairs, their coifs looking like newspapers twisted into sun hats.

The procession was due to arrive in the piazza at six, but one of the *carabinieri* told me it had only just left the Duomo and would be another half hour. The spirit of the crowd had dwindled somewhat, as if, after dressing up and the excitement of getting there, they had really had enough and would have liked to have gone quietly home.

I walked away down a side street to get some air. Outside the piazza it was cool, with the light beginning to go. A merry-go-round had been set up on a piece of waste ground and dozens of children were flying heedlessly along on their grinning mounts. Beyond them the town ended abruptly; miles of bare plain stretched away to where the peaks of the Trebina seemed now only a thickening of the twilight. A few balloons of dust marked the passage of vehicles scurrying in from hill villages.

Back in the piazza the coloured bulbs had been switched on and the plane-trees swarmed with children, all chattering like birds in the bent branches. Neon signs flashed over shops and hotels, and chains of diamond stars were looped between the tall palms. The dust had settled, and the whole crowd was quieter and more expectant. I edged in past the news-kiosk, the top of which was crammed like a rajah's howdah on an elephant, towards the glowing dais. Scrawled along the wall behind me in blood-red ink were the words EVVIVA IL PAPA. EVVIVA LA SARDEGNA MARIANA. EVVIVA IL CARDINALE TEDESCHINI. Village groups, clustered round standard-bearers holding the name of their parish on long poles, began to sing desultorily. A loudspeaker was turned on and an announcer tried a few practice phrases. The dais had a sprinkling of people on it, and a few crows had settled impressively on the canopy. Numerous photographers peered about with light-meters. A slight breeze was ruffling the palms, and illuminated neon bridges over the narrow streets gave the whole thing a Venetian air. In place of gondolas, however, a platoon of outriders on motor-bikes volleyed into the piazza, and now the *carabinieri* started pushing the crowd back in earnest. A man fell off the top of the news-kiosk and a few minutes later a crash, followed by a thud and a roar of laughter, betokened the abrupt end of the circle seats on one of the plane-trees. The crowd had recovered their good humour, singing and calling out '*Evviva il Papa*', and leaning forward hopefully. But nothing happened. Interest subsided again, being diverted to the minstrels playing their flutes and the man with a pointed hat and a parrot in a cage, who told your fortune for ten lire.

Nobody was paying any attention at all, when, suddenly, the procession swung into sight. Led by soldiers in black, with red cocked hats and white shoulder bands, the first sections slowly circled the piazza before reforming round the dais. These were followed by a patrol of minute boy scouts, seemingly blown along by the trombones of the red-faced village band that puffed in their rear.

The noise was tremendous, for the announcer had started a running commentary on a hand microphone, jumping all over the dais like a boxing referee, and the loudspeaker was also blaring. A troop of girls, about fifty strong, in red, blue and gold costumes, now emerged, singing listlessly and darting coy glances at the photographers crouching with flash-bulbs in front of them. Groups of women, in costumes that were individual variations of the basic full skirt, lace blouse and stitched shawl, ambled intoning into the square, succeeded by others in white coifs and black skirts with blue pleats. While these circled rudderless, standard-bearers, carrying the flags and names of their village, each led a section of women, dressed in local costume. Borore, Iglesias, Arborea, Ortueri, whose women wore cream, heraldically embroidered head-scarves, succeeded one another, sweat pouring off them, old sad peasants among young beauties with huge, black eyes. Little shaven-headed boys surrounded a standard bellying out like a red sail; behind them the voices of nuns, starched and cool, were obliterated by the shrill trebles of the bawling youths. The procession was soon hopelessly jammed, and fierce queue-packers in crumpled suits barked '*Avanti!*' at the nuns so brusquely that they shied up from their hymn-books like nervous fillies. I recognized the group from Santa Giusta, flagging a little behind their cross. Men in pale-blue silk, with boaters the same colour, troops of bearded monks, more nuns, dirty, unshaven priests, and finally elegant plump dignitaries in surplices, completed the marchers.

The circling seemed as if it would go on all night. The smell of wine and sweat in the square was now mixed with incense. Flash-bulbs were going off every minute. The commentator had got the wires of his microphone so wound round him that he stumbled about half-trussed. Occasionally the young novices, installed at the best places on the route, called out to the crowd to clap the Cardinal.

At last, with the arrival of bishops in shocking-pink, their yellow shiny hats making them look like fat ladybirds, there were signs that the image of the *Madonna del Rimedio*, behind which would be the Cardinal, was about to reach the piazza. The Archbishops of Oristano, Sassari and Cagliari, flanked by a retinue of handsome young priests, hobbled up the carpeted steps, boys in black velvet, with long white stockings, holding out their vestments like wings.

There was a dramatic pause, the archbishops turning round to gaze benignly through their glasses at the thousands of faces floating up out of the twilight. Cameras clicked, *carabinieri* yelled at the crowds to make way, and suddenly the Cardinal himself, to applause, clapping and whistling of the kind normally reserved for film stars, stepped majestically into view.

Tedeschini, however, was a more imposing figure than any theatrical personage, more exquisitely robed, more fawned on. His impact on the festive Sardinian peasantry, the excited novices and nuns and monks, was such that God himself could not have been greeted with greater acclamation. While the junior clergy clapped and cried '*Evviva il Papa*', the whole crowd genuflected at his approach. With iron-grey face, erect, and with perfect timing, the Cardinal swept forward and then halted. Raising himself on his toes, he stared at the people with piercing eyes, lifted his hand in the blessing, then came down on his highish heels with a snap. Not a muscle moved in his face, the eyes never relinquished their merciless intensity. Old peasants burst out sobbing as he moved round the circle, stopping every few feet to give fresh blessings, pausing with countenance divine and majestic enough to awe the most resolute pagan into submission. This was acting in the great tradition, impossible not to admire. The gaunt, tremendous profile turned this way and that, the high heels clicked, the carmine lips tightened. Cardinal Pirelli himself, had he been raised from the beatitude of his immolation, could never have cut such a figure. The eyes burned holes in their arc of fire, the kneeling figures raised their handkerchiefs to shiny noses, then, the blessing pronounced, the beam switched off, moved on. The priests holding the Cardinal's train stood bemused behind him and, behind the image, now being carried by athletic figures to the dais, gravely walked the Cardinal's attendant—a boy whose pure beauty would have pleased Pirelli's creator as much as it would have His Eminence himself.

As the Cardinal turned to mount the dais, the official Vatican photographer, asserting his precedence, jostled all his colleagues out of the way. The Cardinal climbed up the steps, the backing photographer snapping all the time a few feet off, and behind him the radio commentator bustled aside stout and wilting clerics, with no ceremony at all. The image was somehow crowned, the archbishops nervously insinuating themselves between photographers and commentators and lifting the trailing wires over their heads as if engaged in some ecclesiastical form of 'Ring-a-Ring o' Roses'. Then the Cardinal, resplendent in his Schiaparelli pink against the dark-red and gold canopies, faced the cheering pilgrims, raised his hand like a victorious boxer, and gave a further solemn blessing. It was all over.

The crowd melted away. Satiated with emotion, it poured down side alleys and streets to catch trains and buses. A few hundred waited to file past the Cardinal, looking weary now, like some great tragedian after the last curtain. The photographers scurried off to get their films developed. In half an hour only stragglers remained.

The last pilgrims having done obeisance, the Cardinal and his retinue left in large black limousines which had drawn up in the piazza. Soon there were only empty bottles and drifting paper around the flower-beds and palms. The real stars had now come out above their neon facsimiles, and the bright coloured bulbs swung gently in a cool breeze. The parrot man with the pointed hat tagged dispiritedly after the minstrel troupe, all looking sad, as if at the poverty of their entertainment compared with the sorcery they had witnessed. Incense hung in the air, and the black crows, which had deserted the dais at the approach of the procession, resumed their comfortable dominion.

* * *

I had intended to go on to Sassari that night, the little accommodation available in Oristano having been booked up weeks before. Sixty thousand pilgrims, according to the next morning's *Nuova Sardegna*, were in the town, and it was immediately apparent that most of them had the same idea as we. The moment the proceedings were decently over, there was a mad rush to the station about a mile away. It was already dark, and once the illuminated, flag-hung towers and floodlit central piazzas had been left behind, the road twisted through humble shacks with no lights at all. The bright dresses of the women, glowing like fireflies, spilled thickly across the street, and behind them *carrozze* tinkled as they ploughed with a clatter of hooves through the dividing people. A few cars hooted impatiently, but mostly these were country peasants going back by cart or excursion bus to their outlying *paesi*.

No extra trains were running. An already overcrowded express to Cagliari was drawn up at the single platform, a sweating woman airing her huge breasts out of a compartment window as if they were detachable. Frantic people streamed through the barriers, struggling to wedge themselves in. The carriage doors could not be shut, and those in the centre were levitated as at some powerful medium's behest. Suddenly, with no warning, the train moved out, a litter of tenacious peasants hanging on the running-boards. The rear light trailed away into the sooty plane-trees curving round the track, and soon disappeared.

Only one more train was due, the stopping train to Sassari that took eight hours. There were still thousands on the platform. Most of these had now settled themselves down for the night. Blankets were laid out between the oleanders stretching between two overflowing lavatories. Family groups spread round in circles, matriarchal figures bringing out bread and cheese and bottles from raffia baskets. A man was sick on the line.

A commotion arose in the waiting-room, which was crammed with visiting schoolmistresses, chattering together like magpies. There were cries for a doctor. A woman was about to have a baby. Hot water was wanted, and towels. An old and collarless man, hitherto asleep on a bench, announced himself as a *dottore* and tried to fight his way in. But the schoolmistresses, innocent as they might have been of the initial sexual rites, were not easily going to be deprived of the end-product. As the *dottore* wormed himself through, calling for air, so they closed in round him—rather as do rugger players when a colleague has his trousers torn off. One expected to see a pair of shorts flung high out of the circle in the traditional gesture.

The harrassed narcissistic station-master, queening it in gold and crimson shako, appeared with an attendant female carrying hot water. He ordered the schoolmistresses out; but they made only token movements, craning ostrich-like necks to get a better view. A bottle of orangeade was passed in and a few minutes later a stretcher arrived. '*Morto! Morto!*' one of the mistresses announced. '*La Madre è morta!*' But it was the child, not the mother, who was dead.

I walked back to the town through empty streets. A few couples strolled in the Piazza Roma. Otherwise the town seemed deserted. The illuminated bridges, the red and blue bulbs, the bejewelled palms, made the square look like a ship on a gala night. But the passengers were all below decks. I went into an hotel and was directed to a private house for the night. The room was spotless, but the man in the next room snored like a trombone till the dawn pushed its green-grey light through the shutters. Sleep was impossible, but just as I had given up and was dressing, he turned over and the snoring ceased.

★ ★ ★

Oristano, as I discovered, walking through the streets in the early, salmon light, is a handsome medieval town, whose new subsidiary industries have not destroyed its character. It remains essentially a country town, with a weekly market to which people come from all over the island. It boasts four hotels, a dozen churches (one to a thousand inhabitants), rows of solid stone houses, with wrought-iron balconies and central courtyards, plenty of flowers and trees down the main streets. It is almost circular, a stone oasis in the flattest part of Sardinia, and changes abruptly from neat residential areas to crude huts on the rim of bare plain. To the west the lagoons merge almost imperceptibly into sea, a gun-metal gleam visible only from the thirteenth-century towers or the top floors of the oldest houses. But Oristano gives one no sense of the sea; the lagoons kill it.

As a modern town it exists in the shadow of its greater, now legendary past. For in the fourteenth century, when the Aragonese overran Sardinia and disposed of the three other independent *Giudicati*—Cagliari, Gallura and Logudoro—Arborea, with Oristano as its capital, fought a long, bitter and triumphant war. Various treaties were signed between 1387 and 1395, but ultimately Arborea retained its independence and its territories. It was the great *Giudicessa* Eleonora, daughter of Mariano IV, the first *giudice* to turn against Aragon, who both organized the war and concluded its diplomatic victories. Mariano, Aragon-trained, had returned from Spain to conduct a secret underground movement whose skirmishes were to last for over twenty years. Ugone, his son, took over on Mariano's death—from plague, the usual Sardinian destroyer—and when he was murdered with his daughter in 1383, his sister Eleonora, greater in mental stature than either, governed in the name of her son. Her husband, Brancaleone Doria, deserted to Aragon but Eleonora, surrounded by enemies within, as well as without, placed herself at the head of her few troops, silencing the same rebels who, having murdered her brother, were now clamouring for a republic.

In Sardinian history Eleonora of Arborea is both Jeanne d'Arc and Queen Elizabeth I, deliverer, spiritual inspiration, wise ruler. The *Carta di Logu*—the Code of Laws—framed by her father, she revised, completed and put into effect. The enlightened humanity of this document, far in advance of the social legislation of the period, so impressed Alfonso V that in 1421 its provisions, intended originally only for Arborea, were made law throughout Sardinia. The monument to her memory in the Piazza Eleonora, a marble statue built by Cambi in 1881, shows her holding the *Carta di Logu*—the person and the achievement most respected by the modern Sard.

I left on the first train for Sassari. The crowds of the night before had been magically absorbed, the station was newly washed. The air smelled fresh, the sky was the pale depthless blue that presaged a hot day. We trundled at half-pace through bare, brown plains, stopping at every station, with its water-pump and tired oleanders and ragged urchins. After three hours' meandering, the sun training its beam through the fly-mapped windows, we reached Chilivani. An hour's wait here, the buffet humming with excitement, for bandits had swooped down the night before and made a highly successful raid. Then a small, smoky branch-line train puffed in, reversed, and soon we were cutting north-west, away from the main Olbia line, through the richer, greener valleys of Logudoro.

I was glad to have seen the *festa* and the Firbankian Cardinal at Oristano. There, one had witnessed the mixture of high religious expertise and amateur theatricals by which the Church captivates the poverty-stricken peasants of the south. If you cannot give them land reform, a more even distribution of wealth, a simple rational example of the Church carrying out Christ's teaching in humility and without spiritual pride or corruption, then let them see the Holy Spirit in fancy dress once a year. Perhaps it was better than nothing; the pilgrims, anyway, seemed to think it a good show.

Now we had left the body of Sardinia behind us: the dried-out rivers, the light-filled dusty arenas backed by distant mountains, the industries and iron-ore and ports. The north-west segment, shaped like a goat's head, is different in spirit from the rest of the island. Africa has slipped away, and in its place there is a steeper, more ravaged Provence.

It was suffocatingly hot in the train, the more so for the windows were closed against the constant flow of grit from the engine. A priest opposite me put away his missal and brought out a copy of Moravia's latest novel. But that too remained unread, and a few minutes later his eyelids flopped down like visors behind his rimless glasses.

We were climbing steadily, the train puffing heavily along

slanting chestnut woods. Isolated white villas surfaced through pear and apple orchards, and viridian valleys, coated with sunlight, carried carpets of zinnias at the foot of cypresses. We cruised through steep cuttings before emerging into shallow plains, with *nuraghi* stuck over them like topknots. In the blue heat-haze, small rosy villages, pressed to hillsides in the shape of strewn bouquets, seemed almost to be floating. Shortly after midday we made a final, spiral climb into Sassari.

* * *

Sassari, the second city of Sardinia, with seventy thousand inhabitants as against Cagliari's hundred-and-forty thousand, was the Genoese stronghold in the island. The enmity between Sassari and Alghero, also between Sassari and Cagliari, persisted to such a degree that for a long time no roads or railway lines were laid connecting the towns, for fear of the consequences. At one time any traveller from Sassari to Alghero had to deposit his sword at the outer gate, being allowed to retrieve it only on his departure. The Algherese, on arrival at Sassari, were obliged, like Jews in Nazi Germany, to wear a distinguishing mark, a scabbard on their right side.

There seemed to be no present survival of this conflict, though, one was told, great commercial competition still existed. Sassari, however, is the least typical of Sardinian towns; the Sassarese have uprooted the past to the extent of pulling down the Genoese walls and Aragonese castle. In their place they have built huge piazzas, banks that can be mistaken for palaces, and created handsome tree-lined thoroughfares. The result is a comfortable, modern business centre, with so much space and air that it might have been designed by Le Corbusier. A skyscraper block of flats, the first in Sardinia, towers on arcaded stilts over the shops and hotels that surround it. This, when it was finished, aroused great local opposition, and because of their expense half the flats are still empty. Yet curiously it is a success: the flat grey-green façade, its eleven floors of windows glittering with sun, rises out of palms and judas-trees with an elegant fragility. From the upper storeys you look out on one side over rolling tobacco fields and olives; on the other, almond and cherry orchards spread through wide valleys dotted with orange-trees and pomegranate. The steeper hills have been replanted with pines, appearing from above like forests of toothbrushes. Rare species of roses are grown in the gardens of the many houses dotted on the limestone hill which the town bisects; and the altitude—Sassari is seven hundred feet above sea-level—gives the air unusual sweetness, so that it might be in Switzerland or somewhere near the Italian lakes.

Because, unlike Cagliari, it is a cool, inland town, uninfected by beach life, the people are more formally and better dressed. Girls clatter across the glassy piazzas in high-heeled shoes, nylons, and tailored coats and skirts. Men wear jackets to their suits and their brief-cases are filled with files, not bathing-costumes. Sassari's university, smaller than Cagliari, seems more in character with the atmosphere of civilized well-being that pervades the town.

Perhaps the first things that strike one, pulling up the steep looping road from the station in a flower-twined *carrozza*, are the cleanliness and modernity. Water spills out of shining markets, the shops, subtly window-dressed, are all chromium and glitter, and every street has its orderly line of palms or oleander. The Piazza d'Italia is surrounded by imposing dust-brown buildings in nineteenth-century gothic, some of which, like the Palazzo Provinciale, are official residences and halls. The remainder are various banks, with decorated ceilings, murals on the walls, and marbled interiors. The middle of the piazza—its shiny surface rippling like water with reflected light in the evenings—bears a statue of the second Vittorio Emanuele glaring balefully from an oasis of slim, feathery palms.

We booked into the *Albergo Castello*, a charming, secluded hotel looking over palms and flower-beds, near the site of the Aragonese castle whose five centuries of existence ended in 1877 to make way for a factory. The town sweeps down through narrow, medieval streets to the south, the skyscraper offers its therapeutic austerities the other side of a line of judas-trees, and beyond the rows of *carrozze*, their drivers nodding in the sun-warmed and flower-scented air, the gay Piazza Cavallino opens into the Piazza d'Italia.

We lunched late and heavily on fish soup, roast veal and *zabaglione*, and by the time I reached my bedroom I was nearly asleep.

I opened the local papers to read about the previous night's ceremonies, but I had barely struggled through a paragraph retailing the words used in the coronation, '*Federico del titolo di S. Maria della Vittoria della S. Romana Chiesa, prete Cardinale Tedeschini della S. S. Patriarchale Basilica dei Principi degli Apostoli dell'Urbe, Arciprete della rev. Fabbrica Prefetto* . . .', before the Cardinal's carmine lips and the plump ladybird-Archbishop had somehow got replaced by the Scarborough Festival cricket scores, with which I had at last been able to catch up. The sun had long passed its zenith, buttering the shutters with the softest yellow light, and the only sounds were the occasional stampings of cab-horses restless under cruising flies.

I woke to the first brushing, distant waves of the *passeggio serale*. From my window I could see the crowds making lazily for the Piazza d'Italia, the white suits of the men pressed like cream between the coloured layers of the women's dresses.

It was cool outside, a fresh breeze blowing crisply through the judas-trees. The greenness all round was exhilarating, though it seemed also a reminder that the south, and with it summer, was gradually being shed like a skin.

I dressed and strolled up the steep Corso Umberto to the top of the town. On the east Sassari drops suddenly, the limestone cliffs leaning at acute angles over low tobacco fields. Tobacco has always been one of the great local products, though the high taxes levied on its import by other countries have meant that it is smoked only in the island. 'The habit of smoking is very general,' Tyndale recorded a century ago, 'but that of snuff-taking almost universal, and many ladies of the noblesse, if not avowedly carrying her own tabacchiera, will never refuse a pinch from another's box.'

Sassari, perhaps because it seems like a continental town, has more the air of a capital than Cagliari. As I walked about, through new streets with shuttered houses fronted by large gardens, it was evident that a greater proportion of well-to-do people still lived here. A brass band played in the Public Gardens, fountains spilled amongst geraniums and cactus, dwarf palm and almond. Small children in immaculate white dresses or velvet suits were led obediently by hairy peasant women in black. The cafés round the main piazzas began to fill up, and cars from outlying estates swung like great black beetles over the hill.

Off the thick green rectangle of garden, on a slant like almost everything in the town, the university and cathedral are tucked away in the centre of the old quarter. Sassari has spiralled outwards in the form of a maze, so that the medieval axis has been completely hidden and unbalanced. The university, a rather dull building put up by the Jesuits in the sixteenth century, is flanked by some rather euphemistically termed palazzos, but the cathedral, despite undergoing almost every possible modification in style since the fourteenth century, has agreeable things about it. The baroque façade, built about 1670 and overhung by foaming trees, is ornate but elegant, though most of the additions to the original building, made when the episcopal seat was moved to Sassari from Porto Torres in 1441, are in Spanish gothic. The whole effect is curiously harmonious and solid, as though it were a castle that had passed through the hands of various owners of taste and ambition.

Shop windows spurted down alleyways in the thickening light. There were good, but expensive, antique shops in a quarter of their own, shut away and self-contained like the Palais Royal *quartier* in Paris. Book shops, china shops, shoe shops and restaurants: cafés with lively murals, inlaid in the eighteenth century, tiled billiard saloons and hairdressers. Before, they had been walled off, a fortified hub at the foot of the Palazzo del Duca, but still aloofly independent, islanded in the violent streams of the past, when the shouts of Pisans, Algherese and Spaniards echoed outside the gates jealously watched over by Genoese troops.

The Piazza d'Italia was splashed with light, the streets leading off it shining like canals. The whole town seemed to be out and about, the lines of strollers passing and repassing as if in formal dance. It might have been the prelude to some grand ball, perhaps for the Duca di Vallombrosa's daughter, whose near-by Palazzo now incarcerated civil servants scratching away in triplicate, or the Genoese *podestà* might have been receiving the Malaspina and Doria families on the eve of the *Festa dei Candelieri*. For in the last part of the fifteenth century Sassari, Alfonso V's 'Città Reale', became to all intents the social capital. Now there were fewer nobility, more and more ducal residences had been turned into offices, and only the windy brass band competed with the radio music of cafés and bars.

I had a drink that evening with Antonio Borio, a lecturer at the university, to whom I had been introduced at the *Ente Provinciale per il Turismo*, of which he was president. He was full of praise for the way in which the malaria had been tackled by American research field units. It had given Sardinia a 'second chance'. Because of it the whole economic outlook had improved: subsidiary industries were being developed, the land recultivated on scientific lines, the soil reclaimed and the peasants encouraged to go back and live on their land. New forests had been planted and so on. 'But', Borio concluded rather sadly, 'the Sards are still a poor people. We have made a beginning, that is all. The real wealth has changed hands. It has moved from the old families who lived on these slopes to the new aristocracy of the south-west—the communist industrialists round Iglesias. There is a different class of rich, a less, shall we say, appreciative one: their money is spent on different things. However, it is improving, it will continue to improve.'

The wife of a local surgeon joined us later at the café table. She was Sardinian, pretty and well dressed. I praised Sassari to her, its exhilarating air, greenness and spaciousness, the way in which the past and present had come so harmoniously to terms. Despite its remoteness, I went on, it seemed to me a noble and modern city. 'Oh! Yes,' she said. 'It's all right. But after a bit it gets very boring. I usually go to the cinema every night and stay in bed in the mornings. Gino, my husband, will get to Rome soon. It's very out of it here, the Sassarese are complete provincials. But please let's talk about something more interesting. Which are the best new English films?'

* * *

I went next morning to the Museo Nazionale G. A. Sanna, an oblong yellow building, set low in an exotic garden. This houses the collection left to the state by Giovanni Sanna, a mining engineer, whose family built the museum in his memory.

It is not, of course, on the same scale as the museum in Cagliari

—neither for the various remains from the *nuraghe* period nor for those from the Roman occupation. There were, however, amusing seventeenth-century paintings of the School of Genoa, charming Sardinian panels painted two centuries earlier, and a Corinthian alabaster vase of remarkable indecency. Much more interesting, however, is the collection of Sardinian folk art in a separate building, recently added, called the Sezione Etnografica Gavino Clemente. Carpets and saddle-bags, beautifully woven in wool with horse and rider or heraldic motifs, are hung along whitewashed walls—intricate landscapes in rose and pale green from Oristano, in black and yellow from Bonorva, in turquoise and scarlet from Muravera. Beside these were ranged costumes from all over the island, embroidered skirts and waistcoats, lace blouses, and stiff petticoats draped as if some headless peasant were thrusting them out with robust bosom and flanks. Curious terracotta hot-water bottles, in the shape of priests, were hung next to corn baskets from Castel Sardo, bird-shaped ornamental gourds, flutes and looms.

This was the genuine Sardinian art which, like the wearing of traditional costume, is now dying out. Most of the designs we had seen on contemporary carpets or coverings were mass produced, the beautiful vegetable dyes that created the characteristic Sardinian colours of rust-brown, lemon-yellow and pink, displaced by crude aniline processes. Hand-weaving has practically ceased and the gay birds, trees, stylized deer and horses, traditionally set against black and white striped backgrounds, have given way to picture-postcard tourist designs. Beauty, now regarded as an end in itself, has killed the striking originality of the peasant craftsmen who wove their wool and plaited their palm leaves with only functional ends in view. The Sardinians were probably the most skilled and vital peasant artists in the Mediterranean, instinctively developing the Etruscan and Greek traditions, with their own local variations. The plainsmen inclined to bright, complex colours: those from the hill villages to more austere, simple designs in black and white.

By the time I got back to the hotel, the open car, which Borio had arranged to take us to see the abbey of Trinità di Saccargia, was waiting. The particular objectives of this expedition were, besides the abbey, the Pisan-romanesque cathedral of San Pietro di Sorres, and the S. Antine *nuraghe*, one of the best preserved in Sardinia, near the village of Torralba. All three were roughly in the same direction, south-east of Sassari, the furthest about fifty miles away.

The weather was perfect, with champagne air and hot sun. The road out of Sassari loops steeply downhill, a brilliant white parting spinning through shoulders of rock and levelling out between cultivated valleys. This is the most civilized landscape in Sardinia: a pale froth of Roman pine and tamarisk, seas of olive, square bony arenas of vine. Light fleecy clouds moved diaphanously across the metal disc of the sun, and the green, rolling hills seemed to swim up out of their limestone base to smooth blue curves of sky. It is also the least typical, for landscape in Sardinia normally means colourless sky without depth, heat beating flatly back from level dust-brown earth, dwarf palm, cactus and umbrella pine the only vegetation to withstand wind and sun.

So we drove through a kind of oasis, a segment of northern Italy that had somehow drifted south. Behind us Sassari, splintered against its lime-streaked heights, assumed more and more the appearance of a medieval engraving, marred only by the thin grey slab of the skyscraper flats.

We were cutting now through elbow-shaped slopes, each defile opening on to a larger one and the gaps between the hills revealing distant ranges of mountain. The sun rose high ahead of us, the fine wide road flashing like tin. We passed few villages and these were widely separated, embedded into hills at the end of dusty side turnings far from the main road.

The Abbazia della SS. Trinità di Saccargia lies in the centre of a fertile valley, completely isolated, with only one house, a peasant's red-tiled villa on a remote rocky ledge, in sight. Otherwise, unusually green foothills dip and rise, with fairways, rather as on a golf course, alternating between steep bunkers and sudden bluffs. The wind pours through these channels, open over a radius of several miles, banging up against the chess-board black lava and white limestone of the abbey.

Why, one asks, was the abbey built in this curious position, away from any community? The story goes that the *Giudice* of

Logudoro, Constantino di Mariano, was travelling with his wife Marcusa, in 1116, to the caves of San Gavino, there to intercede for a child to be born to them. But, having to spend a night at the place where the abbey now stands, they received a divine revelation, the result of which was, that in John Warre Tyndale's equivocal terms, 'by some miracle the object of her intended prayers was forestalled'.

The delighted *Giudice* built the church and monastery in acknowledgement of the miracle, which was recognized by the Pope, and gave them to an order of Camaldolite monks. Over the years, however, the monks grew lazier and more indiscreet, and they were finally expelled in the fifteenth century.

Little now remains of the monastery—in the one surviving cloister a peasant family live amongst chickens and cooking utensils. Figs were drying out under clouds of flies, maize spilling over the arcades as hens picked their way through piles of melons and tomatoes to scuttle noisily through the open doors of a chapel. But the church, much renovated, still stands, its slim campanile thrusting upwards into the blue sky, as colourful an example of Pisan-romanesque as any of the striped churches of Florence or Siena. The thick horizontal black and white stripes shimmer in the sun, shadows of surrounding trees lengthening against the mosaics on the triple-arched portico. Inside, it is cool as a well, empty save for some few benches and faded murals. Tall grasses have grown up all round the walls, and patches of sky and hill with grazing flocks, like details from a landscape by Palma Vecchio, form a backcloth to the pillars in the arcades.

We drove back to the main road, turning south into more mountainous country. A high wind was blowing, and along the roads cypresses, long bent over by gales, curled in solemn unison. We flashed past rumbling ox-carts and primitive settlements, maize hanging in the sun like yellow beads from all the houses. The smooth green hills began to fade into a bleak volcanic plain, rocks rearing up at intervals under the burning sun, and small villages perched on the blackened rims of extinct craters. On a holed strip of ground, dotted with volcanic cones, some rising to a height of fifteen hundred feet, the villages of Cheremule and Torralba huddle in clumps of trees just off the road. A side-track leads steeply uphill to a sand-coloured bluff of its own. On the edge of this, the superb romanesque church of San Pietro di Sorres, built, like the abbey of Saccargia, in black and white trachytic lava and limestone, faces away from the plain beneath towards grey lava rocks. Behind it stretches a wide plain, humps of bare earth protruding from it like wading camels. A few olive-trees sprinkle the lower slopes of the mountains.

The present building was begun, on the site of an earlier romanesque church, in the first half of the thirteenth century. At that time it was the cathedral of the diocese of Sorres, suppressed in 1503. Now, wind-swept and surrounded by thick walls made of large white stones, its richly ornamented Pisan arches echo to the shrieks of children. The monastery remains have been converted into a school, though here, as at Santa Giusta and Saccargia, no other building is within miles. Like stone ships these churches have foundered on barren reefs, monuments testifying to the taste and skill of artisans and designers long after their spiritual voyages were abruptly ended.

The *nuraghe* of S. Antine, a mile or two further on, is one of a group of ten spread over the plain of Giave. This particular one, the show-piece amongst Sardinian *nuraghi*, has its own custodian, a spry, grinning figure of eighty-three in stocking cap and black velvet, accustomed to a steady flow of visitors. He had a formal ritual prepared, lighting candles to lead us up a spiral stairway through the circular galleries to the stone parapet on top, then plonking himself down between the architraves of one of the doorways to be photographed. 'I usually sit here,' he said, settling himself comfortably on the stone and blinking in the sun like a benevolent church dignitary.

From the half-demolished third storey, some fifty feet from the ground, the plain tilts its yellow stubble-fields to a lifting horizon of powder-blue hills. *Nuraghi* in various stages of ruin top off bits of rising ground, looking like white chess-men on the stone-walled squares of the plain. The village of Bonorva, whose grottoes are one of the bandit strongholds, is set high up to the east, and one can see here in miniature how exactly the Sardinian landscape is suited to defence in depth and endless withdrawals to prepared positions. Each *nuraghe* is built slightly higher than the one preceding it, each in turn covers a narrower defile. As the ground rises and falls, so is each declivity looked down on by a ring of fortifications. Then, beyond the *nuraghi*, rise the amphitheatres of mountains, villages placed like eyes at various heights. These were the last redoubts, where the Sards, from the *nuraghi* chiefs onwards, kept their counsel and freedom at eagle level. None of these steep hills ever surrendered to invaders. With vultures wheeling over the foothills, the cooped-up defiant Sards gazed balefully at successive colonists who gave up their empires on the lower slopes. The Sards became birdmen, condemned to the upper air, their craggy homes the mauve peaks which once were all that protruded from the sea.

The *nuraghe* of S. Antine has a central domed chamber, eighteen feet wide and eighteen feet high. Off this, five small passageways lead to the corridor which, first circling the central chamber, spirals some seventy yards to the summit. Two more chambers are superimposed on the ground-floor dome, and various recesses at all levels lead off to more domed chambers on the outer corridor. The truncated tower is set in the centre of a large circular terrace, built, like the main structure, of flat volcanic stones, each row overlapping the lower.

These solid blocks, some six foot long, four foot wide and nearly three foot deep, are the main fascination of the *nuraghi*. How were they carried and from where? Apart from tiny vents cut above the architraves over the entrances, no light reaches the cool, dark galleries. Inside the chambers the stone dominates, a giant, protective but also threatening force. The stones of the *nuraghi* convey more than anything else the enigma and mystery of ancient Sardinia, its antique rituals, fierce tribal wars, and careful votive craftsmanship. They are clues whose significance is only partially understood, they point a direction but no more.

The worked, polished stone of S. Antine places it in the Greek age, and of all the *nuraghi* it is the most complete in design. Round its finely poised rampart shards of pottery lay strewn. Thistles and corn-stalks stood upright on the slopes that fell from the clear, converging line of the uncemented walls. Looked at from any angle it thrust nobly against the colourless sky, one of a connecting chain of outposts whose solidity had survived the later wars that found no use for it.

We drove back to Sassari, moved and impressed by these three unique constructions, each affirming, in their present uselessness, the qualities that allow works of beauty to endure in their own right, with no practical purpose whatsoever. The bare, treeless plains were watery with light, the sun spreading over the dry earth a radiance that exhilarated rather than sapped. Near the Fonte Rosello, the late Renaissance fountain made of white inlaid marble on the outskirts of Sassari, women were laying their washing to dry. Water spouted from the lions' faces that grimace from the sides, and in an adjacent building more women scrubbed and rinsed huge baskets of linen. The Fonte Rosello, though it now bears signs of being the centre of an arbitrary lavatory for both men and beasts, is a marvellously suggestive example of Genoese workmanship. The quadrilateral base, with statues representing the four seasons at each corner, is crowned by two crossing arches and through these the tree-brushed crust of white houses ringing the town cuts across oval segments of sky.

There was no one about in the piazzas. Shutters were down and the afternoon siesta made it seem a city under siege.

* * *

The waiter who used to serve me in the *Muroni* restaurant came from Porto Torres, a sea-port about twelve miles to the northwest of Sassari. He was a thin, ravaged man, who mooned about listlessly flapping at flies and who seemed locked in some philosophic speculation that made the duty of waiting a tiresome intrusion. I asked him about Porto Torres, described in the *Guida d'Italia* as a '*grosso e attivo centro, dotato di un buon porto e di spiaggia frequentate per bagnante. Vanta una nobile storia. . . . La bellezza dei resti monumentali, l'eleganza delle iscrizioni e delle sculture provenienti da Turris testimoniano del ricco passato della città.*' 'It's a beautiful place', he said with a faint smile, 'to get away from.' He crooked his little finger in a curious gesture and the nail, which he wore, on that finger only, to a repulsive length of about three inches, reached down to the palm of his hand. 'It is stagnant, quite cut off, like that,' he grinned, pointing to the circle formed by nail and finger. At intervals, in between waiting, he groped with this nail meditatively into his ear.

I went out in the afternoon bus, a rather dull drive through flat fields of cactus and vine, with here and there humps of land covered in dwarf juniper. The sun was again baking, but a slight sea breeze brought with it snatches of thyme and rosemary from the belt of rough cistus fringing the coast.

There was, I quickly discovered, a good deal of truth in the opinions of both the *Guida d'Italia* and the waiter. Porto Torres has a superb basilica, built by the Pisans in their purest style about the middle of the eleventh century, as well as an elegant Roman bridge and a curious ruined Temple of Fortune. It is also one of those places, of hang-dog, dilapidated appearance, which create within five minutes an intense depression, almost a panic, in case by some unforeseen calamity one should be marooned there.

The town, which in its Roman heyday had as many as fifteen thousand inhabitants, now has some eight thousand five hundred pale and emaciated citizens. The dead-straight Sassari road, becoming eventually more thickly balanced with stained, peeling houses, comes to a full stop in the centre of a horse-shoe harbour. The last hundred yards, where fly-blown cafés and tired oleanders break up the bleak grey frontages of granite houses, form the main street of the town. The port, whose ships back almost into the Piazza Cristoforo Colombo at the seaward end, is used mostly by cargo-ships. The air, far from smelling of the sea, is dank, full of dust and grit, and the grind of cranes seems to be the only sign of life.

Few people were to be seen when the bus, commanded by an imperious conductor aged eight, pulled up in the Via Vittorio Emanuele. Two old men were slumped on the ground, sleeping with their backs to a wall. The bead curtains of the café where I drank a warm orangeade, rattled to allow a thin, sore-spotted cat to stalk purposefully out with a large rat in its mouth. A beggar, blinking in the sunlight as he lay, apparently paralysed, on the street corner, was struck by a football kicked by some urchins playing near the dock gates; whereupon he leaped vigorously to his feet and ran swearing amongst them, swinging out with his stick. I finished my orangeade and walked, via some refuse-heaped sidestreets, up the short hill to the Basilica of San Gavino. The red-tiled roofs of the port rippled in the heat below, and the fishing-boats in the bright-blue harbour looked pretty in a squat, stagnant sort of way. Out in the bay seven large cargo-ships lay anchored off the bed-shaped island of Asinara, the thick haze giving them a sinister, mysterious air. Asinara, once possessing a thriving Camaldolian monastery, has since been an international quarantine settlement and a penal colony, so, despite its generations of local fishermen, shepherds and foresters, its name also has a disquieting ring.

The church, built on the site of an ancient pagan burial-ground, was named after one of the great Sardinian saints, a Roman soldier who commanded the garrison at Torres in Diocletian's reign. Ordered to put to death two Christian priests, Protus and Januarius, he was converted by them and himself shared their martyrdom. All three were beheaded on October 25th 300. Their remains were dug up by the ecclesiastical authorities of Sassari in 1614, and the anti-clerical Tyndale quotes with contempt a Sardinian historian's account of the wonderful signs that attended the exhumation. 'The portents accompanying the discovery, the musical harmonies heard in many places, the unexpected splendours appearing in the temple, the frequent perfumes emitted from the tombs, the number of miracles performed upon the devout, drawn by a supernatural force to venerate the sanctity of these bones', etc.

There is, inside the basilica, a painting by Franceso di Castello portraying the beheading of San Gavino, and near by, behind the altar of the crypt, marble statues of various local martyrs. This Tyndale describes as: 'not only the Porto Torres Pantheon of apotheosized ecclesiastics who have suffered corporal torments, but the theatre for the performances of the Frati Filippini, an order of monks residing at Sassari, who, thinking to merit heaven by making earth a hell, perform constant pilgrimages to this spot for the purpose of self-flagellation; of which the effects were shewn to me in a few drops of blood shed three days previously'.

The unimpressed English barrister-at-law continues: 'I saw this ceremony at Rome some years since, but the consciences of the monks at the Eternal City are tougher and their skins tenderer, so they castigated themselves while well protected by their thick clothes; but the more scrupulous race of Sard fanatics strip themselves for the self-infliction, under the impression that the admiring spectators would not be satisfied with mental sufferings unless accompanied by visible signs of carnal torture—advantageous also to themselves, as producing alms and contributions as well as pity.' Also a good example of the critical 'Morton's Fork' Tyndale directed at the Church.

However, be that as it may, the Pisans made a good job of the basilica. Despite much restoration, as well as stout fortifications built against raiding Corsairs, it is a fine embodiment of the austere graces of the romanesque style. A buff-coloured, spacious building, its two dozen or so marble columns, each drawn from a Roman temple, form two main aisles, above which horizontal beams stretch under a lead roof—with room left for light to pour through the interstices. Under the raised choir, a number of sarcophagi and marble statues flank the saint's tomb. There are apses at either end, with swords of sun from the cloisters severing the three naves. The effect is coldly impressive, an imperious testimony to taste rather than to feeling.

The golden light of late afternoon glowed on the blind arcades. A priest reading his Office walked back and forth like a ship's captain, his mouth moving soundlessly, his glasses glinting. Torn political posters flapped on a parapet outside, and the cries of a clothes-seller, nasally Arabic in tone, came up from the mud-built houses below. But the priest paced unheeding, lost in his interior mnemonics. There seemed no connection, if there ever had been one, between this high-floating medieval sanctuary and the depressed, sweating town at its feet.

I went down past the seven-arched Roman bridge, spanning the uneven banks of the trickling Torritano river. Sheets were laid over an upturned boat to dry, and downstream a group of girls, dresses tucked into black knickers, pounded clothes on the wet stones. Huge pink cacti shadow-boxed one another along the seaweed-strewn beach, and where the spilling sun washed the ruined stone of the Palazzo del Re Barbaro, once the Tempio della Dea Fortuna, the mosaic birds tilted their alert profiles on the over-grown pavements. The railway station has so smothered the two-thousand-year-old rock tombs, palaces, basilica and tribunal that lie open to sun and wind at the dreary end of a shunting track, that one can only long now for them to be cleared completely away—useless junk collecting the grime on their stunted columns.

* * *

Castel Sardo, higher up the coast to the east of Porto Torres, is one of those Genoese cliff cities whose beauty has survived their function. The fortified walls ringing the landward side of the citadel have crumbled away, the cannons have rusted, the patter of women swaying on bare feet up the steep stone steps with baskets on their heads, replaces the tramp of soldiers' boots. Castel Sardo, founded by the Dorias in the twelfth century, bore the denoting adjective of its occupants—Castel Genovese, Castel Aragonese—until Carlo Emanuele provided its present, less humiliating name in 1769. But by then this rocky northern outpost, once an important port, independent, with its own statutes and government, had already lost its point. The fortress became a museum, the inhabitants reluctant custodians of a slowly rotting work of art. The green water, looping under its rocks in a series of sandy bays, bore the shivering image, top heavy and unstable, that would one day splinter as reflection and reality collided.

Castel Sardo, whose nearest geographical equivalents are perhaps Tossa de Mar on the Costa Brava or Bonifacio, has some of the qualities of both these towns. But, though its obviously romantic situation seems to have been contrived with tourists especially in mind, it has never had any. The bleak mountains of Anglona and Gallura cut it off—in the way that much of the Sardinian coast is blocked away from the interior—and only winding side roads, through bare, stony country, reach it. For most people, understandably, the effort is not worth while, and Castel Sardo remains an agreeable grey shape humped across a picture postcard. The connoisseur of decline, however, will treasure it, for life is barely perceptible in its tooth-like battlements, and the heart-beat of existence can hardly be heard.

The day I spent there was suitably sultry, the sun worn down to a thin disc by thundery clouds. The sea came in listlessly, lapping its yellowish foam on the narrow strip of sand separated from the coast road by only a thin line of tamarisk and cactus. A few oxcarts, breasting the occasional hills, were all that we passed, dipping quickly down to the coast from Sassari, with miles of coarse scrub spreading out from the scurfy parting of the road. Approaching Castel Sardo the mountains rose more sharply to the south, almost the same shade as the mascara-coloured sea. Then suddenly, framed between the broken arches of a bridge, the castle seemed to be adrift, its shelving outline cutting spray from the sea like the prow of a battleship.

Close at hand, with the road spiralling up into the citadel like a nerve, first impressions were modified. Round the stern, as it were, a new suburb has cemented its flat roofs into the green valley, stretching away into the mountains like a wake. Flocks were grazing on the foothills, softening the harsh, beaten-up appearance of the citadel.

Small piazzas splay out from the old town, their curved balustrades giving different-level views of the sinuous outline of Asinara and the smudge over the horizon that is the southern tip of Corsica. Off these dingy platforms steep flights of steps lead to the citadel. Many of the houses on them have crumbled away, leaving jagged portholes to the sea. In these gutted ruins chickens scuttled over floors of thistle, cats edged silently out of rusted sitting-rooms. Old men sat in groups on the stone stairways, leaning on their sticks, and the only sound was the noise of hammering coming from the church—a late-gothic building of the fifteenth century, with pleasant medieval paintings done by the *maestro di Castel Sardo*, an unknown local painter with Spanish training. Typically the church, perched on the cliff edge, was the single building that money was available to renovate—while whole families lived in the insanitary, fly-covered caves that surrounded it.

The castle is now used as a barracks for the *carabinieri*, a few rooms being kept for prisoners. Coinciding with my arrival at the entrance, an old toothless woman with grey bird's-nest hair appeared, in a great state of agitation, to denounce someone. The man on guard asked her what it was all about, but she would only tell it to the Comandante. 'The Comandante has gone to Sassari,' the guard said. 'He won't be back till the evening.' 'Very well, I'll wait,' the woman replied, considering a little, 'I dare not go back now', and, conserving her secret, she sat down outside the gate, mumbling quietly to herself and shaking her head.

Most of the women in Castel Sardo make baskets—bleaching the wild-palm leaves and plaiting a variety of simple animal designs over a plain background. These baskets, whose heraldic patterns are traditional, we saw all over the island, and they are unusually agreeable. Each house, a madonna hanging in the glassless window, had its group of women working round the entrance. Although the Castel Sardo design is immediately recognizable, individual families produce their own variations, specializing in fish or deer as if it were a patent. The male inhabitants are mostly fishermen whose boats huddle in the dank, shadowed harbour in the lee of the rock. But, as in most isolated Mediterranean villages, the middle generation seems to be missing. The very old and the very young form a permanent freize, as austerely decorative as their raffia borders, to the dipping steps, white as waterfalls from below, but poverty has produced a time-lag too great to unify them. The middle-aged have gone elsewhere.

As I drove back to Sassari heavy single raindrops spattered the dust. Gaudy film posters peeled on the walls of wayside villages, the wind beginning to churn the sea. It seemed suddenly as if summer was running out, the horizon closing in with thunder. The band was just setting up its music as we reached the Public Gardens and then, with a clash of cymbals, they and the storm began. Twenty minutes later the streets were racing with water, the sun shone from a brazen blue sky and the palm leaves in the Piazza d'Italia glinted like swords.

PART FIVE

Alghero and Gallura

THE country between Sassari and Alghero, that latemedieval no-man's land never voluntarily crossed, is some of the bleakest in Sardinia. Once Sassari is left behind, the thin unsubstantial skyscraper the final landmark, bare hummocks, flat on top and ringed with sparse, dark vegetation like giant monks' heads, spin away on all sides to the horizon. The road twists through sheer valleys, across bridged canyons and over dried river beds. It is a Mexican landscape, the sun glinting on precariously perched boulders, the parched brown earth softened only by silver islands of olive round isolated white cottages. Cactus, wild fennel and thyme cover the rocky moorland like unshaved stubble.

Yesterday's rain had cleared the air and it was again baking. We decided to travel the twenty-five miles to Alghero by bus and soon after dawn, in the company of numerous sportsmen, we set off. When we reached open country, the low thick scrub almost treeless, the sportsmen, smelling heavily of sweat, leather, garlic and wine, departed in ones and twos with their game bags and shotguns into the undergrowth.

Near the village of Uri, gleaming high up in the hills, I heard for the first and only time the *launedda*, the ancient reed instrument used by the Sards to accompany the *ballo tondo*, their national dance. Someone was playing in a shuttered cottage, alone on a bare ravine, the notes, soft and wild, being answered by a harsh Arab chanting. In a moment we had rumbled past, the music and the song cut off abruptly in mid-phrase, as though a man was being choked.

The hills grew lower now, shelving into myrtle and artichoke, a pale-green sea beyond which lay the real, glittering sea. Round about here an artichoke apéritif is produced, which tastes as disagreeable as it sounds. However, since with *Villacidro*, a

Strega-type liqueur, it is the only Sardinian-concocted drink, it stands proud, but usually unopened, on every bar counter in the island.

We came down to sea-level, the afternoon light spilling over the red-tiled roofs of new, tidy villas, each with its patch of vine, its oleander and trail of bougainvillea. The bus swung round a wide, tree-lined piazza, grinding to a noisy, whining stop and waking up a row of *carrozza* drivers, asleep on their bridges. A gramophone blared from a café where men were sitting reading newspapers and eating ice-creams. Between the piazza and the harbour, towers, battlements and fortified walls received the gold westering sun on their variously crumbling stone.

★ ★ ★

The first time I saw the name Alghero was on an illustration to Pierre Chevrier's biography of Antoine de Saint-Exupéry. Over the caption *Fête au 2/33 à Alghero (Sardaigne)* there is a picture of an old Sardinian peasant, with dark face and thick walrus moustache, dancing on a table littered with wine bottles. Saint-Exupéry and two or three other French airline pilots stand smirking in the background.

The next time I saw it was in a strange volume of reminiscences by a lady named Amélie Posse-Brazdova, who was interned there during the 1914-18 war. This work almost lives up to its authoress's name, beginning: 'When you leave the Porta del Popolo and follow the Via Flaminia, the pine woods of the Villa Strohl-Fern rise before you like a romantic back-cloth high up on the right', and carrying its splendid cast of central European minor nobility into the wastes of Sardinia. Turning the pages to try and glean some of the flavour of Sardinian life at that period, I came across a whole musical-comedy scenario, dominated by Bohemian poets and painters with names like Oki, Siguard, Chytil, a Czech Jan Autengruber, Countess de Psiakrewskowska and the very *décolletée* Baroness Fanni di Villanova, who liked to be guest of honour at parties, and usually wore 'a huge plumed hat, red satin dress, black *glacé* kid gloves, which she kept on all through dinner, and an enormous feather fan behind which she flirted boldly in the most devastating manner'.

Sharing Frau Posse-Brazdova's internment at Alghero were a number of Polish priests, a Czech photographer and a variety of Croatian sea-captains. Her own great friend was a young Sardinian poet named Conte Amore Giovinetti who turned up to meet her in the noon heat wearing a dinner-jacket, black-and-white check riding-breeches, flowing necktie and red cummerbund. 'Indeed,' notes the authoress, 'from the first moment of my arrival, I received the impression that anything might happen here. This was no ordinary little town.'

So, in fact, it turned out, though the adventures of the artistic Slav baroness did not touch greatly on Sardinian society. Alghero seems to have had a permanent attraction for voluntary or involuntary exiles, and it still remains a more cosmopolitan town than any other in Sardinia. Admiral von Tirpitz bought a large coastal estate just north of Alghero before the first World War, and its caves and bays were subsequently used by submarines which surfaced there in the dark for secret rendezvous.

Our own stay in Alghero was spent at the villa *Las Tronas*, a castellated, baronial mansion of the late nineteenth century, belonging to the Conte Sant' Elia, late Master of Ceremonies to His Majesty King Vittorio Emanuele. This curious chocolate-coloured summer residence had only a few weeks previously been opened as a hotel. It was imposingly placed on its own rocky promontory, the sea breaking at the edge of its terrace. Jetties, where once royal yachts had tied up, reached down into the sea, and cement arms enclosed a private swimming-pool. Huge vases and terracotta pots stuffed with geraniums lined the gravel terrace where striped chairs and parasols were set out in front of the long sea-windows. From these the curving line of alternating cliffs and bays stretched away to enclosing mountains on either side. Half a mile to the north the high harbour walls of Alghero, topped by turrets and domes, clamped to over close-packed whitewashed houses.

On our arrival we had been presented to the Count, just descending the stairs on his way in to dinner. His presence was heralded by the appearance of the major-domo and staff, who, already lined up in the hall, stiffened to attention as a small, tottering figure in a white suit slowly emerged. When we were introduced the Count quavered in his sad squeaky voice, 'My wife, you know, is English. This is the first time I am obliged to let my house. I was at the Italian Court once, Senator and so on, you know, but now I have little means.' He stared a moment, his pale-blue eyes seeming to be straining through their mist to departed splendours. He pointed his stick to the photographs on either side of the hall, where signed portraits of most of the ex-Kings of Europe were interspersed between Sardinian carvings and hunting-prints. 'There,' he said, tapping the nearest one, 'there is your Duke of Windsor, though of course I knew him when he was Prince of Wales. We were great friends.' He broke off suddenly, made a fussy little bow and stumped away, clearing his throat, through his royal gallery. Not one of the seven kings who looked down on him from their sepia mounts still remained on his throne—nor in most cases did the throne any longer exist. Six months later, too, the poor Conte di Sant' Elia was spared the humiliation of having to let his house, for, in the middle of winter, his frail body made its final inspection of the photographs with their sprawling royal signatures, and quietly subsided under them.

There were many engaging things about the villa *Las Tronas*, which consisted of a terraced dining-room, a cocktail bar with a Russian billard table, three large sitting-rooms and about a dozen bedrooms. The drawing-room, for example, was dominated by a pale-blue font-like object, decorated with china ladies of Roman profile squeezing their breasts. The chintz-covered sofas were strewn with beaded cushions, naked Javanese girls held up the table-lamps and posed on the edges of ashtrays, the walls were covered with astonishing oil-paintings. One of these, a landscape showing the cliffs of Capo Caccia just beyond Alghero, bore a silver plaque with the words: *Grazioso dono di sua maestà Vittorio Emanuele III re e imperatore A Don Luigi Arborio Mella Conte di Sant' Elia—Primo Maestro delle cerimonie della Maestà sua. 30 Aprile 1938.* Next to some macabre portraits of be-medalled figures in full uniform hung a painting by Macaroni of Conte Gaspare Serra '*Gentiluomo di Camera di sua Maestà*', a man with romantic, brushed-forward sidepieces, but whose moustache Signor Maca-roni had painted so lopsidedly that it looked like the cork-inscribed appendage of a music-hall comedian's 'feed'. A wall-map concentrated on the eloquently named Sardinian headlands of Capo Buggeru and Capo Soddu, while, amongst a deal of oriental junk, genuine specimens of Sardinian weaving and craftsmanship lay almost unnoticeable.

The staff at *Las Tronas* consisted of the Count's personal valet, a housekeeper, chef, barman, waiter and an extremely beautiful young girl of about sixteen, whose duties were to look after the bedrooms. She was always to be found waiting at the bedroom door, black eyes flashing and mouth a bold carmine bow, and it would obviously not be long before such demanding beauty found its just reward. We were the only guests in the villa, so we had her undivided and disturbing attention. In addition, a few flitting figures were to been seen at meal-times, some women and a young boy, but they played various parts as members of the Count's entourage and *Las Tronas* was their summer home.

The first evening there was another, more violent storm, the heavy rain followed by a gale. The sea boiled all night outside my window, the waves hissing off the rocks, so that it felt like being on an ocean liner.

* * *

By morning the wind had dropped, though there was still a low ceiling of scudding black cloud, and the rock pools were full from the night's overflow. From my balcony I could see the Count, dressed in yachting cap, white trousers and blue blazer, strolling stiffly back and forth along the sea-walk. On his arm walked the stout dark-haired lady who was his constant companion. A few fishing-trawlers were making for harbour, taking a green sea over their bows, and thumping into concealing hollows of waves. Great activity was evident downstairs, for a group of forty Sardinians—the island's *nobiltà*, the major-domo said, whisking his duster briskly over the backs of the dining-room chairs—were expected at midday for their annual lunch. Long before they had arrived the rain came solidly down again, dripping off the pines in the garden and giving the squat domes and ramparts of Alghero a melancholy gloss. Meanwhile, an imported squad of waiters were put to work at once arranging plates of lobster, ham and melon, twisting napkins, and filling vases with flowers. The decorated, biscuity, round Sardinian bread was set out in baskets from Castel Sardo, and immense bowls of salad, grapes and figs were laid in between the bottles of Torbato, the sweet straw-coloured wine of Alghero, that stood sentinel by each place.

One by one the *nobiltà* arrived in cars, scurrying in out of the rain, the men pulling their felt hats down, the women drawing coats tightly round them. All seemed to be in their best clothes, though they were, we felt, rather a letdown as representatives of Sardinian feudal society. The women, well dressed in most respects, had dark furry legs under their nylons and thick sporrans of hair protruding from their armpits. The men, who stood in a little group by themselves, clapped one another on the back, stuck their thumbs into paunchy waistcoasts, and flashed gold-filled mouths at each new arrival. At one o'clock they went in to eat, the doors were closed behind them, and four hours went by before they emerged again.

★ ★ ★

It was the next morning before the rain stopped and the sun reappeared. Alghero now looked bright and clean, a medieval town basking in warm, apricot light. On my way to the harbour I passed the first of the new hotels, whose gaunt scaffoldings stalked the coast like skeletons. By now they will have been finished and Alghero will have taken its place as the first experimental resort of the new post-malarial Sardinia. On the edge of the town, where the sea-walls curved away from the Via Dante with its bandstand and wide esplanade, there were posters advertising a contest for the *Miss Sardegna* beauty title. The Misses Macomer, Nuoro, Cagliari and Iglesias would, it announced, be among the competitors and the winner would ride through the town on a white horse. Unfortunately, it appeared to have taken place a week earlier, which was a great disappointment. Alongside it flapped even older posters for a demonstration of hernia appliances whose salesman had been following us round the island. In every town the word ERNIA, in huge black letters, rose off the walls like an announcement of the farewell recital by some renowned star of the concert-hall.

The centre of the town is compact, dirty and all that is usually meant by 'picturesque'. The narrow cobbled streets are slung with washing, the pale rinsed colours drying out from one wrought-iron balcony to another, giving a perpetual air of *festa*. Pink, green and yellow paint peels on the dark cave-like houses, with arches bisecting the sky, so that the eye is drawn up to beautifully moulded cornices, stone columns and, beyond them, turrets and domes, sand-coloured against the depthless Mediterranean light. From the amorphous, rather mean buildings, in front of which dark Arab-looking children sit mournfully, the spiky, thin campanile of the cathedral, a moderate achievement in late Spanish gothic, rises to dominate the harbour. Most of the roads and alleyways slope down to the port, beautifully set in a wide bay, with sandy beaches curving under the swell of green headlands to the north.

The port was crammed with fishing-boats, gunwale to gunwale, the sun spilling off the glass-green water and the flared, gilded bows of the coral boats shivering in reflection. The fishing at Alghero, for lobster, coral and sardines especially, is renowned. Alongside the larger boats fishermen were selling off sardine and *dentice* from small whalers, the fish gleaming like coins as they were weighed and sold direct to customers. Nets lay out to dry on the hot stone quays and huge plaited lobster-pots hung like bells from the harbour walls. Rows of old, bearded men sat on benches watching the loading of cargo-boats, one of which was just leaving for Trieste. I talked for a while to the owner of a small *dentice* boat. He had been a baker, he said, in New York, where he had lived for eighteen years without a passport. 'I guess I came back home to wash the smell of gasoline out of my nostrils before I die.'

Several of the fishermen spoke a pure Catalan, and Alghero is unique in having retained its Spanish linguistic heritage almost intact. For Alghero—from the Latin *alga*, seaweed, whose brown streamers crackle underfoot in thick swathes along the sea's edge— has been, since the mid-fourteenth century, essentially a Spanish town. Though it was founded by the Dorias about the same time as Castel Sardo, and fortified by them against the Pisans during a period of over two hundred years, from the time of the siege by

Don Pedro IV, of Aragon, which ended after great bloodshed in 1354, it was consistently populated by Catalan emigrants. The character of the modern Algherese is grave, dignified and quite un-Italian in its reserve. A stern observer in the early nineteenth century wrote: 'The state of society at Alghero is formal and vapid, from an inheritance of Spanish with a graft of Italian manners, without the polish which characterizes the best society of those countries.'

The great event in the history of Alghero was the visit of Charles V, in 1541. The Emperor, on an expedition to Algiers, spent a day or two in the Casa Albis, was received with fabulous pomp, and in return treated the Algherese dignities with some levity. He complained of a pain in the chest, excusing himself from the elaborate banquet arranged for him, and his troops slaughtered and stole a great many animals. As a conciliatory gesture the Emperor is supposed, without much authority, to have dubbed all the Algherese knights—*estode todos caballeros*—looking out from the Casa Albis and laughing at the behaviour of the troops. Though there may have been a lack of gravity in the Emperor's proclamation, the punctilious citizens of Alghero took their new titles with great solemnity and never ceased to address one another as *Don*. The window from which the Emperor looked out as he called out his legendary phrase was subsequently blocked up and the room, like a church altar, made into a refuge where anyone might seek asylum.

There is a Sardinian proverb, *Dolori spingi boxi*—grief culminates in song—but Alghero provides little illustration of it. By nine in the evening the town, never very lively, is completely silent, the inhabitants immured behind their dark ramparts. Naked bulbs shine over crucifixes in the thin streets, otherwise there is no light except the moon creaming over the breaking sea, throwing the watch-towers along the Lungomare Dante into brooding relief.

Later that day I took a *carrozza* out to the beaches which run for a mile or so in a straight line to the north. A few villas have been built, on what was Tirpitz's land, and behind the fringe of pines that comes flush to the sand lies some of the most lush land in the island. An airport, Fertilia, is here, on a small plain between hills, and a village has been formed by refugees from the overrun Italian territory east of Trieste. This agricultural Giulian community is one of several settlements in Sardinia, created for one purpose or another, and formed by transporting whole groups from the mainland to an undeveloped site. The Fascists did it before the war, especially for industrial purposes, and a number of towns named in honour of Mussolini and his proconsuls later underwent hasty changes of name.

The beach had a melancholy end-of-season air. The paint on the bathing-cabins was blistered and fading, and the sun had no great strength. The bars and restaurant had taken their chairs indoors and there was only one bather—a powerful, bald-headed hunchback who stood on the edge of the water and threw a huge flat stone about, as if practising for 'putting the weight'. Eventually he lay on his back in a few inches of sea and did bicycle exercises. The sun dropped behind Capo Caccia (whose famous grotto the Duke of Buckingham visited to compare with Fingal and at the entrance to which Admiral Smyth erected Bengal-Lights in 1824), and fishing-boats moved out towards the green sky. But the hunchback continued to pedal tirelessly, as if he could somehow keep night or the summer's end at bay by the revolutions of his bowed and hairy legs.

* * *

It was now mid-September and the golden days, in this pause for an autumnal second wind, had gone. A few straws of sun poked through occasionally from the grey crumbling masonry of clouds, but the heat was over and the sky had a rinsed, English look about it. We were due to leave Sardinia from Santa Teresa, picking up the Maddalena boat for Bonifacio; but I had heard so much about the beauties of Tempio from our commercial traveller friends in Carloforte, that we decided to stay a week-end there on the way. It would mean, at any rate, a journey right through the centre of Gallura, the highlands of Sardinia, and what is generally regarded as the most dramatic of the island's landscapes.

These cross-country journeys have to be made by bus, for the express trains run due north and south—Olbia to Cagliari, Cagliari to Sassari, with a small diversion through the mining centres of the south-west to Iglesias. But buses have their compensations, for they carry about with them the Sardinian peasant background, and, though they are no use to the impatient traveller, they are the most rewarding means of travel.

We drove by car from Alghero, boarding the Tempio bus at Sassari in the early afternoon. The rain had ceased and it had become one of those cool, sunny days, with slow islands of white cloud sailing over freshened green hills.

The first part of the journey was through almost northern country—green, tree-studded plains and jagged granite crests, up and down which ran the white switchback of road. From the higher ridges we looked down on white houses in clusters of oak and aloe, olive-groves glistening on the lower slopes and beyond them the sea beating with light. We wound up to the perched hill-village of Osilo, climbing through cactus hedges with fruit glowing pink in the sun, and the road clinging to the rock as it fell steeply away. Then down again, into a grey-green valley with a skyline of jagged peaks, some of them with ruined watch-towers on their summits, others with the white oblongs of monasteries set against them. Behind us, the campaniles of Osilo looked like factory chimneys, black against the sun. The green had given way to dark-brown soil, the road was edged with sunflowers and fields of yellow stubble swung away into the distance. It was deserted, empty country, the land seeming to work for itself without the help of man. Now and again we rumbled past a solitary man on horseback, his gun glinting on his shoulder, but there were no villages, no houses of any kind. We slipped down into a narrow gorge, with a mauve range of mountains. the Limbara, ahead of us on the horizon and a sharp ridge in between. Half-way up this, we stopped for a few moments at Nulvi, a flowery town with women in yashmaks, squads of bespectacled priests, and men in black doublets or sheepskin *mastrucas*. Gaping youths surrounded the bus, wearing cloth caps, their mouths open like fledglings waiting to be fed, and two girls, with babies at their breasts, swept their long embroidered skirts about them and got aboard. Nulvi is a pretty, rather squalid village, with a wonderful view over the deep bare valley. It is dominated by a tall, octagonal campanile, thrusting out over some cloisters and a public garden, and by its comfortable Capuchin convent. 'It was strange to see', the persistent Tyndale wrote, 'the well-fed clergy, in their silken robes, lounging and chanting in their carved choir, while outside the church all was wretchedness and misery.'

Some way out of Nulvi, once more in bleak, wild country, we came across a small procession: isolated in the landscape it was first a blur of colour, trailing a cloud of dust. Then it shook itself clear into men in the traditional black and white on horseback, women in richly brocaded skirts and white blouses riding sidesaddle behind them, and the leading horsemen bearing a paleblue standard. They were on their way, I learned, to the ruined church on the top of a hill near Martis, a village a mile or two ahead of us. Long after we had swung past them they remained perfectly distinct, picking their elegant way up a steep mountain path, a gorgeous Quixotic retinue materializing out of nothing.

These symbolic mirages one had gradually come to expect as typical. The rolling hills, dun-coloured and scorched as they were, needed just these blobs of brightness to bring them to life. In return they intensified any contrasting image, a solitary palm, an ox-cart, a black-suited man with scarlet cummerbund, so that its clarity was preserved as if through a lens. The pink granitic mountains of Gallura were now shutting off the horizon, great lined rocks as in a Mantegna landscape. The sun dripped its gold light over tilted villages, inset into the foothills of steep, jagged peaks. At Laerru we stopped again, the blue sky seeming very low over the tall campanile of the parish church—yet one more of the sixteenth-century Spanish gothic buildings which seem to grow out of the Sardinian rocks. A mad old figure, in faded uniform of pale blue and black, with clinking medals and peaked cap, came cackling out of a café to join the bus. He had long white hair and an unkempt beard, and every few seconds he crowed like a bird. Once we were moving again he went slowly down the bus, shaking hands and crowing at each of the passengers in turn, suddenly drawing up to beat his medals and scream out commands in dialect. He got out at Perfugas, the next village, humping his sack over his shoulder and stumbling into the first bar like some veteran soldier of the retreat from Moscow. Perfugas is a sloping, one-street affair, shepherds sitting out on the steps of their houses in the dipping sun, sticks in their hands and the pale-green and pink woven saddle-bags beside them. With shouts of '*Guarda povera barba!*' following him, the old man soon staggered out into the road, this time blowing a whistle and dancing a little jig by himself. In the intervals of crowing he drank from the wine bottle he had now acquired, while a whole crowd of laughing urchins formed a circle round him and clapped their hands. Two or three times he fell violently on his back, and then another lunatic was pushed into the circle to accompany him. This one was younger, with mottled, mauve face, hollow eyes and grotesque double rows of teeth. Together they capered, grinning at one another, till the bus, ready to go, hooted noisily at them. Just as we were leaving three drunks flung themselves at the bus door, scraping inside while it was moving. One of them leaned out of the window and, with his finger over the top of the bottle, squirted beer at the group of people waving the bus off.

The pink barrier of the Limbara was only across the valley. We slid across the green banks of the Coghinas river, with bullocks padding through a quick-flowing stream and the sun glistening on the red berries of the overhanging lentisk. Beyond, the iodine trunks of the stripped cork-trees, their long brown stockings reaching up to the grey spraying branches, glowed against the brown of the next hill. We had moved into shadow, the saw-toothed skyline rose-bleached above us and only the foaming cork-trees spreading like skirts round each peak. Boulders, ravines and isolated huts flanked the winding road. One of the women from Nulvi, her child still clasped to her white distended breast, leaned out of a window to be sick and on the other side the drunk from Perfugas hurled his beer bottle into the pink frill of oleanders lining the Coghinas.

It grew fresher and then colder, for we were climbing steadily. Round a bend we turned full against the declining sun, with the buildings of Tempio arched like an eyebrow under the southern dome of the Limbara. The cathedral bells were ringing out over the valley, and as we drove up a long street into the central piazza, we passed groups of people walking up and down in their black Sunday best. Along the walls of the cathedral some targets had been set up and a number of youths were paying a few lire to have ten shots at them with a rifle. The bullets whined and spattered off the masonry, tearing strips off the familiar adjoining posters for *Ernia* and the *Miss Sardegna* contest. One quickly felt at home.

* * *

Tempio, for all the majesty of its situation, and the fact that it is both the capital of Gallura and the seat of a bishop, is a primitive, austere town. I was told that many people came for the air and the water, but it was difficult to see where they could have stayed. The only hotel, the *Carlini*, is tiny and dark, and was full when we arrived. We had been introduced on the bus to a gay, polite architect with a face like Fernandel's and whose felt hat, in Fernandel fashion, had been blown out of a window on one of our steeper descents. He was a friend of Antonio Borio's in Sassari and he now very agreeably found rooms for us. These were in a cave-like house, without much plumbing, but very clean, and made, like almost every building in Tempio, out of grey granite.

The town is two thousand feet up and the difference in temperature was considerable. From November to April the surrounding peaks are snow-covered and the air is then full of the sound of mountain streams. Now it was dry and still, but with a crispness we had not felt before.

It was nearly dark by the time we went to look for dinner. Lights lay in isolated clusters over the valley, as though large shrubs had been illuminated. A man with rifle slung over his shoulder rode by on a wiry Sardinian donkey. The steep, narrow streets, like those in Alghero, were mostly arched, thin bridges of white stone curving against electric-blue sky. The restaurant, to which we were recommended, was small, but the food excellent —melon, smoked ham and olives, roast veal and anchovies, peaches, figs and grapes. The waiter had worked in the British Officers' Club in Padua, and after three years in Tempio, an act of piety for his old mother, was saving up to get back there as quickly as possible. He pointed out a flashing, dark, extremely young girl at the next table. 'That is Miss Tempio,' he said with some awe. 'Fourth to Miss Sardegna.'

Signor Cannas, our architect friend, arrived with his wife and a new hat, which he raised respectfully to Miss Tempio, who managed a gracious nod. After dinner he took us back to his flat to play us Sardinian music on records, for we had complained about its absence. The *ballo tondo*, like the Spanish *sardanas*, imitates the movement of the sea in pattern, the dancers holding hands, advancing and retreating like a slow tide and eventually working up to energetic waves and stormy stampings. The songs are almost uniquely joyless, laments and protestations of love that deny fulfilment. In lonely places, Cannas said, you could still sometimes hear a man singing an old traditional song in dialect to himself, and on days of *festa* everyone danced the *ballo tondo*. But ordinarily it was juke-box music; American rhythms, Italian words and Neapolitan tenors.

It thundered and rained again in the night. I was woken early by a trumpeter, going his rounds yelling out the day's prices for fruit, meat and vegetables. Bullock-carts rumbled under my window, their black-suited, patient drivers outlined against the clear mountain light. The movement in the streets was away towards the slopes of the great granite peaks or down to the valleys where vines, olives and cork-trees spread in squares of contrasting green.

Tempio is a town of terraces and wide promenades that reach out on either side of the old medieval centre and run horizontally across the mountains under thickly planted ilex-trees. On every level there is a dramatic view, the white peaks of the Limbara sawing above a pine forest to the south, and the grey bare ridges of Gallura northwards. Between these the cork forests, the finest in the Mediterranean, swing up and down the valley. Most of the Tempiese work, for a thousand lire a day, in the giant corkfactory which processes and ships the cork from Olbia to ports all over Europe. The cork forests, like most of the corn estates in the centre of Sardinia, are owned by smallholders, but all the produce goes through the Tempio factory.

Cannas called on us after breakfast with the son of the factory owner, a young man who offered to drive us through the cork woods in his large American car. On the northern skyline we could see the village of Aggius, where Cannas had recently built a new bell-tower, and it was up to this that we were soon purring over the rough stony road. The clouds, which had been bandaging the mountains all morning, began to disperse; a hot sun dappled the apple orchards dotted among cork-trees and vineyards.

Aggius is high up under the giant boulders which, from a distance, look like teeth, the whole ridge of hills edged in mouth shape with these bare blocks of granite. It is a miniature, pretty village of pink-washed houses, each with its wrought-iron balcony and flat roof laid out with pimentos and tomatoes. The church, flanked by Cannas' long thin tower, looks over the valley to the white gash of Tempio, and though the houses were small they all had been built as if they were meant to last—as if the men who designed them believed, in essentials anyway, that life was stable and unchanging.

We left the car and climbed behind the village to the enormous rocks, as holed as sponges, that hang threateningly over the upper houses. It was here that the famous *Muto di Gallura*—the Galluran mute—hid out for twenty years of ruthless murder. The mute belonged to a family called Vasa which had long waged a fierce vendetta against the Famiglia Mamia. All the Vasa family had been killed off, one by one, except the mute, who took to the caves above Aggius and came down only to make his killings. His final act, which has given the whole affair a unique place in Sardinian legend, was the murder of the twelve-year-old son of the head of the Mamia family. The boy, so the legend now goes, was of a fair beauty so remarkable that no girl in Aggius dared look at him. He was one day walking through the cork woods, singing a well-known dialect poem by the Tempio poet Don Gavino Pes. One of the verses of this poem begins:

Di la Primavera vinuta è pal me l'ultima sera

'For me this is the last evening of summer'—and the *Muto di Gallura*, who had long been watching for this boy, chose that moment to shoot him. It was said of the Galluran mute, and it has since become a local saying, that he could put a shot wherever he put his eye.

Tempio has always been the centre of Sardinian poetry and Don Gavino Pes has been called by Italian critics the Sardinian Metastasio. The Sards are by nature great improvisers of verse, if not very distinguished poets. Indeed only two of their poets, out of, it must be said, a comparatively huge army of practitioners, have managed to acquire reputations outside the island. Tigellius, patronized by Augustus and Cleopatra, incurred the critical contempt of both Horace and Cicero, though motives of envy at his degree of court favour cannot be quite dismissed. The other Sardinian poet to survive into literary history is Lofraso, a native of Alghero, who figures in the chapter of *Don Quixote* in which the curate and the barber go through the ingenious gentleman's library while he is asleep.

'This', said the barber as he opened another volume, 'is *The Ten Books of the Fortunes of Love*, composed by Antonio de Lofraso, the Sardinian poet.'

'By the holy orders that I have received,' the curate declared, 'since Apollo was Apollo, since the Muses were Muses and poets were poets, so droll and absurd a book as this has not been written; in its own way it is unique among all those of its kind that have seen the light of day, and he who has not read it does not know what he has missed. Give it to me, my friend, for I am more pleased at having found it than if they had presented me with a cassock of Florentine cloth.'

Don Gavino Pes, who wrote during the second half of the eighteenth century, is the Sardinian poet most highly regarded by the intelligentsia of Tempio. He was essentially a political writer, persuaded by his family, against his inclinations, to become a priest. Handsome, passionate and highly attracted to women, he shrank from the required vows of celibacy. One night he dreamed that the Pope was going to pass a law enabling priests to marry. He acceded to his parents' wishes and became a priest. Since no such law was ever passed, the dream turned out to be a nightmare. His poems, as a result, are consumed with melancholy frustration, with regret for the wasted, unappreciated potentialities of youth. *Il Tempo*, written in old age, laments the quick passage of time, the impossibility of valuing it in adolescence.

>Palchi no torri, di, tempu passatu?
>Palchi no torri, di, tempu paldutu?

Back in Tempio I came across an anthology of local poets, most of whom, like Pietro Curuleddu, had written their *Elogio a Tempio*:

> Tempiu beddu, Tempiu amurosu
> No decu sminticatti in vita mai ...

Later that day I sat in a café comparing the dialect poems with their Italian equivalents. A friend of the factory owner, an out-of-work *dottore*, brought me a volume of Don Gavino Pes and tried to render some poems into English, though his knowledge of English was hopelessly imperfect. He explained that a few lawyer friends might be coming later to drink coffee with us and while they were present he would speak only English. Then, rather shamefaced, he asked whether, if I was unable to understand him, I would be kind enough not to show it, for his friends all thought he could speak perfectly and, as he was hoping for a job as an English teacher, he could not afford to lose face.

Before long the friends arrived and I was surrounded by eight youthful *dottori*, all rolling dialect phrases on their tongues, and arguing as violently over poetic ambiguities as do English village boys over football. Occasionally my original friend would enunciate very carefully a sentence beginning 'I opinion you' and ending 'not at all, please'.

He was symptomatic of the Sardinian middle class where the title of *dottore* was the initial step in a life of pretence. Each village had its surfeit of lawyers, in good suits and with empty brief-cases in their hands, who spent the whole day at cafés 'dottoreing' one another while there was no food in their stomachs or their homes. Below them in station, the peasants at least ate.

When I got back to my room there was a lingering smell of cigar. My dispatch-case and suit-case were not as I had left them. From the window I saw two *carabinieri*, guns slung over their shoulders, standing at the corners of a dark street. We were the first foreigners to have been in the town for nearly five years, so it would have been uncharitable to have grudged them this small chance of justifying their authority.

★ ★ ★

The next day was again wet. It seemed that we should arrive in and leave Sardinia in rain. The dead, parched plains of the south, marked only by dusty green stumps of palm and cactus, seemed already as remote as the blue heat-shimmering hills that bordered them. From my window I looked out over the Coghinas valley, foaming grey and silver with cork and olive, as from the bridge of a ship. The pale ribbon of the road to Sassari twisted into the distance. I could see the black dots of men working in their vineyards, sometimes a slash of colour on the flanks of the Limbara, where a costumed peasant led down his brushwood-laden donkey. The granite peaks were under cloud and the air smelt of damp and pine.

The boat for Bonifacio sailed at eleven the next morning, which meant spending the night at Santa Teresa di Gallura, the last Sardinian port of call before Corsica.

The only bus of the day left at dusk and we zigzagged in and out of the sunset, the last sheets of apricot light thinning into lemon and leaving the jagged mountains as though the peaks had been coated with whipped cream.

The road hugged the sides of ravines, the headlamps flicking from the rubbery leaves of cactus and the steely glint of jutting rock, to sudden emptiness as we swerved inwards from precipices. The driver, who had looked rather hilarious in Tempio, seemed full of unusual *joie de vivre* and he drove with his foot hard down and his hand never off the horn. We overtook a lorry on a sharp bend, a volley of stones slithering into the valley with the crack of rifle fire. We had stopped at various places in the darkness, taking aboard peasants loaded with babies and baskets, till the bus was packed solid. At Luogo Santo, which we reached after an hour and a half of screeching brakes and whining hooter, a mad mob tried to fight its way in. Hen coops were thrust through the open window and those unable to wedge themselves in, hauled themselves on to the roof. A few left out altogether beat angrily on the windows till the conductor, ringing the bell, yelled back at them '*Non è Luogo Santo, è Luogo del diavolo!*' and we skidded on, leaving a blue burst of exhaust in their faces.

The inside of the bus had become a sweltering mixture of sweat, garlic, grapes, and thyme—great baskets of which acted as buffers between the pushing passengers. The lorry had now passed us again and the bus-driver seemed determined on revenge. We hurtled up and down apparent switchbacks, fine rain misting up the windows so that it was impossible to see out. The hens scuffled in their boxes, a pregnant woman and then a nun were sick. When the lights of Palau eventually appeared a cry of relief went up from the front of the bus. We stopped by the customs house, where we had taken our first steps on Sardinian soil, and most of the peasants clattered off, muttering, to the Maddalena ferry which lay alongside. Heavy rain was now falling, splintering the reflections of light on the water. The steamer blew its siren impatiently, and then we swung on again, our lamps picking out a solitary foal in the lee of a headland and flashing over the surf breaking at the edge of the road. By the time we reached the few houses of Santa Teresa it was after ten. We found rooms in the only café in the village, ate a hurried meal of spaghetti and raw wine, and were quickly asleep.

The morning was windless and clear. Beyond the gay cinnamon and cobalt-blue church, the mountains of Corsica looked unbelievably near. A couple of yellow fishing-smacks were making their way into the bay, bows cutting the glass-smooth water like diamonds. In the bar, where we drank coffee and munched stale buns, I saw one of the commercial travellers from Carloforte. They had provided a kind of recurring imagery to our trip, solitary representatives of the thin lines of communication to the *continente*.

Punctually at noon the *Gallura* backed into the almost landlocked harbour. The sun had intensified the greenness of the capes and flashed off the cliffs. Five minutes later the ship's head, pointing at Bonifacio, was lifting gently in mid-channel. The towers and campanile of the parish church of Santa Teresa slipped behind the headland. Sardinia began to sink into the sea, a grey dwindling hump with a fret of foam round it. We cut through the bluest water we had seen, with flying fish in scarcely broken curves spinning through the waves ahead of us. To the east rose the green crest of La Maddalena, as tantalizingly beautiful as, ten years ago, I had first imagined it. Now one more of those haunting bays, so inaccessible to me then, was fading in the wake. The ship smelt of soap and tar, and we were the only passengers. The Captain on the bridge, his signet ring glinting, adjusted his dark glasses and lit a cigarette.

FOUR POEMS

A Barman in Cagliari

Blue Curaçao, Glen Mist, Vernaccia, Senancole,
La Trappistine, Kirsch, Crême de Noyau, Anis—
These were his landscape when he turned inward,
Away from the street to the sea flowing in glass,
Mirrored cranes and tents of salt, red sailing boats
Flecking the mountains, the lagoons to the west.
And lower down, because nearer, trams swung
Round the reflected rims of glasses, the necks of soda
Bottles. *Sirops* stood like soldiers on the marble,
Straws at the slope and an armoury of lemons.

He was mostly a smile, with a real animal smile
Inside his professional smile like a lining; he had, too,
A wink for private use, eyes he dilated at will
As some people waggle their ears. The sharp removal
Of crisps and olives, the twist of the hips,
Were indicative enough of disapproval
For the toughest customer, and rarely necessary.

For keeping a bar was to him a philosophy,
A reconciling of opposites, of rest and distraction:
It was a harbour whose craft he, an ex-mariner,
Deftly controlled, an anagram of psychology
And subtraction, an equation the correct
Solving of which took him nightly
Past where the salt works gleamed pale lilac,
To a plump woman who never disturbed him.

Nuraghi near Abbasanta, Sardinia

Here men hunted, fished, shot,
Worked miracles with flint
And obsidian, occasionally got
Drunk, fighting with each other
Or over women. The stone glint
Of forts signalled over plains, bare
Save for boulders, cactus and maize,
A desert-coloured stubble, where
Always mountains stalked under blue haze
In the distance, but never came nearer.
On good days they made out of bronze
Warriors and animals, cutting thin masks
For nights of *festa*; images dearer
To them than the toy amusements
Of city-statesmen. The sun beating
In hammers of light, they waited on rocks
For wild boar, partridge, deer, retreating
When shadows fluted their stone clocks,
To coned forts, these circular look-outs.

Now three thousand of them, that many
Years later, litter the island;
Like crumbling tombs of especially grand
Chieftains they protrude from this granary
Of Rome wherever the land rises.
But the bronze objects, safe under glass,
Still draw their bows, firing at whoever may pass
By them, inquisitive of their delicacy.
Miniature boats, herdsmen, attest their efficacy,
Suggesting how sophisticated was the primitive
Grasp of reality, the visual boldness

Of men for whom art was alive,
Like hunting or building, a process
Necessary for survival, an attempt
At self-knowledge. Revealing to them, in their
    unkempt
Surroundings, their roughshod history,
What manner of people they were,
The nature of their lives, their claims to glory.

Mineral Boats at Carloforte

Green 3-Masters, the green of grass,
Doubling their number on sea-glass,
Till off the salt-white jetty
Fifty silhouettes sit pretty;
Each waits patiently for nightfall
Its daily pregnancy of mineral:
On flaring prows extend long booms
With painted eyes to pierce the gloom.
Their figureheads have bowsprit noses,
Complexions of port and roses.
Brightly they queen it over tunny,
Sardine or coral boats, beside them puny
At their moorings, while like guns
Small waves lick the sun
That lies along the lacquer of their hulls.
Sunset finds them flecked with gulls
Wearing cinnamon and turquoise feathers
Cocking eyes at courteous weather.
Loaded by darkness under lamps
That shadow the salt heaps like the camps
Of some great army, they lift
Their bows, while workmen sift
The broken stone through sieves
Into the holds. The stern ropes give,
And now they tune their anchors
Like an orchestra, stern-down like tankers.
And turning, one by one they shake
Sails free, draw phosphorus from their wakes.
Life-boats for this quarried port
Where Arabs, Turks and Genoese fought
For Empire, they now bear north the spoils

Of pick-axe conflict, drilled-stone toils:
To have, shaded from all prying eyes,
Before the indecency of sunrise,
Their gritty *accouchement* in the torn
Sky of Genoa and Leghorn.

Giuseppe of Carloforte

Head heavy as a cut white chrysanthemum,
Bobbing between masts, as though it were in fact
A flower he was carrying, a gift to be treated
With care, he moves—a professional good fellow—
From boat to boat, unloading anecdotes while others work.
He eases his belly like a faded drum
On sun-warmed decks. And so great is his presence
He seems, a one-man band, to be beating it
To proclaim his arrival, a fanfare of benevolence.
Older than history, his trousers patched sails, he pads
The quay like a bear, striping it with his shadow:
Advancing up gangways, supervisor who does nothing,
He leans over holds glistening with fish,
Port-names rolled round his tongue—Havana,
Buenos Aires, Ferrol, Ragusa—as if they could help
To make work tolerable, at least pay for his upkeep.
The tunny fleet, cadaverous and scrubbed, rides under him,
Bows painted with meticulous faces, unwinking as saints:
And mineral boats, white light on their crucifix mastheads,
Squat like green birds, their bellies full of quartz.
Raised on an elbow, he surveys them as if they were his,
By right of his being there, like the view, the coastline
Of palms, the half-moons of bays under ink-blue rocks—
Common property of those who make imagination work for
    them.
In fact, they are, for he is Giuseppe, retired beggar
Late of the Bronx, who made a fortune hawking matches
And, returned to his birthplace, invested in ships.
Now, athwart decks all day, he lies,
Expert in squandering time, rolling marbles the colours of his
    eyes.

Index

Abbasanta, 90, 117
Accipitrum, 125
Aggius, 188–9
Agincourt Sound, 25, 27–8, 31
Ajaccio, xii, 1–4, 9, 10, 40, 99
Aldington, Richard, 66
Alfonso IV, King of Aragon, 96, 122
Alfonso V, 155, 160
Alghero, xi, 48, 112, 128, 184, 187, 190
Algiers, 23
Anfiteatro Romano, 107
Anglona mountains, 171
Aragon, 97
Aragon, King of, 96
Arborea, 96, 150, 155
Ardara, 57–8
Asinara, 169, 172
Augustus, 190

Baia della Mezzaluna, 133
Baie des Anges, 1
Barbagia, 78
Barbary Coast, 25–6
Barbusi, 121–2
Barcelona, 96, 99, 109
Basra, 53
Bastia, 1, 14
Bastione Santa Caterina, 101
Bavaria, Elector of, 97
Beechey, Sir William, 24
Bey of Tunis, 125
Biche Channel, 28
Boccaccio, 52
Bonifacio, xii, 4, 6–10, 13, 39–41, 171, 183, 192, 193
Bonifacio, Straits of, 1, 7, 13, 27, 39
Bonorva, 60, 162, 165

Borio, Antonio, 161, 187
Borore, 150
Bortigali, 71
Boswell, 2
Bouchier, E. S., x, 88
Brittany, xii
Bromeley, Richard, 25
Buckingham, Duke of, 183
Budelli, 17
Buenos Aires, 33
Busch, Eva, 12

Cagliari, 30, 38–41, 47, 52, 62, 66–7, 80–1, 88, 90–1, 93–4, 96–7, 99–105, 107–13, 119–23, 125, 128, 132, 137, 138
Calabria, 66, 95
Calasetta, 124, 132, 133
Calvi, 4, 9
Cambi, 156
Campidano, the, 90, 121, 140
Cannas, Signor, 187, 188, 189
Cannes, 4
Cape Corse, 23
Cape Longo Sardo, 24
Capo Buggeru, 179
Capo Caccia, 178, 183
Capo Carbonara, 101, 112, 120
Capo Sant' Elia, 101, 105
Capo Soddu, 179
Capo Spartivento, 100, 101, 106, 112, 116, 119
Caprera, 23, 30–7, 39
Capri, xi, 4, 15, 23, 124
Carbonia, 138
Carlo Alberto, King, 34, 98
Carlo Emanuele III, 97, 125, 171
Carlo Emanuele IV, 98

Carlo Felice, King, 93, 98, 117
Carloforte, 52, 112, 119, 125-9, 131-2, 136-7, 183, 193
Carthage, 96
Casa Albis, 182
Casa Cantoniere, 72
Castello di Acquafredda, 122
Castello, Francesco di, 169
Castel Sardo, 24, 162, 171-3, 180-1
Castile, 97
Cato, 95
Cavendish, Lady Elizabeth, x
Cavour, 36
Charlemagne, 96
Charles V, 48, 82
Chaucer, 52
Cheremule, 164
Chevrier, Pierre, 176
Chiesa dei Cappuccini, 107
Chilivani, 59, 156
Cicero, ix, 190
Civitavecchia, 14, 51, 52
Cleopatra, 190
Coghinas, 192
Coghinas, river, 186
Collins, Mr, 33, 35
Colonna-Cesari, Col., 40, 41
Connolly, Cyril, 129
Cornus, 118
Corsica, x, xi, 1, 3, 9, 11, 13-14, 21, 24-5, 31, 37, 38-9, 40, 54, 56, 94, 132, 172, 192
Corso Garibaldi, 79, 82, 85
Corso Umberto, 51, 55, 86, 159
Corso Vittorio Emanuele, 106
Costa, A., x
Costa Brava, xi, 171
Cours Mirabeau, 4
Curruleddu, Pietro, 190
Cyprus, 15

Dante, 78
Darsena, 101, 105
Daudet, 2
De Amicis, 146

Decimomannu, 91, 121
Degas, 146
de Gaulle, 3, 4
Deledda, Grazia, 141, 142, 143
de Maupassant, 2
de Plaisances, Pierluigi and Claudia 133-4, 136-7
Diocletian, 51, 140, 169
Diodorus, 93
Domus dei Gianas, 88, 93
Domusnovus, 121
Donnelly, Capt. Ross, 24
Doria, Brancaleone, 155
Doria family, 160, 171, 181
Douglas, Norman, xi
Dragute, Admiral, 48
Dresden, 59
Dumas *père*, 78
Dürer, Albert, 59

Egypt, 28
Elba, xi, 1, 14, 15
Elector of Bavaria, 97
Eleonora, *Guidicessa*, 155
Elmas, 120
Ennius, 95

Fagioli, Dr, 138-40, 145
Ferraciolo, 35
Fertilia, airport, 182
Florence, 164
Fonte Rosello, 167
France, 27
Frati Filippini, 169

Gallura, 9, 13, 17-19, 88, 96, 171, 183, 185, 187, 188
Gardner, Admiral Alan (Lord Gardner), 24, 27
Garibaldi, Felice, 33
Garibaldi, Giuseppe, 1, 22-3, 32-7, 39
Garibaldi, Menotti, 34
Garibaldi, Teresita, 32, 34
Gennargentu range, 71, 76, 81, 84, 86
Genoa, 32, 38, 53, 134-6

Giave, Plain of, 165
Gibraltar, 30
Giovinetti, Conte Amore, 177
Graves, Robert, xi
Greene, Graham, 130
Grotto de Marcello, 113
Guardia dei Mori, 133

Hamburg, 11, 14
Hamilcar, 94
Hamilton, Lady, 29
Hannibal, 95
Hanno, 47
Hardy, Thomas, 142
Hasdrubal, 94
Hawkesbury, Lord, 27
Heracles, 93
Hieracum, 125
Hobart, Lord, 25, 27
Holbein, 59
Horace, 190

Iceland, 23, 30
Iglesias, 96, 120, 137, 150, 184
Île Rousse, 4
Îles Sanguinaires, 1, 2, 6
Indo-China, 3
Ischia, xi, 15, 124
Isola Bianca, 55

Jackson, Mr, 27
Januarius, 169
Justinus, 93

Karalis, 91, 118

Laerru, 185
La Maddalena, xii, 9, 17–20, 23, 25–31, 33, 37–40, 42
La Marmora, Count Alberto, 117
La Plaia, 138
La Punta, 134
Largo, Carlo Felice, 100, 105–7, 113
Lawrence, D. H., x, xi, 15, 64–9, 72
Lawrence, Frieda, 66, 70

Lear, Edward, 2
Léger, 5
Levisena Islands, 24, 25
Limbara Range, 50, 54, 184, 186, 188, 192
Liona, Emma, 29
Lofraso, Antonio de, 190
Logudoro, 155–6, 164
Lungomare Dante, 182
Luogo Santo, 192
Lyons, 14
Lyons, Gulf of, 28

Macaroni, Signor, 178
Macomer, 52, 60, 62, 64, 71, 76, 86–9, 117
Madao, 87
Madonna del Rimedio, 145, 151
Mago, 94
Majorca, xi, 15
Malaspina family, 160
Malchus, 94
Malta, 25, 26, 34, 65
Mamia family, 189
Mandas, 67
Manet, 146
Marciana Marina, 1
Mariano IV, 155
Mariano, Constantino di, 164
Marinella, 5
Marinetti, 5
Marrubiu, 90
Marseilles, 4
Martha Islands, 25
Martis, 185
Maugham, Somerset, 4, 129–30
Mazzini, 33–4, 36
Melville, Lord, 28
Menotti, Gian-Carlo, 114
Mérimée, 2, 76
Merton, 24
Messina, 23, 25
Milan, 14, 53, 128
Milis, 89, 90
Minto, Lord, 27

Minton, John, 5
Monaco, 23
Monte Acuto, 57
Monte Cristo, 23
Monte Ferru, 89
Montelepre, 74
Monte Pinto, 50
Monte Santo, 58
Monte Urtigu, 89
Monti, 57
Moscow, 126
Munich, 59
Muravera, 162
Murmansk, 31
Murolo, Roberto, 102
Museo Archeologico Nazionale, 115
Museo Nazionale G. A. Sanna, 161
Museum of Antiquities, 93-4
Mussolini, 97, 183
Muto di Gallura, 189

Naples, xi, 32, 138
Naples, Gulf of, 112
Napoleon Buonaparte, 1, 3, 6, 9, 15, 23, 39-41
Narcao, 121
Nelson, Lady, 120
Nelson, Lord, 1, 23, 24-31, 39, 120, 126
New York, 33
Nice, xii, 1
Nicholas, Sir Nicholas, 23
Nora, 117-19, 138, 140
Norris, Admiral, 48
North Africa, 4
Nulvi, 184-6
Nuoro, 53, 61-2, 64, 67-8, 70, 75-9, 83, 85-6, 141
Nuoro, Bishop of, 74

Olbia, ix, xii, 14, 38, 42-5, 47-8, 50, 52, 54, 62, 70, 89, 95, 117, 119-20, 156, 183, 188
Oliène, 73
Ollastra, 90

Orani, 73
Orgosolo, 73-4
Oristano, 82, 89-91, 145-8, 151, 153-6, 162
Orosei, 69, 73, 83
Ortobene, 76, 84
Ortueri, 150
Oschiri, 57
Osilo, 184
Ovid, 78
Ozieri, 57-9

Padua, 187
Palau, 17, 37-39, 41, 43, 193
Palazzo Communale, 101
Palazzo del Duca, 160
Palazzo del Re Barbaro, 170
Palazzo di Giustizia, 148
Palazzo Provinciale, 158
Palermo, 64
Palma, Gulf of, 23, 28
Paoli, 3, 30
Paris, 3, 11, 12, 14, 128
Pausanias, 93
Pedro IV, Don, of Aragon, 182
Pellew, Sir Edward, 28
Perfugas, 185, 186
Pergola, 8
Pes, Don Gavino, 187-91
Peyron, 87
Piaf, Edith, 6, 7
Piana, 4, 125, 133
Piazza Crispi, 82
Piazza Cavallino, 158
Piazza Eleonora, 155
Piazza Garibaldi, 18
Piazza d'Italia, 158-60, 173
Piazza Indipendenza, 101, 115-16
Piazza Plebiscito, 83, 85
Piazza Roma, 147, 148, 154
Piazza San Giovanni, 83
Piazza Vittorio Emanuele, 85
Piazza Yenne, 113
Picasso, 78, 117
Piedmont, 26, 30, 99

Piercy, Mr, 62
Pirelli, Cardinal, 152
Piper, John, 122
Place de Gaulle, 3
Poetto, 38, 93, 102-3, 106, 110, 112, 138, 140
Poggio, 1
Pope Boniface VIII, 96
Pope Pius IX, 34
Porta del Popolo, 176
Porto, 4
Portoferraio, 1, 15
Portofino, 4
Porto Scuso, 137
Porto Torres, 119, 160, 167-9, 171
Porto Vecchio, 8
Porto Vesme, 137
Posse-Brazdova, Amélie, 176, 177
Procida, 128
Promenade des Anglais, 1
Propriano, 4
Protus, 169
Provence, xii, 90, 156
Prunas, Don Pietrino, 60
Pula, 116-17, 139-140
Punta delle Colonne, 132

Quintus, ix

Ravenna, 33
Riviera di Levante, 112
Roccopina, 7
Rockefeller Foundation, 45
Rome, xii, 14, 32-33, 48, 53, 85, 94-5, 98, 126-7, 129, 142, 148, 161, 169
Rosas, 33, 123
Ross, Mrs Alan, x
Rossi, Tino, 6
Rue Buonaparte, 5
Russia, 23, 27

Saint-Exupéry, Antoine de, 5, 176
Saint-Tropez, 4
Sampiero, 3
Sampiero Corso, 1

San Gavino, 91, 164
San Gavino, Basilica of, 169
Sanna, Giovanni, 161
San Pietro, 52, 119, 124-5, 127, 129, 136
San Pietro di Sorres, 165
San Pietro Island, 28
Santadi, 121
Santa Gilla, 119
Santa Giusta, 146-7, 150, 165
Santa Maria, 17, 123
Santa Teresa, 14, 16, 33, 38, 183, 192-3
Santo Stefano, 16, 18, 20, 39-41
Sant' Elia, Conte, 177, 178
S. Antine, 163, 165-6
S. Antioco, 123-5, 132
Santu Lussurgu, 89
Sardus, 93
Sartène, 7
Sassari, x, 59, 145, 151, 153, 156-61, 163, 167-9, 172-3, 175, 183, 187
Savoy, Duke of, 97
S. Bartolomeo canal, 104
Scapa Flow, 30
Scotland, 7, 41
Scipio, Lucius Cornelius, 47-8, 95
Scudo, 5
S. Efisio, 140
Sella del Diavolo, 104
Serra, Conte Gaspare, 178
Seydis Fiord, 23
Sezione Etnografica Gavino Clemente, 162
S. Giovanni, 123
Sherbrooke, Capt., R. St. V., 31
Sicily, 25, 34, 35, 64, 66, 70, 93, 133
Siena, 164
Silanus, 71
Siliqua, 121, 122
Silone, 77
Simenon, 4, 129
Smyth, Admiral, 183
Snipe, Dr, 26
Sorgono, 67, 68

205

Sorres, 165
Spargi, 17
Spanioti, Island, 25
S. Pantaleo, 64
S. Paolo, 89
Spiaggia della Bobba, 133
S. Simplicio, 49–51, 55
SS. Trinità di Saccargia, Abbazia della, 163, 165
Stephanini, 87
Stettin, 14
S. Tomeo, 50
St. Peter, 125
Strabo, 65
Stromboli, 23
Sulcis, 118, 124
Sulpicius, 95

Tabarca, 125
Tamuli, 61, 87–8
Tarragona, 51
Tarshish, 94
Tavolara, Island of, 51
Tedeschini, Cardinal, 148–51, 159
Tempio, 111, 183–4, 186–190, 192
Tempio della Dea Fortuna, 170
Tempio della Dea Tanit, 139
Terranova, 47–8, 90
Terrubia, 123
Tetuan, 23
Tharros, 118, 119, 147
Thousand of Sicily, the, 23
Tigellius, 190
Tigris, 53
Timaeus, 93
Tirpitz, Admiral von, 177, 182
Tombe di giganti, 87–8
Tonara, 68
Toro Island, 28, 123
Torralba, 163–4
Torre dell' Elefante, 93, 101, 106
Torre di San Pancrazio, 101
Torres, 64
Torritano River, 170
Tossa de Mar, 171

Toulon, 23–5, 28
Trafalgar, 24, 29
Tratalias, 121, 123
Trebina, 149
Trevelyan, G. M., 33–4, 36–7
Truyvet, Admiral, 41
Tunis, 5
Tyndale, John Warre, x, 29, 41, 47, 57–8, 87–90, 159, 164, 169–70, 185

Ugone, 155
Uras, 90
Uri, 175
Utrecht, Treaty of, 97

Vacca, 123
Valéry, 133
Vallambrosa, Duca di, 160
Vandals, 96
Vasa family, 189
Vecchi, 34, 35
Vecchio, Palma, 164
Venice, xii
Ventimiglia, xi
Venus Erycina, 103
Verga, 77
Via Aspromonte, 83
Via Attilio Deffenu, 82
Via Barcellona, 107
Via Cagliari, 51
Via Dante, 180
Via Grazia Deledda, 84
Viale Armando Diaz, 103
Viale Fra Ignazio da Laconi, 107
Via Manno, 106–7
Via Mannu, 84
Via Napoli, 107
Via Nelson, 22, 31
Via Ospedale, 107
Via Papandrea, 82
Via Roma, 99–103, 105–6, 108–9, 115
Via Santa Restituta, 107
Via Sardegna, 109
Via Statale, 63
Via Tharros, 147

Via Vittorio Emanuele, 168
Vidal, 87
Villa Strohl-Fern, 176
Villanova, 101, 115
Villasor, 91
Vitello, 123
Vittorio Amadeo II, 97
Vittorio Amadeo III, 97
Vittorio Emanuele I, 36, 98
Vittorio Emanuele II, 98, 158

Vittorio Emanuele III, 177, 178

Warner, Rex, 63
Waugh, Evelyn, 12, 13
Werner, Ilse, 12
West Indies, 24
Windsor, Duke of, 178
Wordsworth, William, 142

Zanotti, Signor and Signora, 128–9, 131, 132–3, 136